MW00581456

ANYTHING'S
PASTABLE

ANYTHING'S PASTABLE

81 INVENTIVE PASTA RECIPES FOR SAUCY PEOPLE

DAN PASHMAN

FOR JANIE,
WHOSE LOVE, SUPPORT, AND
OCCASIONAL SKEPTICISM
MAKE EVERYTHING POSSIBLE.

AND FOR BECKY AND EMILY,
THE BEST TASTE TESTERS,
AND DAUGHTERS, A COOKBOOK
AUTHOR COULD HAVE.
I'M SO PROUD OF BOTH OF YOU.

CONTENTS

FOREWORD

BY J. KENJI LÓPEZ-ALT

Who invents a new shape of pasta? Who looks at the dozens of shapes available at the supermarket, the hundreds of shapes available from specialty markets, and says to themselves, "We can do better," and then actually follows through?

Before Dan created cascatelli, I'd never heard of a brand-new pasta shape that wasn't cartoon-themed and served from a can. When I think of pasta being invented, I picture da Vinci feverishly sketching pen-and-ink technical diagrams of bronze dies, not a podcaster from New Jersey.

But to tell you the truth, I'm not surprised Dan did it. As a longtime friend and even longer-time fan of Dan's work, there is nobody I'd rather debate food opinions with. Whether he's imploring you to fold your New York slice inside out so that the cheese hits your tongue first (if Dan is successfully doing this, my taste in pizza runs greasier than his), or suggesting that you cook your falafel mixture in a waffle iron (we agree on this one), you can always count on Dan to offer passionate, thoughtful-bordering-on-obsessive opinions.

While debating the ideal stacking order of a hard-shell taco (I like to melt a "cheese hinge" into the bottom of the shell first) is fun, it's ultimately trivial. But cascatelli is different. Cascatelli isn't just a different way to grill your cheese. Cascatelli is important. Cascatelli is on the dinner tables of people around the world. Cascatelli is exciting.

Cascatelli is the end point of years of research and effort with a singular goal. Cascatelli is good.

Now, I know Dan will tell us that when he came up with cascatelli, he was merely iterating and refining, combining the best parts of his favorite pasta shapes, all while standing on the shoulders of giants. But here's the thing: any one of the billions of people in the world familiar with pasta could have stood on the shoulders of those same giants. But Dan is the guy who did. (Take the compliment, Dan.)

It's a shape that is so obviously delicious, that so perfectly captures what Dan named as the three most important qualities of pasta (forkability, sauceability, and toothsinkability), that is so versatile, so naturally fun to eat, that it feels like it's existed forever.

So it is with the recipes in this book.

If you want to learn how to make traditional Italian pasta dishes, pick up copies of *Cooking by Hand* by Paul Bartolli and *Essentials of Classic Italian Cooking* by Marcella Hazan and cook from them.

If, on the other hand, you've eaten your share of classic carbonara and lasagna Bolognese and want to level up your pasta game and unlock the full potential of your pantry, if you're interested in learning from a man who's made his entire career out of discovering creative new ways to enjoy a meal, then pick up this book and let Dan be your

shepherd, guiding your mouth into whole new worlds of deliciousness.

Inside you won't find a recipe for red sauce, though you will find a guide for how to doctor up a jar of store-bought red sauce for whatever mood you're in. You'll find recipes for Lime-Corn Nut Pangrattato—perfect for topping your Thai Curry Mac 'n' Cheese. You'll find instructions for the smartest method I've seen for cooking pasta in advance while retaining its eating qualities. He'll show you how to bring some heat to your cacio e pepe with chili crisp, or funky depth to your vodka sauce with Indian pickles.

You'll discover why your pantry should always have preserved lemons in it (hint: they go great with artichokes and cavatelli). How do you feel about mushy, mayo-slicked pasta salads? Me too. Thankfully, Dan has an entire chapter on pasta salads that will have a line circling all the way around the church basement. (His puttanesca pasta salad with

fish sauce and Calabrian chiles is my favorite recipe in the book.)

It's rare that you read a cookbook in which every recipe has an interesting idea, an appealing flavor combination, a clever technique or spark of originality, but that's what Dan has accomplished here through his obsessively hard work.

The ability to come up with excellent ideas and the tenacity to follow through with them. Goodthinkability and sticktoitiveness. That's what Dan has, and that's what this book will help you build in your own kitchen.

Of course, he's also pretty forkable.

—Kenji

P.S. Dan, the last time I made your ingenious pasta pizza recipe, I baked it in a square pizza pan with a circle of cubed brick cheese around the edges to get a Detroit pizza–style caramelized cheese crust. It was amazing.

INTRODUCTION

About six years ago, I decided to invent a new food. In part this was because I wanted to tell an epic, multipart story on my food podcast, *The Sporkful,* and I thought the process would be full of entertaining ups and downs.

But there was another reason.

I launched *The Sporkful* in 2010, and in the early days, the show was largely driven by my many idiosyncratic opinions about eating. (I believe cheeseburgers should be served with cheese on the bottom, to bring the cheese closer to your tongue, which accentuates cheesy goodness and creates a seal that protects the bottom bun from soggage. I've

missed exits on the highway thinking about the best way to dip a tortilla chip to maximize dip load while minimizing the risk of chip breakage. I could go on.)

Over the years *The Sporkful* has evolved, and now uses food to tackle more substantive issues, including culture, identity, science, history, and economics. But our motto remains "It's not for foodies, it's for eaters," and we still make time for debates about the best way to layer the fillings of a PB&J (it's jelly-PB-jelly).

So I remain a food-obsessed weirdo. But I'm not a chef. I have no professional culinary training whatsoever.

When a chef has an idea about how to cook something, they can try it out, refine it, and serve it in their restaurant or put it in their cookbook. If enough people like it, it must have some merit. I'm a pretty good home cook, and before I set out on my food creation quest, I had tried a few of my quirky creations in my own kitchen. But as the years wore on and I became more widely known for my food opinions, I realized I had never truly put any of my ideas to the test, to find out if they had any merit.

I started asking myself, "Do I actually know what I'm talking about?"

I decided the only way to answer this question was to invent a new food, and to see if anybody thought it was any good. This would not be a theoretical exercise. I wanted to not only invent the food but also get it produced and attempt to sell it. I settled on a pasta shape because everyone likes pasta, it's generally affordable, and you can ship it without refrigeration. All this would make it easy to share with *Sporkful* listeners far and wide.

But the main reason I decided to invent a new pasta shape is that I was generally dissatisfied with many of the existing ones. (I'm looking at you, angel hair.)

You see, I've come up with three criteria by which I believe all pasta shapes should be judged. *Sporkful* listeners know these terms well, but if you're new, I'll catch you up. They are:

1. FORKABILITY: how easy it is to get the shape on your fork and keep it there

2. SAUCEABILITY: how readily sauce adheres to the shape

And most important of all . . .

3. TOOTHSINKABILITY: how satisfying it is to sink your teeth into it

THINGS YOU WILL NOT FIND IN THIS BOOK

- HOW TO MAKE FRESH PASTA FROM SCRATCH
- A THREE-HOUR RECIPE FOR TOMATO SAUCE
- PICTURES OF TUSCANY
- ANGEL HAIR
- WAGON WHEELS
- ANY RECIPE I WOULD NOT BE EXTREMELY EXCITED TO MAKE AND EAT AGAIN

Lots of shapes out there are good at one or two of these, but very few nail all three. Spaghetti doesn't even get one of them right, which is why I declared at the start of my journey that it sucks.

Maybe, I thought, I could bring a new perspective to pasta shapes, and create one that does it all.

"I can't even think of a shape that doesn't already exist," my wife, Janie, responded when I told her about my plan. "I think you're a really smart person," she continued cautiously. "Maybe utilize that energy to think of something else other than a pasta shape. A new flavor of ice cream?"

I would not be deterred. If there's greater motivation in life than proving your spouse wrong, I haven't found it. Isn't that why you get married in the first place?!

In the end it took three years. I traveled to the Pasta Lab at North Dakota State University to learn about durum wheat, and interviewed Maureen Fant, who translated the seminal *Encyclopedia of Pasta* by Oretta Zanini De Vita, which attempts to catalog every known shape. Maureen told me there are three hundred to four hundred shapes that go by approximately twelve hundred names—different regions or towns often have different names for the same shape. My family and I ate every obscure shape we could get our teeth on as I methodically isolated variables—Do I like long or short shapes? Tubes or flat ones? Ruffles or ridges?

Pasta shapes were floating through my dreams. I got a graph paper notebook and began sketching new concepts while sitting on the sidelines of my daughter's soccer games, trying to come up with a shape that maximized forkability, sauceability, and toothsinkability like no other before. I thought I had some good ideas, but to know for sure I needed to produce some edible pasta prototypes.

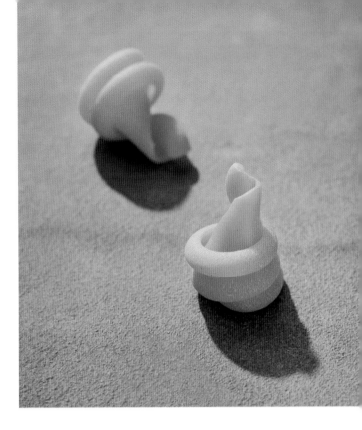

I spent months trying to convince Giovanni Cannata, the only pasta die designer in America, to work with me. (The die is like the mold for the shape.) Giovanni told me many of my sketches would be physically impossible to produce—one idea I had combined a tube with ruffles, but he said the mechanism that creates the ruffles would crush the tube. Meanwhile, I was trying (and failing) to find a pasta company to manufacture my shape once I had it. (You can hear the whole dramatic story, complete with Janie's reservations and me nearly being brought to tears, in *The Sporkful* podcast series "Mission: ImPASTAble.")

On March 19, 2021, the series concluded and my new shape went on sale, produced by an artisanal pasta company in upstate New York called Sfoglini. I named the shape cascatelli—Italian for "waterfalls." And people loved it. The first production run of thirty-seven hundred boxes sold out in less than two hours through Sfoglini's website. Cascatelli and I were featured on *CBS Mornings*, the *Today* show, *Good Morning America,* and NPR, and in the *New York Times* and *Food & Wine.* The story was picked up by news outlets in Italy, France, Germany, the U.K., Spain, and Israel. Sarah Jessica Parker shared it on her Instagram. I even appeared on *Access Hollywood* talking about this pasta shape, which was not on my vision board when my quest began.

At the end of the year, cascatelli was named one of the Best Inventions of 2021 by *Time* magazine, which included it on the cover. THE COVER.

One of the best parts of the experience was that my whole family shared in my success. Janie quickly went from skeptic to talking about the pasta shape that "we" invented. Our daughters, Becky and Emily, ten and seven at the time, heard from their classmates who were loving cascatelli. Normally

when you accomplish something in your job, your kids couldn't care less. But a new pasta shape? That's something they could get excited about.

Another highlight was that *Sporkful* listeners started sending me pictures from all over the country and the world, showing me what they were making with cascatelli. I found this surprisingly moving, to feel as if I'd been invited into people's homes for dinner, a small part of me at the table there with them.

But there was a problem.

Seventy-five percent of the pictures I received showed the pasta with tomato sauce, meat sauce, or mac 'n' cheese. A few party animals made basil pesto. Add in other well-worn classics like carbonara and cacio e pepe, and that was 95 percent of what I saw.

This, to me, was tragic. While I don't think any pasta shape will work with every conceivable preparation, I believe a great shape will work with a wide range of them, and I believe cascatelli is a great shape. It wasn't being used to its full potential.

And beyond cascatelli, this showed me that many people seem unaware of all the glorious ingredients they can and should be putting on all their pasta shapes.

So in 2021, I began work on this cookbook—my first cookbook. My goal was to create a pasta cookbook that I had never seen before, one for home cooks who are less concerned with old traditions and more interested in new combinations, using a variety of ingredients and pasta shapes that I love to cook with in my own kitchen. To do that, I collaborated with a team of incredibly talented recipe developers with experience across a range of cuisines. Each of them is credited alongside the recipes they worked on, and you can read more about them on page 262. Together we came up with dozens of pasta dishes that I think stand out from the old standbys.

So there's no recipe for marinara sauce in here—although I will give you tips on how to jazz up a store-bought jar in my Jarred Tomato Sauce Decision Tree (see page 30).

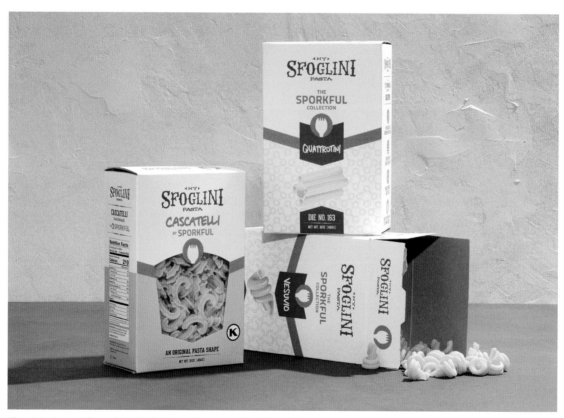

The original cascatelli, made by Sfoglini, is now in stores nationwide, and there are some store brands that make their own versions of the shape (which I've licensed to them). Quattrotini and vesuvio are in select stores, coming to more. All three are also available directly from Sfoglini.com.

What you'll find instead is my spin on a range of lesser-known Italian classics, alongside dishes like Kimchi Carbonara (page 125), Cacio e Pepe e Chili Crisp (page 69), Shrimp and Andouille Mac 'n' Cheese (page 180), Mexican Wedding Soup with Chipotle Turkey Albóndigas (page 168), Shells with Miso Butter and Scallions (page 42), and Keema Bolognese (page 160). These dishes reflect the way many Americans already use pasta at home—as a comforting, starchy base for the range of flavors and ingredients that infuse much of our other cooking.

Pasta is incredibly adaptable. As I'll argue in several essays throughout the book, the idea that Italy's iconic pasta dishes have always been done one way is incorrect, and the notion that Italians object whenever anyone tries to do anything different with them is overly simple. Pasta has evolved and continues to evolve all over the world, and I hope this book will become some small part of that ongoing evolution.

As you go through the recipes, I suspect some of them will feel familiar to you and some will feel different, regardless of what spices or ingredients you typically cook with. But I hope you'll find all of them incredibly delicious. (Every one passed my highly rigorous and scientific Can I Stop Eating It Test, which means I could not stop eating any of them.)

While cascatelli gets a starring role, there are thirty-four different pasta shapes featured in this book, including quattrotini and vesuvio—two obscure Italian shapes that I teamed up with Sfoglini to produce and launch in 2023—plus many other lesser-known favorites of mine. (I also provide more common substitutes for your convenience. You can search for recipes by pasta shape in the index.)

While people call me the "inventor" of cascatelli, the truth is that the shape represents more of

THE SLEEPER HITS OF THIS COOKBOOK

Friends keep asking me which recipes in here are my favorites, but of course I can't choose. I will, however, tell you the five dishes I'm naming my Sleeper Hits. They may not seem as novel or eye-catching as some others, but these are dishes I was still daydreaming about months after testing them and that I know I'll be making in my own home for years to come. They are:

TAGLIATELLE WITH PROSCIUTTO, NUTMEG, AND PARMESAN [PAGE 39]

CAVATELLI WITH ROASTED ARTICHOKES AND PRESERVED LEMON [PAGE 112]

SWORDFISH WITH SALSA VERDE SAGNE A PEZZI [PAGE 115]

TORTELLINI IN KIMCHI PARMESAN BRODO [PAGE 182]

RAW HEIRLOOM PUTTANESCA WITH FISH SAUCE AND CALABRIAN CHILI [PAGE 204]

an evolution. After all my research, I ended up combining the best elements of two of my favorite shapes—mafalde and bucatini. I was building on what came before, taking inspiration from those around me. I've done the same in this book, and have tried to credit my inspirations throughout.

There are many similarities between this project and cascatelli. There's been deliciousness and frustration. Becky and Emily, now thirteen and almost eleven, were eager taste testers, and at times Janie questioned whether it was all worth it, especially when I insisted on testing the Cavatelli with Roasted Artichokes and Preserved Lemon recipe on page 112 for the thirteenth time (not exaggerating).

I took another research trip, this time to Italy, to sample pasta dishes that are unknown even to many Italians. In Bari I learned to make spaghetti all'assassina, or "assassin's spaghetti," from chef Pietro Lonigro, the eighty-year-old who pioneered the dish more than a half century ago.

As with cascatelli, I agonized over small decisions, like whether to use Morton or Diamond Crystal kosher salt. (It matters because different salts have different levels of saltiness. I went with Diamond Crystal in all my recipe testing, so if you use a different salt, please adjust accordingly—more on this on page 7.)

As with cascatelli, it's taken three years to create this book, and I'm sharing the behind-the-scenes story of the process in more detail in a special *Sporkful* podcast series, complete with recordings of all the highs and lows, which I think will give you a new appreciation for how cookbooks are actually made. Through it all, I found myself motivated once again by a desire to prove that I might actually know what I'm talking about.

I'm incredibly proud of the result, and I can't wait for you to start cooking these recipes. I hope this book earns me another invitation into your home for dinner, and that you'll share pics with me when it does. Just don't tell me you made tomato sauce.

REALLY IMPORTANT STUFF TO KNOW BEFORE YOU START COOKING
ON CONVENIENCE AND DELICIOUSNESS

As a working parent myself, I know how it feels to frantically squeeze the preparation of a decent meal in between pickups, drop-offs, and my own attempts to actually make a living.

As a food-obsessed person who wants to wake up every morning giddy about what meals the day has in store, I also know how it feels to trudge into the kitchen staring down another plate of the same old, same old.

I've worked hard to create a book that addresses both of these feelings simultaneously. I tested every recipe in here in real-world conditions—with the kids wandering in and out of the kitchen whining about when dinner will be ready while I frantically text Janie, who's at the store, and ask her to pick up the one ingredient I forgot.

Most of these recipes can be made in less than an hour. There are a few projects, for the days when you have the time and desire. There are dishes for a crowd that you can make in advance in any season. And there are pastas you can whip up on a weeknight for your family, or just for yourself, to eat on the couch in your pajamas.

I've taken inspiration from a range of cuisines, so no matter what you typically cook at home, there will probably be some ingredients in here that you don't already have. I've tried to use many items in multiple dishes, so if you buy something for one recipe, you'll be able to use it in others.

On page 259 I've included lists of the recipes that fall into key categories:

- 45 minutes or less
- 5 ingredients or fewer (not including pantry staples)
- Make ahead
- Vegetarian

READ THIS: A MAKE-OR-BREAK WORD ABOUT SALT

Every recipe in this book was developed and tested using Diamond Crystal kosher salt, and yes, it really matters.

Did you know that some salts are much saltier than others? That's because there's wide variation in the size and shape of different salt crystals. Finer salts will be more tightly packed, and you'll get more granules in a teaspoon—meaning more actual salt. Also, some shapes of crystals have more surface area than others, so more of the salt lands on your tongue and you register it as saltier.

Here's why most recipes call for kosher salt:

1. It has a purer flavor, unlike sea salt (which tastes like the sea) and table salt (which has iodine, which can affect flavor).

2. Its larger, flakier granules are easier to control as you sprinkle them. Larger granules also means less salt per teaspoon, which allows you to use more of it—so you can spread it evenly throughout a dish. (It's very easy to accidentally use too much table salt because it's so fine. One errant pinch can throw off the whole enterprise.)

But even among kosher salts there's variation. I decided to go with Diamond Crystal over Morton kosher salt because I like the way the Diamond Crystal flakes feel in my fingertips when I sprinkle them. To me the Morton salt feels like the stuff you put on your driveway when it snows. (In her book *Salt Fat Acid Heat*, my friend Samin Nosrat also points out that Diamond Crystal dissolves much faster, and as she says, "The more quickly salt dissolves, the less likely you are to overseason a dish, thinking it needs more salt when actually the salt just needs more time to dissolve.")

That said, you can use Morton for any recipe in this book, but note that MORTON IS ALMOST TWICE AS SALTY. So if you're using Morton, cut the salt quantity in half, then add a pinch. And as always, taste before serving and if your reaction is, "Yeah, that's good" but not "Wow, I love this!" then you probably need to add more salt.

All that being said, I hope these recipes will inspire you to put in a little extra effort. Plan a day or two in advance, so you can get those couple of ingredients that may be new to you. Set aside the time to cook. I can honestly say that working on this book has forced me to do just that, and I'm so happy it did. It's made me a better cook and brought whole new levels of deliciousness into my home. Put in that bit of effort and I'm confident it'll do the same for you.

HOW TO BUY DRIED PASTA

Cascatelli is a very good pasta shape, but part of the reason it blew people's minds when it first came out is that many folks had never cooked with high-quality pasta made by a company like Sfoglini. Now I have parents telling me that their kids will only eat cascatelli! That's partly because it's a fun shape and they got into the story, but it's partly because even kids can taste the difference between ordinary pasta and the good stuff.

Ordinary pasta is bland, with a texture that's often rubbery instead of chewy. The really good stuff has a nutty flavor reminiscent of fresh bread and tends to be sturdier, giving you more margin for error when cooking, more toothsinkability when eating, and more durability if it sits in sauce for a while or even in the fridge overnight.

But to spot the difference in the store based only on the package, you need to look for certain clues about a pasta's quality . . .

BRONZE DIE VS. TEFLON DIE

More traditional pasta makers use a bronze die, which gives the pasta surface a chalky white, sandpaper-like texture, which grips the sauce. (As I said, the die is like

BLACK PEPPER WILL CHANGE YOUR LIFE IF YOU LET IT

For many years, whenever a recipe told me to add ¼ teaspoon or ½ teaspoon of black pepper, I'd think to myself, "That's such a small amount, I'm not going to bother to measure it because then I'll have to wash a measuring spoon. I'll just hold my pepper grinder over the bowl and crank it a few times and that'll be close enough."

Then I started working on this book and actually measuring how much pepper I was putting into recipes, and it turns out I have never in my life put enough pepper into anything.

When I went to Italy, I saw how they not only use lots of freshly ground pepper but they also sprinkle big chunks of cracked peppercorns on finished pasta dishes. These peppercorns are so fragrant, so earthy and full of flavor, that I spent several bites mourning all the underpeppered years of my life that I can't get back.

So please don't skimp on the pepper, and be sure to add cracked whole peppercorns wherever I ask you to, and even in a few places where I don't.

One tip: To save time you can grind ½ cup of peppercorns in a spice grinder and keep it in a bowl next to the salt on your counter. That makes it easy to grab a pinch, or dip a measuring spoon in, and it's still freshly ground and much better than store-bought ground pepper.

the mold for the shape.) When found alongside other key attributes below, the use of a bronze die can also indicate an overall commitment to quality from the manufacturer, because using a bronze die makes the process more expensive.

You see, when that sandpaper-like surface is created, small particles of pasta dust fly all over the factory. Being caught in a pasta dust storm may sound dreamy, but containing those particles and making sure they don't get into the machinery requires extra equipment (which costs money) and limits how much pasta you can crank out per hour. It's a slower process.

The alternative to bronze is Teflon. A Teflon die produces pasta with a smooth, slightly yellow surface, which is what you'll see on standard supermarket pastas. Machines that use Teflon dies can produce more pasta per hour without any concerns about dust, so it's more cost effective.

Pastas made with bronze dies tend to be better, but there are very good ones made with Teflon that you can find in most supermarkets. Among those, De Cecco is my favorite, and I would take it over any bronze die pasta that costs less, because as I'll explain, the bronze die is not the only sign of quality. When buying Teflon pastas, look for ones with a rich amber-yellow color, which tends to indicate better semolina that's been dried more slowly.

You'll be able to recognize bronze die pastas by their rough surface, which should be visible through the packaging (see photo). Brands that use bronze dies will also often market that feature on the label, sometimes with the Italian phrase *trafilata al bronzo*.

In recent years, as American consumers have become more educated about quality pasta, some of the biggest pasta brands in the world have launched new lines of bronze die pastas at lower prices. While their flavor and texture may not match the better bronze die pastas, they do have that rough, sauceable surface, and I'm excited to see so much improvement in the overall quality of the American supermarket pasta aisle!

SLOW-DRIED VS. FAST-DRIED

As I learned when I started talking with pasta producers to get cascatelli made, there's as much skill involved in drying pasta as there is in extruding it. When pasta is dried quickly, at higher temperatures, the gluten in the pasta dough stiffens more, trapping starch in its web. When the pasta is cooked, it's then harder for the starch to gelatinize, so the pasta loses some of its chewiness and instead turns rubbery—a

Mafalde, a shape that was a major inspiration for cascatelli, extruded from a bronze die (lower right) next to one made with Teflon

devastating blow to potential toothsinkability. Some brands will say "slow-dried" on their packaging. If not, you can infer a lot about the drying process by checking the other criteria on this list, including price. (Because slow-dried pasta takes more time to yield the same amount of product, it costs more to produce.)

COOKING TIME

One of the key determining factors of toothsinkability is the thickness of the pasta itself, and it can vary widely among different versions of the same shape. Giovanni Cannata, creator of the original cascatelli die, tells me the thickest rigatoni on the market is about 50 percent thicker than the thinnest.

A GRATE CHEESY NOTE ABOUT GRATED CHEESE

We're going to be using a lot of grated cheese in this book, mostly Parmesan and Pecorino. When they're produced in the Italian tradition and in certain approved regions, they're called Parmigiano-Reggiano and Pecorino Romano. While I'm not going to stop you from seeking out these high-quality, pricier cheeses labeled DOP, or protected designation of origin, for the purpose of these recipes, regular old Parmesan and Pecorino are just fine.

I use fairly high-quality store-bought pregrated cheese from an Italian market because I love the flavor and I'm too lazy to grate my own. (Grated is much finer than shredded.) At the very least I encourage you to buy your grated cheeses from the refrigerated section of the store and avoid the ones labeled "cheese product." More processed cheeses have their place—I'm a huge defender of American cheese and call for it in several recipes here—but the super-processed grated cheeses just don't have much flavor, and in many of these recipes that flavor is crucial.

That said, some of the Parmesan sold in containers at the grocery store will appear ground, or almost powdery, like granules as opposed to small oblong shreds. (It likely won't be labeled "ground" but it will *look* ground.) This is fine as long as it's real cheese! The volume will be about the same as (store-bought) grated, and it actually dissolves into sauces better, which is why we specifically recommend it in the carbonara recipes, as well as the Cacio e Uova on page 36. Still, regular grated will work in all cases.

So whenever I call for grated cheese, I'm referring to pregrated cheese. If you're grating the cheese yourself, use a Microplane or the small holes of a box grater and note that it comes out much fluffier than the store-bought stuff, so double the volume I call for in the recipe. (The big holes in the box grater are for shredding cheese, not grating it.)

Of course, when you look through the window on the package, you can't tell which one is 0.032 inches thick and which one is 0.048. But when you bite into it, you can FEEL the difference. And thicker, more toothsinkable pastas take longer to cook. (They also take longer to dry, which is why companies focused on keeping prices low tend to cut their shapes thinner.)

The other advantage to pastas with longer cook times is that they give you more margin for error in cooking. Being off by 30 seconds when the cook time is 12 minutes is less distressing than being off by 30 seconds with a cook time of 8 minutes. So look for brands with consistently longer cook times across various shapes—and if you're debating between two different versions of the same shape, use this as a tiebreaker.

PRICE

While doing R&D for cascatelli, I visited North Dakota State University's Durum Wheat Quality and Pasta Processing Laboratory, better known as the Pasta Lab. (North Dakota grows most of the durum wheat used in pasta made in America.) I met professors Frank Manthey and Elias Elias, two of the world's leading experts on durum wheat, which is milled into semolina flour for pasta. If you've eaten pasta in America, you've almost certainly eaten semolina they had a hand in developing.

Because most pasta is made with nothing more than semolina and water, the semolina is very important. Professor Manthey explained that it can be ground so it's especially coarse, or more powdery and fine. The powdery version is easier to work with on a mass scale, and it's cheaper, so that's what most big companies use. But it can compromise flavor.

Cascatelli rolling off the press at the Sfoglini factory

"The finer you grind, the more surface area is exposed" to air, he told me. "You start getting oxidation on the surface." That oxidation means many of the natural compounds that produce aroma escape long before they make it to your mouth. When you grind semolina more coarsely, on the other hand, it retains more of its natural flavor.

"If I was going to make the highest-quality pasta," Professor Manthey told me, "I would use a coarser grind."

While the difference may be microscopic to your eyes, it's massive on your tongue. But short of sampling a cooked pasta plain, to check for that flavor and aroma of fresh bread, there really is no way to gauge semolina quality in a pasta other than looking at the price and presuming that it correlates to the cost of ingredients.

Now, you may have noticed a pattern here. In every step of pasta production, the option that produces a better product also costs more.

Of course, you should buy and eat whatever pasta tastes good to you and fits within your budget. There are certainly good pastas out there for a couple bucks (like the aforementioned De Cecco), and when you're just trying to throw a meal together on a weekday night, don't break the bank. But I would encourage you to adjust your expectations of what really good pasta should cost. If you'll pay five dollars for a pound of ground beef, why not pay the same for a box of amazing pasta?

My favorite brands tend to sell in the five- to eight-dollar range. There are some that go for more, but I don't think they're worth it. (I'm looking at you, Benedetto Cavalieri.) My all-time favorite pasta companies are Rustichella d'Abruzzo, whose pastas are in some U.S. specialty stores and available online through Market Hall Foods, and the American company Sfoglini, who make many excellent pastas in addition to the original version of cascatelli and our other pasta shape collaborations, vesuvio and quattrotini.

PACKAGE SIZE

Most pasta sold in America comes in one-pound (16-ounce) packages, but the ones imported from Italy often come in a half kilo, which is 17.6 ounces. Almost every recipe in this book calls for one pound of pasta, but you'll be fine using a half kilo. (You could choose to nibble on a few plain cooked pieces to bring it closer to 16 ounces.) Italian companies sell certain bulky shapes in quarter kilos—8.8 ounces. If that's what you're buying, you'll need two packages.

HOW TO BUY GLUTEN-FREE PASTA

There have been great advances in gluten-free pasta technology in recent years, but these pastas are made in different ways, with a range of different substitutes for the gluten. To figure out which ones to look for when shopping, it's helpful to understand the science behind these products. Want to nerd out with me? Great!

Gluten is a protein found in wheat, barley, and rye. Because pasta is traditionally made from wheat, it's full of gluten, which plays a key role in pasta's texture. When you exert force on a mixture of flour and water—as with kneading or extruding it through a die to form a shape—the gluten in the flour changes, forming a microscopic network that gives dough its structure. Food scientists say this network is "viscoelastic" because it's kind of viscous (thick and oozy) and kind of elastic (stretchy).

The viscoelastic structure of gluten is responsible for the pasta's all-important toothsinkability. But researchers, especially in Italy, have figured out how to hack certain starches so they mimic that viscoelastic web, without gluten.

That being said, not all starches are created equal. Rice and corn work pretty well for gluten-free pasta, but the best method is to use starches from legumes like peas, lentils, and chickpeas, according to Dr. Alessandra Marti, a food science researcher at the University of Milan. That's because legumes are high in protein—and remember, gluten is a protein. So legumes not only provide starches that can be hacked to act like gluten, they also bring more protein to the table, which, while not the same protein, is a good substitute, especially if you need to eat gluten-free.

That's why I teamed up with the folks at Banza to make a gluten-free version of cascatelli—all Banza's pastas are made from chickpeas!

RED PEPPER FLAKES (OR: SPICINESS IS IN THE EYE OF THE SPICE-EATER)

Few aspects of writing this book have been more stressful than figuring out how hot to make the spicy dishes. Because when it comes to spiciness, one person's mild may be another person's five-alarm fiasco.

In most cases here, when I offer you a range for how much of the spicy ingredient(s) to add, the low end is what I consider mild to medium, and the high end is what I consider to be hot. If there is no range, that means I feel that the flavor that comes from the spicy components is really integral and it's probably in my medium to hot range. (I think I have a pretty high spice tolerance, at least for a person who didn't grow up eating hot foods.)

Once you've tried a couple of the spicier dishes, you'll figure out how your spice preferences match up to mine and be able to adjust future recipes accordingly.

As for red pepper flakes, even when I've tried buying fancy ones, to my taste they provide little more than a pesky, grating heat without much flavor.

That being said, I know many people like them, and if that includes you, knock yourself out. Many recipes in this book call for them, and you're always welcome to increase or decrease the quantity to your taste. But if you feel as I do, you're also welcome to leave them out entirely or replace them with chopped jarred pepperoncini, which contribute much more flavor in addition to spice.

HOW TO COOK DRIED PASTA

For most of the recipes in this book, if you simmer the sauce for an extra minute or forget a clove of garlic, you'll still have great results. But cooking dried pasta just right requires precision. If there's one lifelong skill that you acquire, or refine, as a result of reading this book, I hope this is it.

In most recipes here, I tell you to take the pasta out of the water 1 or 2 minutes before the low end of the cooking time listed on the box, because you'll finish cooking the pasta in the sauce. I've found

REALISTIC RECIPE TIMES

Did you know that often, when you see a time frame attached to a recipe, it does not include the prep? The clock only starts from the first instruction. I just learned this while working on this book. So if the ingredient list says, "6 carrots, peeled and roughly chopped," the minutes spent peeling and chopping aren't included in the time estimate. What a stupid system! All these years I thought I was just the world's slowest cook!

This book is different. I try to give you a realistic estimate for how long each recipe takes from start to finish, so you don't end up as I have so many times—embarking on a "45-minute" recipe when I have 46 minutes available, only to find out it actually takes more than an hour.

basing my instructions on the package's timing to be effective, but it's not perfect, because every brand of pasta calculates its cook times a little differently. (The imported Italian brands generally use times that yield firmer pasta—sometimes too firm for me.)

There is no one level of pasta doneness for all people. Some Italians think even al dente is overcooked—they prefer it al chiodo, or like a nail you'd use with a hammer. Over time you'll see what you like, figure out which brands work for you, and decide whether you should adjust the cook times in this book at all.

Most important, remember that pasta should be chewy to the point of being almost meaty. Sinking your teeth into it should feel extremely satisfying, like eating the perfect steak while laying your head on a cool pillow after a long day.

Here's how to do it:

1. **BUY GOOD PASTA.** See above!

2. **A WATCHED POT NEVER BOILS, BUT A COVERED ONE DOES.** Covering your pot while you heat the water helps it boil about 8 percent faster, according to America's Test Kitchen. If your water is boiling but you're not yet at the step in the recipe where you add the pasta, keep the pot covered and reduce the heat to low. When you're ready to cook the pasta, just crank it back up to high and it'll return to a boil quickly.

3. **PUT MORE SALT IN THE WATER THAN YOU THINK YOU NEED.** For a pound of pasta I generally recommend 4 quarts of water with 2 tablespoons of kosher salt. The salt seasons the pasta and the pasta water, which is often used at the end of a recipe to adjust the consistency of the sauce. The salt does not, however, have any material effect

THE PARSLEY IS (PROBABLY) DEAD, LONG LIVE THE PARSLEY

When I see a small amount of parsley on an ingredient list, I immediately get annoyed. My mind flashes forward to the moment when I'll find the remaining 90 percent of the bunch of parsley that I bought for the dish in the back of the fridge, brown and mushy, and throw it out.

But at the moment when I'm finishing the dish and I sprinkle on those bright green bits, I'm always glad I bought it, because it makes the food look so much fresher and more colorful. There is no easier cheat for improving the appearance of your food. You could sprinkle chopped parsley over McDonald's fries and you'd think you were at a five-star steakhouse.

So anytime you see ¼ cup chopped parsley in a recipe in this book, consider it optional, or add more so you can feel like you're doing something worthwhile. If the recipe calls for ½ cup or more, then it's doing more important work for the actual flavor, so keep it in. And remember that to keep your parsley (and any fresh herbs) fresh longer, trim the stems and wrap them in a damp paper towel, place the whole herb in a zip-top bag, gently press out as much air as possible, seal it, and keep it in the fridge. This will extend the parsley's life, but if you forget about it for long enough, it'll still meet the same sad fate.

---

on how long it takes the water to boil. As Bill Nye explained when I had him on *The Sporkful,* you'd have to add a TON of salt to noticeably change the boiling point. When you add salt to very hot water and it fizzes up, that is not actual boiling—it's the salt crystals creating something called nucleation sites, which is a term you are welcome to google.

4. STIR IT UP. This is key in the first few minutes to prevent the pasta from sticking together. It's even more vital with flat shapes like fettuccine and lasagna, which are most prone to fusing to each other.

5. NOTE THE COOK TIME ON THE BOX AND SET A TIMER. As I said, different brands calculate cook times differently, and everyone has their own preferred pasta doneness, so you need to monitor the process to get your ideal results. I typically set the timer for 2 minutes less than the lowest time on the box and begin checking then. (This info is less important for recipes in this book, where I'll tell you when to take the pasta out. It's more of a general principle or a tip to use if the recipes here aren't producing pasta cooked to your liking.)

6. RESERVE YOUR PASTA WATER. It's used in many recipes to get your sauce to the right consistency and adds more flavor than plain water. If like me you sometimes forget to do this, leave the measuring cup in the colander in the sink. Then when you go to drain the pasta, you'll be reminded. (But if you still forget, just use hot water. It'll be fine!) When reserving a large amount of pasta cooking water from the pot, use a ladle or a 1-cup liquid measuring cup to scoop it out and transfer it to a larger (4-cup) liquid measuring cup.

7. CHECK YOUR PASTA EARLY AND OFTEN. The obvious way to do this is to eat a piece, but you can also bite or cut a piece in half and look at the cross section. The bright white line in the center is the uncooked portion. For me the pasta is done when that line is faint but still visible. If the pasta tastes just right when you check it, then it is overcooked, because . . .

8. THE COOKING DOESN'T STOP WHEN THE BOILING DOES. When you drain pasta, its residual steam continues to cook it in the colander. When you transfer pasta from the pot to a hot pan full of sauce, it continues to cook. Even once the pasta has been put on the plate and served, it continues to soften. I've tried to take all this into account in these recipes.

9. ERR ON THE SIDE OF EARLY. It's always better to take your pasta out a little too soon and let it cook in the sauce for an extra minute or two. If the sauce gets too thick or dry, add a splash of reserved pasta water or, if you drained the pasta water, plain hot water. But if you overcook your pasta, there is no going back. All is lost. The only thing you can do at that point is slam your colander down, run to your bedroom, and cry into your pillow.

10. YOU CAN COOK PASTA IN ADVANCE! In many of the "Make Ahead" recipes in this book (see page 260), you'll pause the recipe before you cook the pasta, so the sauce is pretty much ready and all you do at the last minute is cook the pasta and combine it with the sauce. I believe this is the make-ahead option that will give you the best possible results. But I understand that we all have to balance quality and convenience, so you can choose to cook the pasta ahead of time and your dish will still be delicious. Just be sure to reserve 4 cups of pasta water and drain the pasta in a colander 1 minute sooner than instructed in the recipe. Spread it on a rimmed sheet pan to stop the cooking and keep it at room temperature for up to 3 hours, or cover and refrigerate if reserving it for longer. When you resume the recipe and combine the pasta and sauce over heat, just note that you may need to add a little extra pasta water to get the right consistency, and be sure to check the doneness of your pasta before serving. Also note that higher-quality pasta will hold up better when precooked.

11. TOSS WITH SAUCE AND KEEP IT SAUCY. Few images are more heartbreaking to me than a big bowl of plain pasta with a pile of red sauce glopped on top. Combining the pasta and the sauce in the pan fully coats the pasta (tubes don't fill themselves!), allows the pasta to absorb the flavors of the sauce, and gives you a chance to adjust the consistency of your sauce before serving. As noted above, the cooking process continues even after you take the pasta out of the pan, so when it's in the pan, you always want the sauce to be just a little looser and more watery than your ideal. As soon as it's served it will begin to "tighten up," and you want to take that into account.

THE BARE MINIMUM KITCHEN GEAR

I hate extraneous kitchen gadgets. I don't like clutter, and I don't really get excited about *things*. I do not need a lemon squeezer that looks like some kind of citrus torture device when I can squeeze lemons with my hands. Instead of crushing peppercorns with a mortar and pestle, I put them on a cutting board and grind them with the bottom of a pot.

But there are a few pieces of kitchen gear that are absolutely essential for this book:

A LARGE, HIGH-SIDED SKILLET: I recommend any 11- to 12-inch pan that holds at least 3 quarts and has sides at least 2½ inches high. A basic 12-inch frying pan with low, slanted sides will probably not be deep enough to hold a pound of pasta and everything else we'll be adding to it, especially when you start stirring it vigorously to bring the sauce together.

A MESH SPIDER (OR "ASIAN STRAINER," WHICH IS SIMILAR): This is basically a cross between a strainer and a giant spoon. It allows you to transfer short pastas directly from the cooking water to the pan where your sauce is waiting, which is something we'll be doing A LOT in this book. Make sure to get one that's at least 7 inches in diameter. An Asian strainer is typically made with wire instead of mesh, so it has a bigger "weave," meaning that very small pasta shapes may fall through the gaps a little, but it will work.

A MICROPLANE, RASP GRATER, OR BOX GRATER WITH A FINE GRATING SIDE: Grated means small bits, shredded is bigger pieces (like the cheese on a pizza). You can't use the big shredding side of a box grater for grating. We will be using a lot of citrus zest, and while it may seem like a small thing, it's often the ingredient that takes a dish to the next level.

A FOOD PROCESSOR OR BLENDER OR IMMERSION BLENDER: I actually made it through this entire cookbook without buying a proper food processor, although I did break down halfway through and invest in a fancy Breville immersion blender, which has an attachment that functions like a food processor.

Update: My mom bought me a lemon squeezer and it's actually pretty nice. It strains the seeds for you and squeezing it is very satisfying. But still, you don't NEED it.

PESTOS, PANGRATTATOS, AND THE JARRED TOMATO SAUCE DECISION TREE

1

E PESTOBUS UNUM: OUT OF ONE FORMULA, MANY PESTOS

I'm starting with pesto because it's a perfect example
of what I hope this book will do for pasta dishes
overall—take something you think you know, that
you probably like just fine, and show you that you
could be enjoying it in so many more ways.

THE PRESTO PESTO FORMULA

MAKES ABOUT 1½ CUPS (ENOUGH TO SAUCE 1 POUND OF PASTA) • TOTAL TIME: 15 MINUTES • DEVELOPED WITH REBECCAH MARSTERS

You're likely familiar with the classic Genovese pesto made with basil, pine nuts, a hard cheese like Parmesan, garlic, and olive oil. But *pesto* literally means "pounded" or "crushed," because this sauce is traditionally made in a mortar and pestle and pounded by hand. So it's really about the technique, not the ingredients. The truth is that with this formula, you can make an incredibly tasty pesto from almost any combination of herbs, nuts, and cheese.

Think of a pesto as having an herb or vegetable base that provides the dominant flavor and color. Most leafy herbs or baby greens will work, but if you want to add woody herbs like rosemary or thyme (which are more potent), choose a neutral-flavored green like parsley, spinach, or baby kale as the main component and start by adding a few teaspoons of leaves from the woody herb, increasing the amount until you're happy with the flavor.

Then there are the supporting ingredients, usually nuts and cheese, that add fat, flavor, salt, and more bulk. If there's a nut allergy in your household, you can substitute pumpkin or sunflower seeds, or nix them altogether and adjust the mixture with extra cheese and/or oil. To make a vegan pesto, just omit the cheese, though you may have to increase the salt and/or oil to make up for it.

Think of the next component as your flavor infusion: something small but mighty. Garlic, anchovies, Calabrian chilies, and so on. And finally you have the oil/fat. Extra-virgin olive oil is classic, but you can also use a combo of EVOO and a neutral oil like canola to temper the bitterness of extra-virgin, or all neutral oil for flavor combos like the cilantro and cotija one (see Suggested Pesto Variations, next page), where you want the other ingredients to take center stage. Any oil that's liquid at room temperature will work!

This formula has endless plug-ins and combinations, and even works with the classic Genovese ingredients. The bottom line is always to taste for seasoning and adjust the textures as necessary. To make any pasta and pesto dish more substantial, you can add a can of tuna, leftover roast chicken or veggies, tofu or seitan, or a soft-boiled egg or two.

For a slightly more elaborate but still simple and delicious pesto, see the Cascatelli with Spicy Broccoli Rabe Pesto on page 214. And you can use any pesto you like in the Pesto Ricotta Baked Cavatappi with Half Veggies on page 225!

½ cup coarsely chopped unsalted nuts (or whole pine nuts, see note)

4 cups (about 2½ ounces) lightly packed fresh herb leaves (see note)

1¼ teaspoons kosher salt

1 garlic clove, coarsely chopped

¾ cup oil

½ cup (2 ounces) finely grated, ground, or crumbled cheese

(continued)

1. If using raw nuts, toast the nuts in a small, dry skillet over medium-low heat until fragrant and darkened a shade, 4 to 6 minutes, stirring and shaking the pan often and decreasing the heat to low if they start to brown too quickly.

2. Transfer the nuts to the bowl of a food processor and let cool slightly. Add the herbs, salt, and garlic and pulse until finely chopped, 8 to 10 one-second pulses, scraping down the bowl once or twice. With the processor running, slowly drizzle in the oil and process until a loose paste forms. Add the cheese and pulse until just combined, 3 to 5 pulses. (If you want a thinner pesto, add more oil or drizzle in some water or citrus juice. If your pesto seems too loose, add more nuts or herbs.)

3. Use immediately or transfer to an airtight container and refrigerate for up to 2 weeks or freeze for up to 3 months.

NUTS NOTE: We developed these pesto recipes using raw, unsalted nuts; if using salted nuts, reduce the salt to 1 teaspoon and taste the finished sauce before adding more. If using roasted nuts, skip the toasting step.

HERBS NOTE: Make sure your herbs are well cleaned and dried. For soft herbs like cilantro, it's okay to include the tender stems in there too.

SUGGESTED PESTO VARIATIONS

PRIMARY GREENS: basil, cilantro, parsley, baby arugula, baby kale, baby spinach

OPTIONAL SECONDARY GREENS: rosemary, thyme, sage, tarragon, dill, marjoram, oregano (these are more potent so start small and work up in quantity)

NUTS: pine nuts, walnuts, almonds, pecans, hazelnuts, cashews, peanuts

CHEESES: Parmesan, Pecorino, Asiago, Manchego, cotija, aged Gouda, Piave

ADD-INS: lemon or lime zest, smoked paprika, cumin, cayenne, black pepper, capers, olives, anchovies

So for instance . . .

CILANTRO + CASHEWS + COTIJA + LIME ZEST

PARSLEY + WALNUTS + PECORINO + PAPRIKA

ARUGULA + ALMONDS + ASIAGO + LEMON ZEST

FUN WITH PANGRATTATOS

Sporkful listeners know that I've long been obsessed with the phenomenon sensory scientists call dynamic contrast. It's the combination of multiple, contrasting textures in the same bite, and while you may not have thought much about it, you probably love it. (There's a reason why all the best candy bars combine crispy, crunchy, chewy, and gooey.)

Many great pasta dishes in Italy, as well as so many Asian noodle dishes, bring together a variety of textures to create dynamic contrast. But sadly, the most common pasta dishes in America didn't get the memo.

In the Carby and Crispy chapter, we'll dive deep into a variety of ways to incorporate more dynamic contrast into your pasta game. And throughout this book we'll turn to one of the easiest and most effective methods: adding a pangrattato.

Traditionally pangrattato is a simple combination of toasted bread crumbs and seasonings, which you can sprinkle over pasta to add crisp and flavor. We're going to use some nontraditional ingredients, but the pangrattatos will be doing the same work they've always done. (The correct plural is *pangrattati*, but I've taken some linguistic liberties for clarity. Did you know that one strand of spaghetti is a spaghetto?)

A few tips . . .

- Cooled pangrattato can be kept in an airtight container or zip-top bag at room temperature for up to 2 days or frozen for up to 3 months, except for a couple noted below that shouldn't be frozen. To use frozen pangrattato, just let it come to room temperature, then taste for crispiness. If it needs a boost, toast it in a dry skillet over medium heat for a minute.

- Each of these recipes makes about ½ cup of pangrattato, which is enough to top 4 to 6 servings of pasta, except the Ritz cracker one, which makes quite a bit more because it's used to top an entire casserole dish. Feel free to double these recipes and freeze the leftovers as noted so you always have some handy.

Lemon-Herb

Lime–Corn Nut

Garlic Bread

Za'atar

Furikake

Ritz Cracker
and Chive

Everything

LIME–CORN NUT PANGRATTATO

MAKES 1 CUP • TOTAL TIME: 10 MINUTES • DEVELOPED WITH ASHA LOUPY

You'll find this in the Shrimp with Ají Amarillo, Olives, and Lime–Corn Nut Pangrattato on page 71, and as an optional addition to the Thai Curry Quattrotini Mac 'n' Cheese on page 58. You can also just eat it by the spoonful. If you're making this right before the Shrimp with Ají Amarillo and Olives, just use the same pan you'll build the pasta sauce in, wiping it out with a paper towel after making the pangrattato.

½ cup corn nuts (see note)

1 tablespoon unsalted butter

2 teaspoons finely grated lime zest

Kosher salt, as needed

1. Place the corn nuts in a zip-top bag, press out the air, and seal. Use a rolling pin to crush the corn nuts into a medium coarse powder about the size of large bread crumbs.

2. Melt the butter in a medium skillet over medium-low heat. Add the corn nuts and cook, stirring and shaking the pan often, until fragrant and darkened a shade, 3 to 5 minutes. Transfer to a heatproof bowl or container, stir in the lime zest, and let cool completely. When cool, taste and season with salt, if necessary.

NOTE: Any corn nuts will work, but try to find quality ones that taste good right out of the bag; these crunchy snacks are also sometimes called giant Inca (or Inka) corn or Quicos. Since they can vary widely in sodium content from brand to brand, make sure to taste your pangrattato before adding any salt in step 2.

FURIKAKE PANGRATTATO

MAKES ½ CUP • TOTAL TIME: 10 MINUTES • DEVELOPED WITH JAMES PARK

You'll use this in the Pan-Seared Mushroom Quattrotini with Furikake Pangrattato recipe on page 97. It's also amazing on top of a fried egg with rice.

1 tablespoon extra-virgin olive oil

½ cup panko bread crumbs

4 teaspoons furikake

Kosher salt, as needed (see note)

Heat the oil in a medium skillet over medium-low heat. Add the panko and cook, stirring and shaking the pan often, until the crumbs are spotty brown and have darkened to the color of peanut butter, 3 to 5 minutes. Remove the pan from the heat and stir in the furikake, then transfer to a heatproof bowl or container and let cool completely. When cool, taste and season with salt, if necessary.

NOTE: The sodium content will vary depending on the brand of furikake you use. Your pangrattato may not need any extra seasoning, but it's always good to taste the cooled mixture; it should taste flavorful but not explicitly salty.

RITZ CRACKER AND CHIVE PANGRATTATO

MAKES ABOUT 2 CUPS • TOTAL TIME: 10 MINUTES

Find this in the Cauliflower and Beer Cheese Mac with Ritz Cracker and Chive Pangrattato on page 238. It's also really nice on salad in lieu of croutons, especially with Caesar or ranch dressing.

3 tablespoons unsalted butter

1 full sleeve Ritz crackers (32 crackers), crumbled but not crushed

½ cup minced fresh chives

Melt the butter in a large skillet over medium-low heat. Add the crackers and cook, stirring and shaking the pan often, until darkened a shade, 3 to 5 minutes. Transfer to a heatproof bowl or container, stir in the chives, and let cool completely. (If freezing the pangrattato, wait to add the chives until you're ready to serve.)

ZA'ATAR PANGRATTATO

MAKES ½ CUP • TOTAL TIME: 10 MINUTES • DEVELOPED WITH ASHA LOUPY

We use this in the Zucchini and Feta Pasta with Za'atar Pangrattato on page 99. It's also great on plain yogurt.

1 tablespoon extra-virgin olive oil

½ cup panko bread crumbs

5 teaspoons za'atar

¼ teaspoon kosher salt

Heat the oil in a medium skillet over medium-low heat. Add the panko and cook, stirring and shaking the pan often, until the crumbs are spotty brown and have darkened to the color of peanut butter, 3 to 5 minutes. Transfer to a heatproof bowl or container, stir in the za'atar and the salt, and let cool completely.

GARLIC BREAD PANGRATTATO

MAKES ½ CUP • TOTAL TIME: 10 MINUTES • DEVELOPED WITH KATIE LEAIRD

For this spin on a red-sauce joint staple, we found that fresh garlic alone tasted a bit harsh, but a combination of fresh and dried garlic gave us that "garlic bread" flavor we know and love. This one's in the Orecchiette with Merguez and Broccoli Rabe on page 83. It's also a perfect addition to plain old pasta with tomato sauce, as noted in the Jarred Tomato Sauce Decision Tree on page 30.

1 tablespoon unsalted butter

½ cup panko bread crumbs

1 garlic clove, minced

¼ teaspoon garlic powder

¼ teaspoon kosher salt

Melt the butter in a medium skillet over medium-low heat. Add the panko and cook, stirring and shaking the pan often, until the butter has been absorbed and the crumbs are just starting to turn golden, about 2 minutes. Stir in the garlic, garlic powder, and salt and cook, stirring often, until the crumbs are spotty brown and have darkened to the color of peanut butter, 2 to 4 minutes. Transfer to a heatproof bowl or container and let cool completely.

LEMON-HERB PANGRATTATO

MAKES ½ CUP • TOTAL TIME: 10 MINUTES • DEVELOPED WITH LINDA PASHMAN

You'll find this one in the Shrimp Scampi with Lemon-Herb Pangrattato on page 105. You'll also love it on cooked green beans tossed with olive oil and lemon juice.

1 tablespoon extra-virgin olive oil

½ cup panko bread crumbs

3 tablespoons finely chopped fresh leafy herbs (see note)

2 teaspoons finely grated lemon zest

¼ teaspoon kosher salt

Heat the oil in a medium skillet over medium-low heat. Add the panko and cook, stirring and shaking the pan often, until the crumbs are spotty brown and have darkened to the color of peanut butter, 3 to 5 minutes. Transfer to a heatproof bowl or container, stir in the herbs, lemon zest, and salt, and let cool completely. (The cooled pangrattato can be kept in an airtight container or zip-top bag at room temperature for up to 2 days like the others, but because it includes fresh herbs, this one shouldn't be frozen.)

NOTE: For the herbs in this pangrattato, use leafy ones such as parsley, mint, basil, cilantro, dill, or tarragon, or any mix of those. Avoid woody herbs like rosemary. And make sure your herb leaves are well dried before chopping so they don't make the bread crumbs soggy.

EVERYTHING PANGRATTATO

MAKES ½ CUP • TOTAL TIME: 10 MINUTES • DEVELOPED WITH KATIE LEAIRD

No recipe in the book uses this pangrattato because I think it's best on plain buttered pasta, which makes it like a toasted bagel with butter, but pasta. Use salted butter and add a sprinkle of grated Parmesan if you want. Get really freaky and add some lox. This will work well with any thick and hearty pasta shape!

1 tablespoon unsalted butter

½ cup panko bread crumbs

4 teaspoons everything bagel seasoning

1 garlic clove, minced

¼ teaspoon kosher salt

Melt the butter in a medium skillet over medium-low heat. Add the panko and cook, stirring and shaking the pan often, until the butter has been absorbed and the crumbs are just starting to turn golden, about 2 minutes. Stir in the everything bagel seasoning, garlic, and salt and cook, stirring often, until the crumbs are spotty brown and have darkened to the color of peanut butter, 2 to 4 minutes. Transfer to a heatproof bowl or container and let cool completely.

THE JARRED TOMATO SAUCE DECISION TREE

Early in the process of testing recipes for this book, I tried a sirloin ragù—steak slow-cooked in a tomato sauce with white wine. It was delicious. But it wasn't exciting. It tasted like a slightly better version of something I've eaten many times before. And it took several hours to make it.

I decided then that if there would be any tomato sauce recipes in this book, they had to be either ridiculously easy or truly different from any tomato sauce I'd had before.

Welcome to the ridiculously easy section.

Why make your own tomato sauce when there are so many high-quality jarred varieties available today? I like Carbone, Rao's, Victoria, and Rustichella d'Abruzzo, but I'll buy other good ones when they're on sale. There really is no wrong jarred tomato sauce—use whichever one tastes good to you!

For me, though, my jarred tomato sauce must meet two criteria:

1. The first ingredient should be TOMATOES. This may be written as "whole peeled tomatoes" or "crushed tomatoes" or "Italian plum tomatoes" or "San Marzano tomatoes" or "oven-roasted tomatoes" or whatever, as long as the first ingredient is not "tomato puree." Tomato puree is typically tomato paste mixed with water, and often preservatives—it's the sauce equivalent of juice made from concentrate instead of fresh squeezed. It's okay if some tomato puree is included, but I want a sauce that starts with actual tomatoes.

2. There should be no added sugar. This is not for health reasons—it's because if the manufacturer is using good tomatoes, they won't need to add sugar.

The two most common varieties of jarred tomato sauce are marinara and tomato and basil. Traditionally, marinara is cooked quickly with fewer ingredients. It's smoother, thinner, and has more of a fresh tomato flavor. Tomato and basil has more Italian seasonings and is cooked for longer, making it thicker and chunkier, more like a Sunday gravy. Many brands also make roasted garlic and spicy arrabbiata tomato sauces.

Except in the case of Spaghetti all'Assassina (page 86), where I specifically call for marinara, you can use whatever kind you like.

Here are more tips for using jarred tomato sauces and the Jarred Tomato Sauce Decision Tree:

- Please do not put the pasta on the plate, glop the sauce on top, and call it a day! Always toss the sauce with the pasta in the pot or pan to fully coat it. (More on this on page 16.) To reduce dirty dishes I drain the pasta a minute early, pour the jarred sauce into the same pot I used to cook the pasta, add the pasta back into that same pot with the sauce, toss to coat, and simmer for a minute.

- If you finish a jar of sauce, after you dump it into the pot, put a bit of water in the jar, close the lid, and shake it up to release the residual sauce. Dump that in the pot too. Any excess liquid will cook off when you simmer.

- With all the ideas in the Jarred Tomato Sauce Decision Tree, you're welcome to mix and match. Add ricotta *and* chili crisp. Add eggplant *and* sambal oelek. You pretty much can't go wrong.

- Almost every sauce addition in the JTSDT is also called for in at least one other recipe in this book. So if you don't already have one of these ingredients and you go out and buy it, you'll get plenty of use from it.

- The only time it's acceptable not to sauce your pasta in advance is when you're having a Tomato Sauce Dipping Party. To do that, make several of the sauces in the JTSDT, set them out in bowls, and serve with plain pasta. Fork individual pieces of pasta and dip them in different sauces to try them all. That's how my kids and I tested the options in the JTSDT!

HOW DO YOU WANT TO IMPROVE

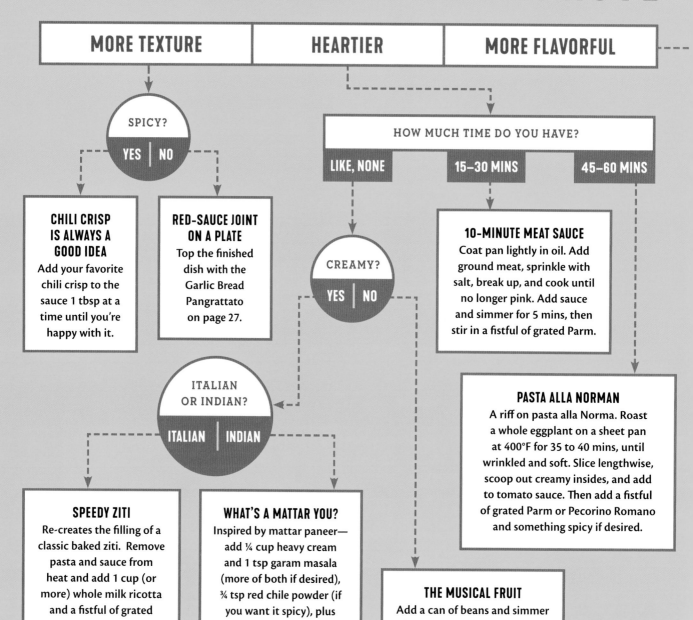

MORE TEXTURE | **HEARTIER** | **MORE FLAVORFUL**

SPICY?
YES | **NO**

CHILI CRISP IS ALWAYS A GOOD IDEA
Add your favorite chili crisp to the sauce 1 tbsp at a time until you're happy with it.

RED-SAUCE JOINT ON A PLATE
Top the finished dish with the Garlic Bread Pangrattato on page 27.

HOW MUCH TIME DO YOU HAVE?
LIKE, NONE | **15–30 MINS** | **45–60 MINS**

CREAMY?
YES | **NO**

10-MINUTE MEAT SAUCE
Coat pan lightly in oil. Add ground meat, sprinkle with salt, break up, and cook until no longer pink. Add sauce and simmer for 5 mins, then stir in a fistful of grated Parm.

PASTA ALLA NORMAN
A riff on pasta alla Norma. Roast a whole eggplant on a sheet pan at 400°F for 35 to 40 mins, until wrinkled and soft. Slice lengthwise, scoop out creamy insides, and add to tomato sauce. Then add a fistful of grated Parm or Pecorino Romano and something spicy if desired.

ITALIAN OR INDIAN?
ITALIAN | **INDIAN**

SPEEDY ZITI
Re-creates the filling of a classic baked ziti. Remove pasta and sauce from heat and add 1 cup (or more) whole milk ricotta and a fistful of grated Parm, plus a dollop of chili crisp (if desired).

WHAT'S A MATTAR YOU?
Inspired by mattar paneer—add ¼ cup heavy cream and 1 tsp garam masala (more of both if desired), ¾ tsp red chile powder (if you want it spicy), plus frozen peas and cubed paneer or halloumi cheese.

THE MUSICAL FRUIT
Add a can of beans and simmer for 5 mins, partially mashing the beans into the sauce.

YOUR JAR* OF TOMATO SAUCE?

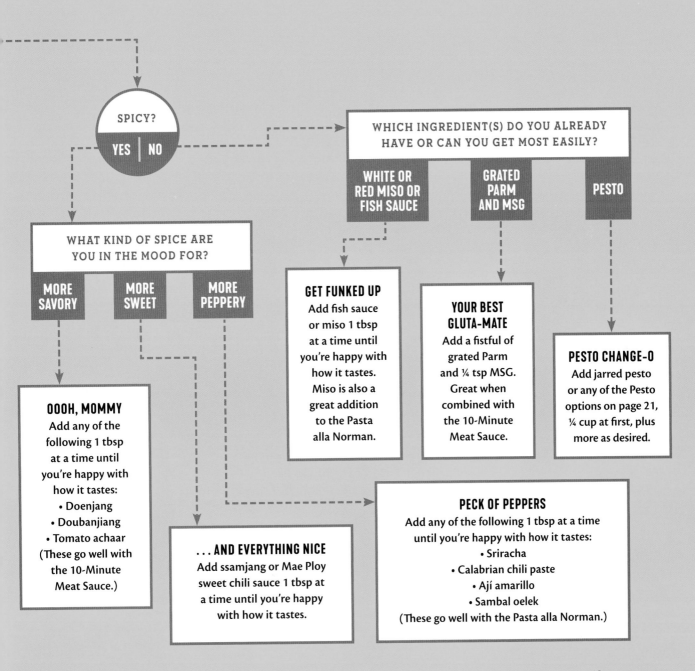

SPICY?
YES | NO

WHICH INGREDIENT(S) DO YOU ALREADY HAVE OR CAN YOU GET MOST EASILY?

WHITE OR RED MISO OR FISH SAUCE

GRATED PARM AND MSG

PESTO

WHAT KIND OF SPICE ARE YOU IN THE MOOD FOR?

MORE SAVORY

MORE SWEET

MORE PEPPERY

GET FUNKED UP
Add fish sauce or miso 1 tbsp at a time until you're happy with how it tastes. Miso is also a great addition to the Pasta alla Norman.

YOUR BEST GLUTA-MATE
Add a fistful of grated Parm and ¼ tsp MSG. Great when combined with the 10-Minute Meat Sauce.

PESTO CHANGE-O
Add jarred pesto or any of the Pesto options on page 21, ¼ cup at first, plus more as desired.

OOOH, MOMMY
Add any of the following 1 tbsp at a time until you're happy with how it tastes:
• Doenjang
• Doubanjiang
• Tomato achaar
(These go well with the 10-Minute Meat Sauce.)

. . . AND EVERYTHING NICE
Add ssamjang or Mae Ploy sweet chili sauce 1 tbsp at a time until you're happy with how it tastes.

PECK OF PEPPERS
Add any of the following 1 tbsp at a time until you're happy with how it tastes:
• Sriracha
• Calabrian chili paste
• Ají amarillo
• Sambal oelek
(These go well with the Pasta alla Norman.)

*Measurements are based on using a whole 24- to 25-oz jar of sauce. For any combo where you're adding significant unseasoned volume to the sauce (like an eggplant or a pound of ground meat), also add salt to taste.

CLASSIC COMFORT: HUGS ON A PLATE

MAPO TOFU CASCATELLI (PAGE 165)

2

CACIO E UOVA (PASTA WITH PECORINO AND EGGS)

SERVES 4 TO 6 • TOTAL TIME: 35 MINUTES • DEVELOPED WITH KATIE LEAIRD

Italians may not love this comparison, but to me this is kind of the world's easiest mac 'n' cheese, just lighter and silkier. *Cacio e uova* translates to "cheese and egg," and that's pretty much all you need. (You could think of this as a meatless carbonara—it's the same dish without guanciale.)

Traditionally this would be sprinkled with parsley at the end, which adds some nice color but not much flavor in such a small amount. And then you have 99 percent of a bunch of parsley dying in your fridge. After testing a lot of options, I settled on replacing parsley with scallions, which provide not just color but also more flavor and a light crunch. But if you want to whip this up right now and you don't have scallions, you can leave them out. And if you want to add some extra punch, sprinkle the finished dish with whatever hot sauce you like on eggs—I go for Cholula or Crystal.

Here this dish is paired with vesuvio, a relatively new shape in the pasta canon, named for its resemblance to Mount Vesuvius, the volcano that buried Pompeii. As I said, in 2023 I teamed up with Sfoglini, who make the original cascatelli, to launch vesuvio and quattrotini, two obscure Italian shapes that I love that are difficult to find in America. (More on quattrotini on page 58.) Vesuvio is incredibly sauceable, and its rolls and folds are pure joy in your mouth. There are a couple of other versions of it out there (some of which came along after stores saw the response to our vesuvio), but you can get ours at select stores or through Sfoglini's website!

2 tablespoons kosher salt

4 large eggs

1 cup (4 ounces) store-bought grated Pecorino Romano (see tip)

½ teaspoon freshly ground black pepper

3 tablespoons unsalted butter

1 tablespoon extra-virgin olive oil

2 garlic cloves, minced

1 pound vesuvio pasta (a.k.a. girelle or trottole; or use cavatappi or rigatoni)

2 scallions, thinly sliced

Hot sauce, for serving (optional)

(continued)

1. Bring 4 quarts of water and the salt to a boil in a large pot.

2. In a large heatproof bowl, vigorously whisk the eggs, Pecorino, and pepper until smooth and consistent; set aside.

3. Heat the butter and oil in a large, high-sided skillet over medium heat. When the butter has melted, add the garlic and cook, stirring, until fragrant but not browned, about 1 minute; remove the pan from the heat.

4. Add the pasta to the boiling water and cook for 1 minute less than the low end of the package instructions. Use a mesh spider to transfer the pasta directly to the skillet. Place the skillet over medium-high heat and cook, stirring constantly, until any water has evaporated and the pasta is evenly coated with the garlic-butter mixture, about 2 minutes (see cooking tip).

5. Immediately transfer the pasta to the bowl with the egg mixture, scraping out the skillet. Add 1 tablespoon of the pasta cooking water and use a rubber spatula to rapidly toss everything together until the pasta is well coated, the cheese is dissolved, and the sauce is smooth and glossy. (There should be extra sauce pooling in the bowl at first, but it should all cling to the pasta after 1 to 2 minutes of stirring. If the sauce looks too thick after 1 minute, add more pasta water 1 tablespoon at a time until silky smooth and creamy.)

6. Transfer the pasta to a serving dish or individual bowls, sprinkle with the scallions, and serve with hot sauce, if desired.

CHEESE TIP: Do your best to find cheese that's grated as finely as possible, which will dissolve into the egg mixture more readily—as long as it's still real cheese (see page 10).

COOKING TIP: I know cooking the pasta in the garlic butter seems like an annoying extra step that dirties another pan, but it's really crucial to getting the pasta nice and hot so it warms the egg and cheese and transforms the mixture into a silky smooth, melty sauce.

TAGLIATELLE WITH PROSCIUTTO, NUTMEG, AND PARMESAN

SERVES 4 TO 6 • TOTAL TIME: 35 MINUTES • DEVELOPED WITH ASHA LOUPY

For years I've heard people describe prosciutto and Parmigiano-Reggiano as "nutty." And when I ate them on their own and concentrated really hard, I thought to myself, "Okay, yeah, I guess that's nutty." Then I went to a restaurant in New York called Via Carota, where I had pasta with prosciutto, Parmigiano-Reggiano, and *nutmeg* and I was like, "THIS IS SO NUTTY AND I LOVE IT!" That tiny bit of fresh nutmeg accentuated the nuttiness in the prosciutto and Parmigiano in a way I had never experienced.

Asha has had that same dish at Via Carota and feels the same way about it, so this is our version of it, and it's one of my five Sleeper Hits of the cookbook (see page 5). When I eat it, I feel like I'm frolicking in a meadow with the pigs and cows that supplied the bounty of prosciutto and Parm, all of us feeding each other acorns and clover, collapsing in a heap of laughter, then lying on our backs and looking for shapes in the clouds. That's how good this is.

Note that this dish comes together quickly, so be sure to have all your ingredients prepped before you start.

2 tablespoons kosher salt

1 pound (or two 8.8-ounce packages) dried egg fettuccine (see note)

¼ cup heavy cream

¾ teaspoon freshly grated nutmeg (or ¼ teaspoon ground nutmeg), plus more for serving

½ teaspoon ground white pepper (or black pepper)

8 tablespoons (1 stick) cold unsalted butter, cut into 8 pieces

1½ cups (6 ounces) finely grated Parmesan

6 to 9 ounces sliced prosciutto, at room temperature (12 to 18 very thin slices, see note)

1. Bring 4 quarts of water and the salt to a boil in a large pot. Add the pasta and cook for 2 minutes less than the low end of the package instructions. Reserve 3 cups of the pasta cooking water (see tip on page 16), then drain the pasta. Immediately return the pasta to the pot, cover, and set aside.

2. In a large, high-sided skillet, combine 1½ cups of the pasta water, the cream, nutmeg, and pepper and bring to a simmer over medium-high heat, then reduce the heat to medium. Whisking constantly, add the butter 1 tablespoon at a time, waiting for each tablespoon to melt before adding the next. Continue whisking and slowly sprinkle in the Parmesan until fully incorporated.

(continued)

3. Pour the sauce into the pot with the pasta, scraping out the skillet. Place the pot over medium heat, add ½ cup of the pasta water, and stir vigorously until the sauce is glossy and clings to the pasta, 2 to 4 minutes. (If the sauce seems too thick, add more pasta water 2 tablespoons at a time until it's the consistency of heavy cream and pools slightly in the bottom of the pot.)

4. Transfer the pasta to a serving platter or individual plates, drape with the prosciutto, sprinkle lightly with nutmeg, and serve.

PASTA NOTE: If you can't find egg fettuccine, use extra-wide egg noodles instead of regular fettuccine. Tagliatelle and fettuccine are almost identical and for our purposes interchangeable. Fettuccine tends to be a tiny bit thicker and narrower, tagliatelle is a bit thinner and wider, but the difference is more regional. In northern Italy they call long, flat, medium-width pasta tagliatelle, while in central and southern Italy they call it fettuccine. Because most Italian immigrants to America came from the south, it's usually called fettuccine in the U.S. This recipe calls for fettuccine because it's easier to find, but the title references tagliatelle because your friends will be more impressed when you tell them you're making tagliatelle.

PROSCIUTTO NOTE: You want 3 slices of prosciutto per serving to make the dish feel substantial without overpowering it, so the amount you'll need to buy depends on how many servings you're shooting for. That said, nobody's ever complained about having leftover prosciutto.

SHELLS WITH MISO BUTTER AND SCALLIONS

SERVES 4 TO 6 • TOTAL TIME: 35 MINUTES • DEVELOPED WITH ASHA LOUPY

If you just came home from a long, stressful day at work and you're starving, and all you want is to sit on the couch and eat something incredibly delicious and comforting and watch bad TV, this is the dish for you. And if, on top of all that, you have kids to feed? This is STILL the dish for you. The sauce is layered with rich, roasty nuttiness from toasted sesame oil, sweet, umami-rich miso, and lots of allium goodness from scallions and garlic, all made silky and spoonable with butter and Parmesan.

My daughter Becky's review: "Amazing. Buh-ro. No words except for *amazing* and *bro*. I didn't know something this amazing could actually exist."

2 tablespoons kosher salt

1 pound small or medium pasta shells

8 tablespoons (1 stick) cold unsalted butter, cut into 8 pieces

1 tablespoon toasted sesame oil

2 garlic cloves, thinly sliced

12 scallions, thinly sliced, dark green parts separated

¼ cup white or yellow miso (see tip)

1 cup (4 ounces) finely grated Parmesan

Roasted sesame seeds, for serving (see tip)

1. Bring 4 quarts of water and the salt to a boil in a large pot. Add the pasta and cook for 2 minutes less than the low end of the package instructions. Reserve 2½ cups of the pasta cooking water (see tip on page 16), then drain the pasta. Immediately return the pasta to the pot, cover, and set aside.

2. Heat 3 tablespoons of the butter and the sesame oil in a large, high-sided skillet over medium heat. When the butter has melted, add the garlic and cook, stirring, until the edges just begin to color, 30 to 60 seconds. Add the white and light green parts of the scallions and cook, stirring occasionally, until the scallions have softened, 4 to 6 minutes. Add 1½ cups of the pasta water, all but ⅓ cup of the dark green parts of the scallions, and the miso and stir until the miso dissolves, about 30 seconds. Whisking constantly, add the remaining 5 tablespoons of butter 1 tablespoon at a time, waiting for each tablespoon to melt before adding the next.

(continued)

3. Pour the miso butter mixture into the pot with the pasta, scraping out the skillet. Place the pot over medium heat, add another ½ cup of the pasta water, and stir vigorously until the sauce is glossy and clings to the pasta, 2 to 4 minutes. (If the sauce seems too thick, add more pasta water 2 tablespoons at a time until it's the consistency of heavy cream and pools slightly at the bottom of the pot. If it looks too thin, continue stirring over the heat until the sauce clings to and coats the pasta.) Remove the pot from the heat and stir in the Parmesan until fully incorporated.

4. Transfer the pasta to a serving bowl or individual bowls, sprinkle generously with sesame seeds and the reserved scallion greens, and serve.

MISO TIP: If you don't frequently cook with miso, don't worry about ending up with a lot after making this. It's fermented, so it lasts a very long time, and is a key ingredient in countless delicious dishes, including the Linguine with Miso Clam Sauce on page 138. It's also a perfect way to take a plain old jar of tomato sauce to the next level, as detailed in the Jarred Tomato Sauce Decision Tree on page 30!

SESAME SEEDS TIP: Most sesame seeds at the grocery store are raw, but you can find packaged roasted sesame seeds at your local Asian market or H Mart, or online. Or you can toast raw sesame seeds in a dry pan over medium heat until golden, shaking the pan often and watching carefully to make sure they don't burn, 2 to 4 minutes.

MAC 'N' DAL

SERVES 4 • TOTAL TIME: 1 HOUR (PLUS 30 MINUTES TO 6 HOURS LENTIL SOAKING TIME) • DEVELOPED WITH ASHA LOUPY

Dal on pasta with a spoonful of achaar is one of my go-to weekday work-from-home lunches, but I admit I usually do it with packaged dal from the supermarket. Of course, doing it from scratch gives you even more depth of flavor—and it's very easy.

Dal refers to a subset of dried legumes as well as the dish that's made with those legumes. Recipes vary from region to region and even family to family, and you can make this recipe with any kind of dal you like, though cooking times may vary with larger varieties. Asha and I love a saucy mix of masoor and toor dal that's rich in turmeric, coriander, and cumin, with a touch of heat from Kashmiri chilies and herbaceous flavor from curry leaves. The red lentils (masoor dal) bring an earthy sweetness and cook up quickly, while the split pigeon peas (toor dal) offer a silky, almost buttery flavor and a luscious mouthfeel. We pair the dal with lumache ("snails"), a big, ridged elbow macaroni that's pinched at one end, which gives it a pouch-like quality, making it more sauceable than macaroni.

⅔ cup red lentils (masoor dal)

⅓ cup split yellow pigeon peas (toor dal, see note)

4 cups (32 ounces) vegetable stock

2½ teaspoons plus 2 tablespoons kosher salt

1½ teaspoons ground turmeric

2 teaspoons coriander seeds (see note)

1 teaspoon cumin seeds (see note)

3 tablespoons ghee (or a neutral oil, like canola)

12 to 16 fresh curry leaves, patted dry if necessary

1 teaspoon black mustard seeds

2 shallots, finely chopped

½ teaspoon Kashmiri chili powder (see note)

2 plum tomatoes, cored and diced

8 ounces lumache pasta (a.k.a. pipe rigate; or use ditalini or medium shells)

1 cup roughly chopped cilantro leaves and tender stems, plus more for serving

2 tablespoons freshly squeezed lemon juice

Plain whole-milk yogurt, for serving

Tomato or garlic achaar, for serving (optional; see note on page 53)

1. Rinse the lentils and peas in a fine-mesh strainer until the water runs clear. To cook on the stovetop, soak the rinsed lentils and peas in cold water for at least 30 minutes and up to 6 hours, then drain and transfer to a medium saucepan along with the stock, 1½ teaspoons of the salt, and 1 teaspoon of the turmeric. Bring to a boil over high heat, then reduce the heat to medium-low, cover, and cook, stirring

(continued)

DAL NOTE: In place of the yellow pigeon peas you can use split yellow peas—just note they'll likely make the dal thicker. Use hot water or reserved pasta water to thin the dal to your desired consistency.

KASHMIRI CHILI POWDER NOTE: This spice really shines in this dish, and you can also use it for the Keema Bolognese on page 160. But hot paprika will do in a pinch.

CUMIN AND CORIANDER NOTE: Whole spices are preferable because they're more potent and offer textural pops of spice, but you can also use ground cumin and coriander, reducing to ¾ teaspoon ground cumin and 1 teaspoon ground coriander. If you don't have a mortar and pestle or spice grinder, you can put the seeds on a cutting board and use the bottom edge of a small pot to grind them.

occasionally, until the lentils are cooked through and starting to fall apart, 30 to 40 minutes; it's okay if not all of the liquid has been absorbed. (To use a pressure cooker, transfer the rinsed lentils and peas to an electric pressure cooker—like an Instant Pot—along with the stock, 1½ teaspoons of the salt, and 1 teaspoon of the turmeric. Cook on high pressure for 20 minutes and allow to naturally release for 10 minutes. Release the pressure and keep warm.)

2. Meanwhile, bring 3 quarts of water and 2 tablespoons of the salt to a boil in a pot.

3. Use a spice grinder or mortar and pestle to pulse or pound the coriander and cumin seeds until very coarsely ground (see note).

4. Heat the ghee in a Dutch oven or large pot over medium heat until shimmering. Add the curry leaves, mustard seeds, and crushed coriander-cumin mixture and cook, stirring often, until fragrant and the coriander and cumin turn a shade darker, 30 to 45 seconds. Add the shallots and cook, stirring often, until golden around the edges, 4 to 7 minutes. Add the chili powder and remaining ½ teaspoon of turmeric and cook, stirring, for 30 seconds. Stir in 1½ cups of water, the tomatoes, and the remaining 1 teaspoon of salt. Increase the heat to medium-high and bring to a simmer, then cover and cook, stirring occasionally, until the tomatoes start to break down, 4 to 7 minutes. Stir in the cooked lentil mixture and any residual cooking liquid, cover, and reduce the heat to medium-low. (The sauce can be made ahead and refrigerated for up to 3 days or frozen for up to 2 months. Reheat before proceeding with step 5 and note that it may tighten up quite a bit, so will need to be thinned with some pasta cooking water before serving.)

5. Add the pasta to the boiling water (remember, it's only half the package!) and cook for 1 minute less than the low end of the package instructions. Reserve 1 cup of the pasta cooking water, then drain the pasta, shaking off the excess water, and immediately transfer it to the pot with the lentil mixture. Increase the heat to medium-high and cook, stirring often, until the pasta is firm and meaty (al dente), 2 to 4 minutes. (If necessary, add the reserved pasta water 2 tablespoons at a time to loosen the sauce to your desired consistency.)

6. Remove the pot from the heat and stir in the cilantro and lemon juice, then transfer the pasta and dal to a serving bowl or individual bowls. Dollop with yogurt, sprinkle with more cilantro, add a spoonful of achaar, if desired, and serve.

GREEN FETTUCCINE WITH CHORIZO VERDE

SERVES 5 OR 6 • TOTAL TIME: 1 HOUR 30 MINUTES • DEVELOPED WITH ASHA LOUPY

My friend José Ralat is the taco editor at *Texas Monthly*. (Yes that's a job, and no I don't expect him to vacate it anytime soon. But if you need to know where to get tacos anywhere in Texas, he's your guy.) When I told José about the concept of this cookbook, his first question was, "Are you going to include green spaghetti?"

As he explained, green spaghetti (or espagueti verde) is a dish found along the Texas-Mexico border that typically includes roasted poblano peppers, cilantro, crema, and sometimes cream cheese. While it's traditionally vegetarian, here we're bulking it up with a homemade green chorizo, and pairing it with egg fettuccine, which we think holds a meat sauce better than spaghetti and has a flavor that comes through very nicely. The sauce gets a little extra acidity—balancing the richness of the meat—from roasted tomatillos and a hearty squeeze of lime juice. The end result is bright and luscious, with a kiss of heat.

4 poblano peppers

5 medium tomatillos (8 to 10 ounces), dry leafy husks removed

2 jalapeño peppers

5 garlic cloves, unpeeled

Cooking spray

1½ cups finely chopped fresh cilantro leaves and tender stems, plus more for serving

1 cup Mexican crema (see note)

¾ cup chicken stock

3 scallions, cut into 1-inch pieces

3½ teaspoons plus 2 tablespoons kosher salt

1 pound ground pork (or beef or turkey)

2 teaspoons finely grated lime zest and 2 tablespoons freshly squeezed lime juice, plus lime wedges for serving

1 tablespoon ground cumin

2 teaspoons dried oregano (good-quality Mexican or Sicilian if possible)

2 teaspoons garlic powder

2 teaspoons ground coriander

Canola or other neutral oil, as needed (if using turkey)

1 pound (or two 8.8-ounce packages) egg fettuccine (or regular fettuccine or pappardelle)

Crumbled cotija cheese, for serving (see note)

1. Place an oven rack 4 to 5 inches from the broiler element and heat the broiler to high. Spread the poblanos, tomatillos, jalapeños, and garlic on a rimmed sheet pan and spray with cooking spray on all sides until lightly coated. Broil, flipping halfway through, until the pepper skins char and blister and the tomatillos soften

(continued)

and slump, 10 to 20 minutes. (If the garlic skins start to darken too quickly, remove at about 6 minutes.) Transfer the poblanos, jalapeños, and garlic to a medium bowl, cover with plastic wrap or a large plate, and let steam for 15 minutes (the poblanos will eventually look totally collapsed and wrinkly). Transfer the tomatillos to a blender.

2. Working with 1 pepper at a time, rub the thin film of charred skin off the poblanos and jalapeños, then remove the stems and seeds, discarding everything but the flesh. (You may want to wear gloves for this step as the capsaicin in the chiles can irritate skin. Leave the jalapeño seeds in if you want extra spice.) Peel the garlic, discarding the skins. Add the garlic, 3 of the poblanos, and 1 of the jalapeños to the blender with the tomatillos, along with ¾ cup of the cilantro, the crema, stock, scallions, and 1½ teaspoons of the salt. Blend until smooth, about 30 seconds.

3. Finely chop the remaining poblano and jalapeño and transfer them to a medium bowl. Add the pork, lime zest, cumin, oregano, garlic powder, coriander, the remaining ¾ cup of cilantro, and 2 teaspoons of the salt and use your hands to mix until just combined.

4. Bring 4 quarts of water and the remaining 2 tablespoons of salt to a boil in a large pot.

5. Meanwhile, heat a large, high-sided skillet over medium-high heat. (If subbing in turkey, add a glug of oil.) Add the meat mixture, breaking it into large pieces with a spoon and spreading it out in the pan, and cook undisturbed until it starts to brown on one side, 6 to 9 minutes. Stir, breaking the meat into small crumbles, and continue to cook until no longer pink, about 5 more minutes. Reduce the heat to medium, add the pureed pepper mixture, and cook until the sauce is heated through and thickens slightly, 2 to 4 minutes. Cover and reduce the heat to low. (At this point the sauce can sit, covered and off the heat, for up to 2 hours. Warm over low heat before proceeding with the recipe. If making ahead, refrigerate the meat mixture until ready to proceed.)

6. Add the pasta to the boiling water and cook for 2 minutes less than the low end of the package instructions. Use tongs to transfer the pasta directly to the skillet and set it over high heat. Stir until the sauce clings to the pasta, 2 to 4 minutes. (If the sauce seems too thick, add pasta cooking water 2 tablespoons at a time until it's the consistency of heavy cream and pools slightly in the bottom of the pan.)

7. Remove the pan from the heat and stir in the lime juice. Transfer the pasta to a serving dish or individual bowls, sprinkle with cotija and cilantro, and serve with lime wedges.

CASARECCE ALLA VODKA WITH TOMATO ACHAAR

SERVES 4 TO 6 • TOTAL TIME: 40 MINUTES • DEVELOPED WITH ASHA LOUPY

I was already adding Brooklyn Delhi's tomato achaar to tomato sauce, so when I saw them share a vodka sauce with their achaar on Instagram, I knew I had to team up with Asha to create our own version. I'm pairing it with casarecce, one of my favorite short shapes, which are flat rectangles that have been rolled up onto themselves from different directions, producing folds, crevices, and twists that are perfect for holding sauce. It's one of the few machine-made shapes that tends to vary slightly from one piece to the next, which contributes to dynamic contrast, the aforementioned technical term for multiple textures coming together in the same bite. That being said, because this sauce has high viscosity and low chunk factor (terms discussed in more detail in my rant on page 154), almost any shape will work. Make a pot, cozy up on the couch, and enjoy!

2 tablespoons kosher salt

4 tablespoons (½ stick) unsalted butter

8 to 12 fresh curry leaves, patted dry if necessary (optional; see note)

1 teaspoon black mustard seeds (optional; see note)

2 large shallots or 1 small yellow onion, finely chopped

4 garlic cloves, minced

2 teaspoons ground cumin

1 cup (or one 9-ounce jar) tomato achaar (see note)

¼ cup tomato paste

1 cup heavy cream

¼ cup vodka

Pinch of MSG (optional)

1 pound casarecce pasta (or strozzapreti, gemelli, campanelle, or rigatoni)

½ cup (2 ounces) finely grated Parmesan, plus more for serving

1. Bring 4 quarts of water and the salt to a boil in a large pot.

2. Melt the butter in a large, high-sided skillet over medium heat. Add the curry leaves and mustard seeds, if using, and cook until the seeds start to sputter and the leaves turn bright green, about 1 minute. Add the shallots and cook until translucent, 4 to 6 minutes, stirring occasionally. Add the garlic and cumin and cook, stirring, until fragrant, about 1 minute. Add the achaar and tomato paste and cook, stirring occasionally, until the mixture darkens and starts to fry around the edges, 2 to 4 minutes. Carefully stir in the cream, vodka, and MSG, if using, bring to a simmer, and cook until the sauce thickens and a spoon leaves a trail in the bottom of the pan when the sauce is stirred, 1 to 3 minutes.

(continued)

3. Cover and remove the pan from the heat. (At this point the sauce can sit, covered, for up to 2 hours. Warm over low heat before proceeding with the recipe.)

4. Add the pasta to the boiling water and cook for 2 minutes less than the low end of the package instructions. Use a mesh spider to transfer the pasta directly to the skillet and place the skillet over medium-high heat. Add ¾ cup of the pasta water and cook, stirring constantly, until the sauce clings to the pasta but still pools at the bottom of the pot, 3 to 5 minutes. (It should look a little too soupy at this point but will thicken when you add the cheese. If the sauce seems too thick, add more pasta water 2 tablespoons at a time until the sauce loosens to the consistency of heavy cream.)

5. Remove the pan from the heat and stir in the Parmesan. Transfer the pasta to a serving dish or individual bowls, sprinkle with more Parmesan, and serve.

CURRY LEAVES AND MUSTARD SEEDS NOTE: You can order curry leaves and mustard seeds online or find them at South Asian markets or spice shops. While you don't need them, I do love the flavor they add. (The curry leaves are also a key component of the Spaghettoni alla Tadka on page 63.) If you leave both out, add the shallots to the butter as soon as it melts and proceed with the recipe as written.

ACHAAR NOTE: Achaar, also known as Indian pickle, is a savory, spicy-sweet relish that I love with pizza, eggs, the Mac 'n' Dal on page 45, as an addition to jarred tomato sauce (page 33), and on almost anything else I might ever want to shove in my face. My friend Chitra Agrawal's company Brooklyn Delhi makes the aforementioned fantastic tomato achaar that's available online and in stores across the country (including Whole Foods), and this recipe is designed to use one full jar of it. You can find other brands of tomato achaar online and at South Asian markets, as well as at some other supermarkets.

WHEN FOOD CULTURES—AND PEOPLE— MERGE

How does an Indian condiment end up in an Italian pasta sauce?

"South Asians in diaspora have a lot of pasta recipes," Khushbu Shah, cookbook author and restaurant editor at *Food & Wine*, told me when I started working on this project. "It's just the natural evolution of Indian cooking, given how common pasta is in American households, restaurants, and grocery stores."

Speaking more broadly, I think this is the natural evolution of many foods. As people migrate around the world—by choice, out of necessity, or because they were forced—they bring their recipes and ingredients with them, and take inspiration from the foods they find in their new homelands. It works in the other direction too—the foods that come with a newer group inspire those who are already there. (That process has certainly inspired me—I cook and eat a much wider range of flavors and cuisines than I grew up eating.) This mashing up happens organically over time in kitchens everywhere, as chefs and home cooks alike create new combinations. Sometimes it's very intentional, other times we're just trying to get dinner on the table using whatever we have in the pantry.

Eventually, some ingredients and dishes cross into the mainstream, some evolve, and others are lost to trends or convenience or the preferences of the majority. Bagels, which my Jewish ancestors brought to America, are now everywhere. Pickled herring? Not so much. At times I feel disappointed that many bagels today are fluffy rolls that happen to have holes in the middle, instead of the crusty, chewy breads they were originally. But I also take pride in this Jewish contribution to "American" food, and I get excited when I see interesting new ideas in bagels, at least when they come from knowledgeable people who care about the craft of bagel making. (A few examples: Shelsky's in Brooklyn, who incorporate a sourdough starter in their dough for a hint of tang; Benchwarmers Bagels in Raleigh, NC, who make a za'atar bagel; and Call Your Mother in Washington, DC, who do a maple salt and pepper, which sounds like the bagel cinnamon raisin wishes it was.)

So when food cultures merge, the results can be delicious and thrilling. But the process is imperfect. Some nuance is often lost. And there are pitfalls, less so for home cooks who can really do whatever they want, more so for chefs and those of us in food media who may be perceived as experts, or representatives of a culture's food. In my years working on *The Sporkful,* I've seen plenty of people who learn about cuisines that are not their own, treat them with care, and credit their sources of inspiration. I've also seen people thoughtlessly glop trends together, acting as if they've invented a concept from whole cloth. (Naturally I'm doing my best to take my cues from the former.)

Even when food cultures are brought together thoughtfully, it's important to acknowledge that there remains a double standard. I talked with Professor Krishnendu Ray of the NYU Nutrition and Food Studies Department on *The Sporkful* a few years ago. He said in the restaurant world and food media, white people (like me) tend to get more leeway to play with other cuisines, while people of color are more often expected to cook the food that matches their skin tone.

We see a double standard at play in the grocery store as well. Foods associated with many Americans of color continue to be placed in the international or "ethnic" aisle of the grocery store, which effectively means they're categorized as "not American." This contributes to a perception that the people associated with these foods are also not fully American, no matter how long they've been here. Meanwhile, foods that came from Europe are readily accepted as part of American cuisine. (There's no German aisle where you find the hot dogs.) This despite the fact that, as Professor Robert Ku of Binghamton University told me on *The Sporkful,* wonton soup has been in America much longer than hot dogs. So maybe we should all be eating wonton soup on the Fourth of July!

Point is, while some of the combinations in this book may be new to some people, these types of mash-ups have been happening in kitchens across America for years—and they're increasingly making their way into restaurants, as anyone who's eaten the malai rigatoni or tandoori spaghetti at the Indian sports bar Pijja Palace in L.A. can attest.

All this is part of the ongoing evolution of pasta, a centuries-old process that continues not only in America but also in Italy. For more on this see "Carbonara, Italy's Hot New Pasta Trend" on page 128.

SSAMJANG AGLIO OLIO

SERVES 4 TO 6 • TOTAL TIME: 40 MINUTES • DEVELOPED WITH JAMES PARK

Aglio e olio is about as simple a dish as you'll find in Italy—it literally means "garlic and oil." In Rome they add crushed red pepper and refer to it in Roman dialect: ajo ojo e peperoncino. In this version of the dish we get that spice, and much more, from ssamjang.

A thick, savory bean paste made with gochujang, doenjang, and toasted sesame oil, ssamjang is a delicious flavor bomb. (We like Sempio brand or Chung Jung One Sunchang Seasoned Soybean Paste.) It plays a vital role in Korean barbecue to create the perfect lettuce ssam—a Korean term for a wrap—along with grilled meat, and makes for a great addition to jarred tomato sauce. Here this mildly spicy and salty Korean condiment transforms a classic pasta dish into something familiar yet special.

This dish benefits from some crunch, but the type is up to you. If you want max crunch, and to push this more in the direction of an Asian noodle dish, top it with crushed peanuts at the end. If you want to further emphasize the aglio, top it with fried garlic. To do that, reduce the garlic in the main recipe to 10 cloves (5 each minced and sliced in step 2) and thinly slice a separate 6 cloves. Heat ¼ cup of neutral oil in a medium skillet over medium heat until shimmering, add the 6 separate cloves of sliced garlic, and cook, stirring often, until golden brown. Transfer to a plate lined with paper towels and let cool, then sprinkle on the finished dish. (You can use the leftover garlic-infused oil in any vinaigrette.)

2 tablespoons kosher salt

14 garlic cloves, peeled

⅓ cup extra-virgin olive oil

⅓ cup ssamjang

½ teaspoon red pepper flakes, plus more for serving (optional)

1 pound mafalde (a.k.a. mafaldine or riccia; or use bucatini, fettuccine, or spaghetti)

½ cup roasted unsalted peanuts, crushed (or 6 fried garlic cloves, see above)

1. Bring 4 quarts of water and the salt to a boil in a large pot.

2. Mince 7 of the garlic cloves and set aside; thinly slice the remaining 7 garlic cloves. Heat the oil in a large, high-sided skillet over medium-low heat until shimmering. Add the sliced garlic and cook, stirring often, until just golden around the edges, 2 to 4 minutes. Carefully add the ssamjang and red pepper flakes, if using, and cook, stirring constantly, until the sizzling subsides and the mixture is fragrant and evenly combined, 1 to 2 minutes; remove the pan from the heat. (At this point the sauce can sit, covered, for up to 2 hours.)

3. Add the pasta to the boiling water and cook for 2 minutes less than the low end of the package instructions. Reserve 2 cups of the pasta cooking water, then drain the pasta. Immediately return the pasta to the pot, cover, and set aside. Add 1 cup of the pasta water to the skillet along with the reserved minced garlic, set over medium-high heat, and simmer, stirring occasionally and scraping up any browned bits from the bottom of the pan, until slightly thickened and the spoon leaves a trail in the bottom of the pan when the sauce is stirred, 5 to 7 minutes. Add the pasta to the skillet along with another ¾ cup of the pasta water and toss over the heat until the sauce is no longer watery and just coats the pasta, 2 to 4 minutes. (If the sauce seems too thick, add more pasta water 2 tablespoons at a time until the sauce loosens but still clings to the pasta.)

4. Transfer the pasta to a serving dish or individual bowls, top with crushed peanuts or fried garlic, and serve with more red pepper flakes, if desired.

THAI CURRY QUATTROTINI MAC 'N' CHEESE

SERVES 4 TO 6 • TOTAL TIME: 35 MINUTES • DEVELOPED WITH IRENE YOO

I am a strong proponent of finding deliciousness alongside convenience in the form of jarred and canned foods. So when Irene Yoo told me that her husband has long incorporated jarred curry into boxed mac 'n' cheese, I was like, "Yes please!" We call for Thai green curry, which tends to be more herbaceous because of the inclusion of basil and coriander, but you can use Thai red curry, which is typically spicier, with a slightly more peppery flavor.

    I'm pairing this with quattrotini, the other obscure Italian shape, along with vesuvio, that Sfoglini and I launched in 2023, also available in select stores or through Sfoglini's website. It's a variation on a shape called cinque buchi ("five holes"), which is only made in Sicily, only during carnival. (When I was in Italy, I couldn't find a single Italian on the mainland who had heard of it.) I added ridges to the outside to increase sauceability and changed the name to make it easier to pronounce and remember for English speakers. When it comes to sauceability, this shape is a beast.

2 tablespoons kosher salt

Lime–Corn Nut Pangrattato (page 25; optional)

1 pound quattrotini (or vesuvio, cascatelli, or rigatoni)

4 tablespoons (½ stick) unsalted butter

5 tablespoons all-purpose flour

One 4-ounce jar Thai green (or red) curry paste

4 cups (32 ounces) whole milk

12 ounces American cheese, shredded (3 cups; see tip)

1 cup (4 ounces) finely grated Parmesan

1. Bring 4 quarts of water and the salt to a boil in a large pot.

2. Make the pangrattato, if using, and set aside.

3. Add the pasta to the boiling water and cook until just al dente (the low end of the package instructions). Reserve 1 cup of the pasta cooking water, then drain the pasta. Immediately return the pasta to the pot, cover, and set aside.

4. Melt the butter in a large, heavy-bottomed saucepan over medium heat. Whisk in the flour until no lumps remain, then cook, whisking constantly, for 1 minute. Whisk in the curry paste, then very slowly whisk in the milk until smooth. Bring to a simmer and cook, whisking often and scraping the corners of the pan, until thickened enough to coat the back of a spoon, 3 to 5 minutes.

TIP: You can buy a block of American cheese at the deli counter of your supermarket and shred it using the big holes of a box grater, or buy sliced American cheese singles and tear them into small pieces with your hands.

5. Remove the pan from the heat and add the American cheese a handful at a time, whisking thoroughly to incorporate between each addition, until the sauce is completely smooth. Slowly sprinkle in the Parmesan and whisk until melted.

6. Add the sauce to the pasta in the pot along with ½ cup of the pasta water and stir until evenly coated. (If necessary, add more pasta water 2 tablespoons at a time until the sauce is creamy and loose but clings to the pasta.)

7. Transfer to a serving dish or individual bowls, sprinkle with the pangrattato, if using, and serve.

CAMPANELLE WITH SQUASH, WALNUTS, AND SAGE BROWN BUTTER

SERVES 4 TO 6 • TOTAL TIME: 1 HOUR • DEVELOPED WITH ASHA LOUPY

Peanut butter and jelly, broccoli and Cheddar, cookies and cream—some combinations are classics for a reason. Winter squash and sage is one of those pairings. The hearty earthiness of the herb complements the sweetness of the squash, making the duo tastier than the sum of its parts. (We're using delicata squash because you don't have to peel it.) Here the sauce gets some extra richness and roasty-toasty flavor from brown butter and walnuts, a bit of freshness from parsley, and a hit of brightness and tang to balance everything out courtesy of both lemon juice and zest.

2 tablespoons plus 2¼ teaspoons kosher salt

1½ pounds delicata squash (2 to 3 squash), stemmed, halved lengthwise, seeded, and cut into ½-inch slices

3 tablespoons extra-virgin olive oil

2 teaspoons finely chopped fresh rosemary

½ teaspoon freshly ground black pepper

½ cup raw walnut halves (or pine nuts, hazelnuts, or pecans)

8 tablespoons (1 stick) unsalted butter

14 to 16 sage leaves

2 garlic cloves, finely grated

½ teaspoon red pepper flakes (optional)

½ cup chopped fresh parsley

2 teaspoons finely grated lemon zest, plus ¼ cup freshly squeezed lemon juice

1 pound campanelle pasta (a.k.a. gigli or trumpets; or use gemelli or cascatelli)

½ cup (2 ounces) finely grated Parmesan, plus more for serving

1. Heat the oven to 425°F.

2. Bring 4 quarts of water and 2 tablespoons of the salt to a boil in a large pot.

3. In a large bowl, toss the squash with the oil, rosemary, 1¼ teaspoons of the salt, and the black pepper until evenly coated. Transfer to a rimmed sheet pan and spread into a single layer. Roast until tender and deeply golden on the bottom, 18 to 24 minutes. (At this point the squash can sit, covered loosely with aluminum foil, for up to 2 hours.)

(continued)

4. Use a mortar and pestle to pound the walnuts and remaining 1 teaspoon of salt into a coarse powder. (Alternatively, combine the walnuts and salt in a zip-top plastic bag, seal, and use a rolling pin or the smooth side of a meat mallet to crush into a coarse powder.)

5. Melt the butter in a large, high-sided skillet over medium heat. When the butter starts to foam, add the sage and cook, stirring occasionally, until the foam subsides and golden brown particles start to form, 2 to 4 minutes. Reduce the heat to medium-low, add the walnut mixture, garlic, and red pepper flakes, if using, and cook, stirring occasionally, until the sauce turns a shade darker and very fragrant, 1 to 3 minutes. (Don't worry if the sauce looks cracked and dry at this point.)

6. Remove the pan from the heat and stir in ¼ cup of the parsley and the lemon zest and juice. (At this point the sauce can sit, covered, for up to 2 hours.)

7. Add the pasta to the boiling water and cook for 1 minute less than the low end of the package instructions. Use a mesh spider to transfer the pasta directly to the skillet and return to medium heat. Add ¾ cup of the pasta cooking water and the Parmesan and toss until the sauce coats the pasta but still pools slightly in the bottom of the pan, 2 to 4 minutes. (If the sauce doesn't pool at all after 2 minutes, add more pasta water 2 tablespoons at a time to loosen.) Add the squash and stir gently until heated through, then remove the pan from the heat and stir in the remaining ¼ cup of parsley.

8. Transfer the pasta to a serving dish or individual bowls and serve with more Parmesan.

SPAGHETTONI ALLA TADKA

SERVES 4 TO 6 • TOTAL TIME: 35 MINUTES • DEVELOPED WITH ASHA LOUPY

As my friends at the Indian pantry staple company Brooklyn Delhi explain, tadka is the technique of tempering or blooming spices (and sometimes herbs, chilies, ginger, onions, or garlic) in hot fat and adding them to a dish. (It's also the name of the infused fat that results from the process.) In different regions of India it may be called vagarne, oggarane, chaunk, or baghaar. The process intensifies the flavor of the spices while infusing their flavor into the oil. Tadka is traditionally used in dal, curries, salads, rice dishes, and chutneys, but it's also great on pizza, mixed with butter and drizzled on popcorn, or . . . can you guess where this is going? Yes . . . ON PASTA.

All the ingredients in this dish can be found online or at any South Asian market. For the smoked chili flakes here I love Diaspora Co.'s Sirarakhong Chillies. If you can't find any smoked chili flakes, Aleppo pepper is a good stand-in, and regular crushed red pepper flakes will work in a pinch. As for the curry leaves, I don't know how to describe how they taste—I just know that they are one of my favorite flavors and aromas in the world.

Finally, the pasta shape referenced here is not a typo. Spaghettoni is thicker than, and superior to, spaghetti, and really shines with this thin, light sauce. For more on this shape, see my rant on page 151.

This recipe moves quickly once you start, so be sure to have everything prepped in advance.

2 tablespoons plus ¾ teaspoon kosher salt

½ cup extra-virgin olive oil

20 fresh curry leaves, patted dry if necessary

5 garlic cloves, thinly sliced

2 teaspoons black mustard seeds

2 teaspoons cumin seeds

¾ teaspoon nigella seeds (a.k.a. nigella sativa or kalonji)

¾ teaspoon smoked chili flakes (see above)

1 pound spaghettoni (a.k.a. "thick spaghetti"; or use regular spaghetti)

Lime wedges, for serving

1. Bring 4 quarts of water and 2 tablespoons of the salt to a boil in a large pot.

2. Line a plate with a layer of paper towels. Heat the oil in a large, high-sided skillet over medium heat until just shimmering. Add a curry leaf to the oil; if the oil begins to pop and sputter, add the remaining curry leaves and fry until bright spotty green, 30 to 45 seconds. (If the first curry leaf does not begin to fry right away, leave it in the pan and continue heating the oil until it sizzles and pops.) Use a slotted spoon to transfer the curry leaves to the prepared plate.

(continued)

3. Add the garlic to the skillet and cook, stirring, until just starting to color around the edges, about 1 minute. Add the mustard seeds, cumin seeds, nigella seeds, and chili flakes and cook until the garlic is evenly golden and the seeds are fragrant, about 1 minute; remove the pan from the heat. (At this point the sauce can sit, covered, for up to 2 hours.)

4. Add the pasta to the boiling water and cook for 2 minutes less than the low end of the package instructions. Use tongs to transfer the pasta directly to the skillet and set over high heat. Add ¾ cup of the pasta cooking water and the remaining ¾ teaspoon of salt and cook, stirring vigorously and continuously and using the tongs to turn the pasta over several times, until the sauce just clings to the pasta, 2 to 4 minutes. Remove the pan from the heat and stir in half of the curry leaves.

5. Transfer the pasta to a serving dish or individual bowls, top with the remaining curry leaves, and serve with lime wedges.

CARBY AND CRISPY: ADVENTURES IN TEXTURE

3

CACIO E PEPE E CHILI CRISP

SERVES 4 TO 6 • TOTAL TIME: 35 MINUTES • DEVELOPED WITH JAMES PARK

I knew from the beginning this book would include multiple recipes with chili crisp, so I knew I wanted to work with my old friend James Park—a former *Sporkful* intern turned recipe developer, social media star, and author of a whole book about chili crisp, entitled *Chili Crisp: 50+ Recipes to Satisfy Your Spicy, Crunchy, Garlicky Cravings*. There are many chili crisps out there, but James says they all include three basic components that can be combined in infinite ways.

"There's an oil, there's a chili, and there's flavoring," he told me. "If you're using peanut oil versus mustard oil, it's a different base. And the pepper flakes: Are you using gochugaru? Are you using Sichuan peppercorns? Are you using Aleppo pepper? So that alone can be chili crisp. But the exciting part also comes in the flavoring. Are you adding soy sauce? Are you not adding soy sauce? Are you adding MSG? Are you adding fried garlic? Are you adding fried shallots? There are literally so many ingredients that change the flavor. You can create whatever chili crisps your heart desires."

For all the chili crisp recipes in this book we call for Lao Gan Ma, a Chinese brand that's one of the best known. It has a high proportion of crisps—pepper flakes and soybeans in this case—and less oil. But you can substitute any kind you like, just note that different versions vary in spice levels, so taste before you add the full amount. For less heat with loads of fried garlic crunch, try KariKari or S&B Chili Oil with Crunchy Garlic. Fly By Jing's is a bit saucier and leans into the numbing Sichuan peppercorn spice I love. I have two or three different jars of chili crisp open in my fridge at all times—it's a great way to live.

"That's what I love about the chili crisp world," says James, who was initially reluctant to put his own spin on the condiment as a recipe developer. "I always thought chili crisp was Chinese. So as a Korean immigrant, I felt partially like it's not something I could touch. But as I started learning more and more, there's a Moroccan chili crisp, there's a Filipino chili crisp. So many chefs and companies are really infusing different kinds of ingredients to create a new blend of flavor. It's just like everyone is trying to say their stories and flavors in a jar, and all of those deserve to be here."

In conclusion James tells me, "I am here to break the rules of what chili crisp can do."

Just like I want to break the rules of what pasta can do!

In this dish as in so many others, chili crisp pairs beautifully with dairy. (It's also great on vanilla soft serve.) It's the perfect addition to cacio e pepe because it amplifies and deepens the smoky spice from the pepper and contrasts perfectly with the Pecorino. As I write this, I cannot wait to eat it again.

I'm pairing it with mafalde, a very special shape for me because it was a key inspiration for cascatelli. It's like fettuccine but with ruffles down the edges. This is the shape that showed me not only how good ruffles are at holding sauce but also how fun they are in your mouth. More shapes should have ruffles! Try to get the long version as opposed to the short one sometimes labeled mafalda (with an *a*) or mafalda corta.

(continued)

2 tablespoons kosher salt

1 tablespoon coarsely cracked black peppercorns (see tip)

2 teaspoons cracked Sichuan peppercorns (optional, see note)

3 tablespoons unsalted butter

3 tablespoons Lao Gan Ma chili crisp, plus more for serving

1 pound mafalde pasta (a.k.a. mafaldine or riccia; or use bucatini, pici, or cascatelli)

1 cup (4 ounces) finely grated Pecorino Romano, plus more for serving

TIP: Use a mortar and pestle, rolling pin, or the bottom of a pot or pan to crack whole black peppercorns (and Sichuan peppercorns, if using) into chunks. You want them coarser than if you had ground them in a pepper mill or spice grinder.

NOTE: You don't have to use the Sichuan peppercorns to get great results, but they do add a depth to the heat that I think takes this dish to the next level. Plus you'll need them to make Mapo Tofu Cascatelli (page 165), my all-time favorite way to have cascatelli!

1. Bring 4 quarts of water and the salt to a boil in a large pot.

2. Toast the black and Sichuan peppercorns, if using, in a large, high-sided skillet over medium-low heat, shaking the pan frequently, until fragrant, 1 to 2 minutes; transfer to a bowl, reserving the skillet.

3. Melt the butter in the reserved skillet over medium-low heat. Add 2 teaspoons of the pepper mixture and cook, stirring, until the butter just begins to brown, 1 to 2 minutes. Add the chili crisp and cook, stirring occasionally, until the chili flakes become fragrant and sizzle, 2 to 3 minutes; remove the pan from the heat. (At this point the sauce can sit, covered, for up to 2 hours.)

4. Add the pasta to the boiling water and cook for 1 minute less than the low end of the package instructions. Meanwhile, place the Pecorino in a large heatproof bowl and set aside. A few minutes before the pasta is done, transfer ½ cup of the pasta cooking water to the bowl with the Pecorino and whisk until no lumps remain.

5. Use tongs to transfer the pasta directly to the skillet and place it over medium-high heat. Cook, stirring constantly, until any water has evaporated and the pasta is evenly coated with the chili mixture, 1 to 2 minutes.

6. Immediately transfer the pasta to the bowl with the cheese mixture, scraping out the skillet. Add ¼ cup of the pasta water and use the tongs to rapidly toss everything together until the pasta is well coated and the cheese is dissolved. (There should be extra sauce pooling in the bowl at first, but it should all cling to the pasta after 1 to 2 minutes of stirring. If the sauce looks too thick after 1 minute, add more pasta water 1 tablespoon at a time until smooth and creamy.)

7. Transfer the pasta to a serving dish or individual bowls, sprinkle with more Pecorino and the remaining pepper mixture, and serve with more chili crisp, if desired.

SHRIMP WITH AJÍ AMARILLO, OLIVES, AND LIME–CORN NUT PANGRATTATO

SERVES 4 TO 6 • TOTAL TIME: 50 MINUTES • DEVELOPED WITH ASHA LOUPY

I showed this recipe to my mom and she was skeptical of the ají amarillo, because she wasn't familiar with it. "I don't want to buy a whole jar of something if I'm only going to use it once," she said. Then she tasted the finished dish and fell in love with it. By the next day she had googled five more uses for it.

Ají amarillo is a Peruvian yellow hot pepper paste. You can find it at Latin American markets as well as some well-stocked supermarkets, but you may need to source it online (trust us, it's worth it). The chiles it uses are bright and fruity with a gentle acidity. We developed this recipe with Zócalo Gourmet Costa Peruana ají amarillo, but any high-quality version will work. Ají amarillo can range from mild to medium heat depending on the brand, so try to find one that's right for you!

As for your leftover ají amarillo . . . Add a spoonful to liven up dressings, mix it into mayonnaise for a zesty spread, combine it with lime juice as a base for ceviche, or just make this pasta again!

Lime–Corn Nut Pangrattato (page 25)

2 tablespoons plus 1 teaspoon kosher salt

1 pound jumbo (21/25) shrimp, peeled, deveined, and tails removed (see note)

⅓ cup extra-virgin olive oil

5 garlic cloves, minced

1 cup pitted green olives, like Castelvetrano or Manzanilla, torn in half

¾ cup dry white wine

⅓ cup jarred ají amarillo paste

1 pound mezzi rigatoni (or mezze maniche, casarecce, or rigatoni)

⅓ cup chopped fresh cilantro leaves and tender stems

3 tablespoons freshly squeezed lime juice

2 tablespoons unsalted butter, cut into 8 cubes

1. Make the pangrattato and set it aside.

2. Bring 4 quarts of water and 2 tablespoons of the salt to a boil in a large pot.

3. Pat the shrimp dry, then toss them in a bowl with the remaining 1 teaspoon of salt until evenly coated; set aside.

4. Add the oil and garlic to a large, high-sided skillet and cook over medium heat until the garlic is just golden around the edges, 2 to 4 minutes, stirring often. Add

(continued)

the olives, wine, and ají amarillo, bring to a simmer, and cook, stirring occasionally, until beginning to thicken and a spoon leaves a brief trail when the sauce is stirred, 4 to 6 minutes. Stir in the shrimp and remove the pan from the heat.

5. Add the pasta to the boiling water and cook for 1 minute less than the low end of the package instructions. Use a mesh spider to transfer the pasta directly to the skillet and set it over high heat. Add ½ cup of the pasta cooking water and stir until the shrimp are just cooked through, about 2 minutes. Remove the pan from the heat and add the cilantro, lime juice, and butter. Stir until the butter is melted. (The sauce should pool slightly at the bottom of the pan and be about the consistency of heavy cream; if it seems too thick or dry, add more pasta water 2 tablespoons at a time.)

6. Transfer the pasta to a serving dish or individual bowls, sprinkle with the pangrattato, and serve.

NOTE: Thawed frozen shrimp work great for this recipe (most shrimp behind the fish counter is previously frozen anyway). The numbers 21/25 refer to the range of how many shrimp make up 1 pound. The lower the number, the bigger the shrimp, because it takes fewer to get a pound. If, like me, you love a lot of shrimp with your pasta, you can increase the quantity to 1½ pounds.

CICERI E TRIA (FRIED AND BOILED NOODLES WITH CHICKPEAS)

SERVES 4 TO 6 • TOTAL TIME: 45 MINUTES • DEVELOPED WITH KATIE LEAIRD

Ciceri means "chickpeas," and *tria*—which comes from the Arabic word for "string"—was the generic Italian word for "pasta" centuries ago. Now it refers to a specific shape found in southern Italy: a wide, flat noodle similar to what we would recognize as pappardelle. When I came across this dish in my research, sometimes also called ceci e tria, I knew immediately it was perfect for this book. By combining fried and boiled pasta in a chickpea broth, it offers crispy and chewy textures together in one bite (dynamic contrast!). It's beautiful in its simplicity, bursting with flavor, and almost impossible to find outside the area of southern Puglia called the Salento, the region of Italy where it's from.

Katie Leaird, who has lived and worked as a chef in that region, developed this recipe. "Up until recently, I'd never had it in a restaurant," she told me. Even after spending so much time living, working, and eating in Puglia, "I'd only had it at friends' homes in the area. It's funny because it was always something that people would kind of apologize for serving me. They'd say, 'I don't really have anything in the house, but let me just make some pasta dough, cut it up, boil it, fry it. I'm so sorry that that's all I can provide you with.' And of course it was spectacular."

2 tablespoons plus ½ cup extra-virgin olive oil (see note)

4 garlic cloves, minced

1 rosemary sprig

½ cup dry white wine (see note)

4 cups (32 ounces) chicken or vegetable stock

Two 15-ounce cans chickpeas, drained and rinsed

1½ teaspoons kosher salt

¼ teaspoon freshly ground black pepper

1 pound fresh pappardelle, cut into 2- to 3-inch pieces (see note)

⅓ cup (1⅓ ounces) finely grated Pecorino Romano

1. Line 2 plates with a double layer of paper towels. Heat the 2 tablespoons of oil in a medium saucepan over medium heat. Add the garlic and rosemary and cook, stirring, until the garlic is fragrant but not browned, about 1 minute. Add the wine and simmer until reduced by half, 2 to 4 minutes. Stir in the stock, chickpeas, 1 teaspoon of the salt, and the pepper, increase the heat to medium-high, and bring to a simmer. Reduce the heat to medium-low, cover, and cook for 20 minutes. (The mixture should be at a gentle simmer; if necessary, reduce the heat to low.)

(continued)

IN SEARCH OF CICERI E TRIA

I t's the summer of 2022, and I'm making my way to Lecce, more than six hours southeast of Rome by train. As I travel south, Italy's mountains and hills flatten. The olive trees and vineyards give way to cacti. The air is sepia toned, dusty. (I spend a lot of time on the train trying to figure out whether Italy has actual deserts, but that proves challenging because Google refuses to believe I don't mean to be searching for Italian desserts.)

Lecce is the heart of a region called the Salento—the tip of the heel of Italy's boot, a peninsula surrounded by the Ionian Sea on one side and the Adriatic on the other. Even if you've never been to Italy, you've heard of Rome, Venice, Milan. Sicily, Tuscany, the Amalfi Coast. The Salento is not near any of those places.

The buildings of Lecce's old city are made with limestone, giving everything a golden hue. I've come here to meet Silvestro Silvestori, a cooking teacher and culinary anthropologist of the Salento.

Silvestro explains that two key factors define the food of this region. It's historically been one of Italy's poorest, and one of its driest. "What makes the Salento special is we don't have any groundwater," he tells me. Without water, you can't have animals. That means the food here has much less meat and cheese, more vegetables and legumes that do well in dry climates. "The pig of the Salento is actually probably the chickpea or the lentil," he says. Over the years the people here have found creative ways to add flavor, and texture, to their pasta dishes.

As Silvestro shows me how he makes ciceri e tria, he tells me a frequent source of debate among locals is whether it's better to simmer the pieces of fried pasta in the broth with the boiled pasta just a little before serving, so the fried pieces soften slightly and soak up some flavor, or whether that fried pasta should be added just as the dish is served, to preserve crisp. He likes to let the fried pasta soak just a bit. "That's how I've always eaten it, and it becomes this sort of pleasantly, vaguely meaty texture," he says.

I agree it gives the fried pasta a unique chewiness, but why pick between the two techniques? For my version I use both, so that the pasta comes in three textures instead of two. (In case you're keeping score, that's a 50 percent increase in pasta textures, which means even more dynamic contrast.) And while the textures are the standout feature here, I also love a pasta dish cooked and served in broth, which to me is a little different from a soup that happens to have pasta in it. The pasta in the latter is a limp afterthought. The pasta in ciceri e tria is the star. Still, as with any soup, I like to eat it with a spoon, which Silvestro says is an accepted method, though the ideal utensil remains another source of disagreement among locals in the Salento.

Silvestro and his assistant, Anna Presicce

2. Meanwhile, heat the remaining ½ cup of oil in a medium skillet over medium-high heat until shimmering. Add one-fourth of the pasta pieces and cook, stirring often, until crisp and starting to brown, 6 to 9 minutes. Use a slotted spoon to transfer the pasta to one of the prepared plates, letting any excess oil drip back into the pan and spreading the pasta into a single layer. Sprinkle the fried pasta evenly with ¼ teaspoon of the salt and set aside. Add another one-fourth of the pasta to the hot oil in the pan and cook until crisp and starting to brown, 3 to 5 minutes (the second batch will cook quicker than the first). Use the slotted spoon to transfer to the second prepared plate in a single layer and sprinkle evenly with the remaining ¼ teaspoon of salt; discard any excess oil. (If making in a humid environment, don't let the fried pasta sit for more than 1 hour as it will lose its crisp.)

3. Remove the rosemary sprig from the chickpea mixture and discard. (At this point the chickpea mixture can sit, covered, for up to 3 hours.)

4. Uncover the saucepan, increase the heat to medium-high, and bring the chickpea mixture to a boil. Stir in the remaining uncooked pasta and cook until tender, about 2 minutes. Remove the pan from the heat and stir in the first batch of fried pasta and the Pecorino. Let the mixture sit for 5 minutes, stirring occasionally (it will thicken but still be brothy).

5. Ladle the chickpea-pasta mixture into individual bowls, top with the remaining fried pasta, and serve. As you eat, I suggest you spoon some broth and cooked pasta over the crispiest fried pasta to add flavor and soften the pasta ever so slightly. Over time you'll find your own ideal texture for this dish and manage your broth absorption accordingly.

OLIVE OIL NOTE: Since this recipe calls for a lot of olive oil, a basic variety will work—no need for the expensive stuff.

WINE NOTE: Use a dry (not oaky or overly fruity) white wine such as Sauvignon Blanc or Pinot Grigio; dry vermouth will also work.

PASTA NOTE: You can find fresh pasta in the refrigerated aisle of your grocery store. If you can't find fresh pappardelle, use fresh fettuccine. Silvestro told me to cut the pieces of pasta to the size of sticks of gum (see photo). You can use a knife, kitchen shears, or just tear them with your hands. It's okay if they aren't perfectly uniform.

At the Awaiting Table Cookery School in Lecce, Silvestro Silvestori teaches his students that the fresh pasta for ciceri e tria should be cut into pieces the size of sticks of gum.

ORECCHIETTE WITH SALAMI, FENNEL, MANCHEGO, AND WHITE WINE

SERVES 4 TO 6 • *TOTAL TIME: 40 MINUTES* • *DEVELOPED WITH KATIE LEAIRD*

One sign of a great dish is that you wake up the next morning still thinking about it. That's what happened to me with this one. Fortunately I had leftovers, so I ate it three days in a row.

    I chose to include this in the texture section even though it doesn't include any obvious sources of crisp or crunch because I wanted to make the point that there are other types of textures worth appreciating. In this case I love the way the chewy, salty salami contrasts with the bursts of juicy, sweet fennel. Then you have the light creaminess of the Manchego balanced with the acidity of the white wine and plenty of pepper. Flavor contrast. Texture contrast. The only place where you won't find contrast is in the reaction you'll have when you eat it, because it's 100 percent delicious.

1 tablespoon kosher salt

3 tablespoons extra-virgin olive oil

6 ounces (about 1¼ cups) hard salami, diced (see note)

1 fennel bulb, cored and diced, fronds reserved and roughly chopped (see tip)

2 cups dry white wine

½ teaspoon freshly ground black pepper

1 pound orecchiette (or mezze rigatoni, calamorata, or medium shells)

3 ounces Manchego, shredded (¾ cup)

1. Bring 4 quarts of water and the salt to a boil in a large pot.

2. Heat the oil in a large, high-sided skillet over medium heat. Add the salami and fennel and cook, stirring often, until the fennel is softened and evenly browned, 7 to 10 minutes. Add the wine and pepper, bring to a simmer, and cook for 15 minutes, stirring once or twice toward the end; remove the pan from the heat. (At this point the sauce can sit, covered, for up to 2 hours. Warm over low heat before proceeding with the recipe.)

3. Add the pasta to the boiling water and cook for 2 minutes less than the low end of the package instructions. Use a mesh spider to transfer the pasta directly to the skillet and place it over medium-high heat. Add ½ cup of the pasta cooking water and toss until the sauce is creamy and the pasta is well coated, 2 to 4 minutes. (If the sauce seems too thick, add more pasta water 2 tablespoons at a time until the sauce is about the consistency of heavy cream and pools slightly at the bottom of the pan as you stir.)

4. Remove the pan from the heat, add the Manchego, and stir until it begins to melt. Transfer the pasta to a serving dish or individual bowls, sprinkle with the fennel fronds, and serve.

NOTE: I love the licorice-like flavor of finocchiona salami in this dish, but if you can't find it, use whatever high-quality hard salami you can get your hands on. Depending on the brand, you may need to remove the thin casing on the outside of the salami before dicing it. We made an exception to our typical ratio of salt in the pasta cooking water for this recipe since the salami adds so much salinity to the finished dish.

TIP: To prep the fennel, you first want to remove and discard the tough core. The easiest way to do this is to quarter the bulb lengthwise, then make a slice on the diagonal to remove the solid triangle at the bottom of each wedge that holds the onion-like layers together. Discard that solid part along with the tough stalks that look a bit like celery (or reserve those for stock), but keep the wispy fronds that resemble dill—they can be used like an herb, as we do here.

SCALLION OIL BUCATINI WITH RUNNY EGGS

SERVES 4 • TOTAL TIME: 50 TO 55 MINUTES (SEE NOTE) • DEVELOPED WITH JAMES PARK

This dish is a celebration of all the crunchy, nutty, pungent facets of scallions, tied together by a lazy river of creamy, runny eggs with crispy edges. Or instead of fried eggs, you can choose to put a raw yolk on top of each serving and mix it in as you eat. That's a common and delicious technique in many Asian noodle and rice dishes that will make the sauce richer, and it'll save the time it takes to fry the eggs.

10 scallions

⅓ cup extra-virgin olive oil, plus more as needed

2 tablespoons kosher salt, plus more for the eggs

4 garlic cloves, minced

½ teaspoon red pepper flakes (optional)

1 pound bucatini (or fettuccine, spaghettoni, or spaghetti)

4 to 8 large eggs (see note)

1 teaspoon finely grated lemon zest, plus 2 tablespoons freshly squeezed lemon juice

2 tablespoons soy sauce

1 tablespoon unsalted butter

½ teaspoon freshly ground black pepper, plus cracked black peppercorns for serving

Finely grated Parmesan, for serving

1. Line a plate with a double layer of paper towels. Thinly slice 5 of the scallions and set aside. Cut the remaining 5 scallions into 3-inch segments, then thinly slice them lengthwise to create 3-inch matchsticks. Combine the scallion matchsticks and the oil in a large, high-sided skillet and place it over medium heat. Cook, stirring occasionally, until the scallions are browned, 5 to 7 minutes (reduce the heat if the scallions begin to darken too quickly). Remove the pan from the heat and use a slotted spoon or tongs to transfer the scallions to the prepared plate. Remove and reserve 1 tablespoon of the scallion oil from the skillet, leaving the remainder in the pan.

2. Bring 4 quarts of water and the salt to a boil in a large pot.

3. Place the skillet with the scallion oil over medium-low heat. Set aside 3 tablespoons of the sliced scallions, then add the remainder to the pan along with the garlic. Cook, stirring often, until the mixture is fragrant and the garlic is just beginning to color, 1 to 3 minutes. Add the red pepper flakes, if using, and cook, stirring, for 1 minute; remove the pan from the heat.

(continued)

4. Add the pasta to the boiling water and cook for 2 minutes less than the low end of the package instructions.

5. Meanwhile, heat the reserved 1 tablespoon of scallion oil in a large nonstick skillet over medium-high heat until shimmering. Working quickly, add 4 eggs to the pan, season with salt, and cover. Cook for 1 minute, then uncover and continue to cook to desired doneness (about 1 minute for sunny-side up, or flip and continue to cook for over easy, medium, or hard). Use a spatula to transfer the eggs to a plate; if frying more eggs, repeat as necessary, adding a bit more olive oil to the pan if it looks dry.

6. Use tongs to transfer the pasta directly to the skillet with the scallion-garlic mixture and place it over high heat. Add ¾ cup of the pasta cooking water, the lemon zest and juice, the soy sauce, butter, and black pepper and toss until the sauce just clings to the pasta but still pools slightly in the bottom of the pan, 3 to 5 minutes. (If the sauce seems too thick, add more pasta water 2 tablespoons at a time until the sauce loosens but still clings to the pasta.)

7. Transfer the pasta to individual bowls and top each serving with 1 to 2 fried eggs. Sprinkle with the fried scallions, reserved sliced scallions, Parmesan, and cracked black peppercorns, and serve. When you eat it, break the yolk and let it run into your pasta, mixing it around to thicken the sauce.

NOTES: This recipe has you fry the eggs while the pasta is cooking because that's the most efficient use of your time, but it does mean you'll have to work quickly. If that's going to stress you out, you can fry the eggs before putting the pasta in the water, but that will add 5 to 10 minutes to the process. When I make this for my family, we each have two sunny-side up eggs on top, which makes it a hearty entrée, but you can do one egg per serving if you prefer.

ORECCHIETTE WITH MERGUEZ AND BROCCOLI RABE

SERVES 4 TO 6 • TOTAL TIME: 50 MINUTES

If you go to Puglia, the region in Italy's southeast corner, and wander the narrow streets of Bari's old city, on most days you'll find the "orecchiette ladies" sitting outside at tables, making piles of the region's most famous pasta shape by hand. Orecchiette, which means "little ears," is classified by Oretta Zanini De Vita and Maureen Fant's *Encyclopedia of Pasta* as strascinati, meaning it's a shape that's pressed or rolled over a textured wooden board to impart a pattern on one side. The pattern on orecchiette looks like veins on the back of an ear, which makes this shape a little creepy if you think too much about it. Orecchiette to me is like little disks of pure toothsinkability—it may be small but it tends to have thick walls and long cooking times. It's great when eaten with a spoon with sauces that have low viscosity and high chunk factor because you can get all the components in the spoon and the shape stands up to those chunks. (Find more on viscosity, chunk factor, and pairing shapes with sauces on page 151.)

In Puglia, orecchiette is famously paired with sausage and broccoli rabe. Here we draw from the flavors of North Africa, substituting merguez (a spicy lamb sausage) for the classic sweet Italian and adding in briny feta cheese and a sprinkle of lemon zest, which provides a bright foil for the rich lamb.

2 tablespoons plus 1 teaspoon kosher salt

Garlic Bread Pangrattato (page 27)

2 bunches broccoli rabe (about 2 pounds), ends trimmed

½ cup extra-virgin olive oil, plus more for serving

12 ounces raw merguez sausage, casings removed (see tip)

6 garlic cloves, minced

2 teaspoons finely grated lemon zest

1 pound orecchiette pasta (or fusilloni, strozzapreti, casarecce, or cascatelli)

3 ounces feta cheese, crumbled (¾ cup; see tip)

1. Bring 4 quarts of water and 2 tablespoons of the salt to a boil in a large pot.

2. Make the pangrattato and set aside.

3. Add the broccoli rabe to the boiling water, pressing it down to submerge it, and cook until the stems are tender and easily pierced with a fork, 5 to 7 minutes. Use tongs to transfer it to a colander (it's okay if a few bits remain in the water). Cover the pot and reduce the heat to medium (or turn the heat off if making ahead as

(continued)

detailed at the end of step 4). Rinse the broccoli rabe with cold water until cool enough to handle, then squeeze out as much moisture as possible. Transfer to a cutting board and chop as finely as possible, until it almost resembles a coarse paste. (This will take several minutes and some elbow grease.)

4. Heat ¼ cup of the oil in a large, high-sided skillet over medium-high heat until shimmering. Add the sausage, breaking it into large pieces with a spoon, and cook undisturbed until starting to brown on one side, 4 to 7 minutes. Stir, breaking the meat into small crumbles and scraping up any browned bits from the bottom of the pan, and cook until fully cooked through, about 2 more minutes. Add the garlic and cook, stirring, until fragrant, 1 to 2 minutes. Reduce the heat to medium, add the rabe, remaining ¼ cup of oil, remaining 1 teaspoon of salt, and the lemon zest and cook until heated through, 2 to 4 minutes. Cover and reduce the heat to low. (At this point the sauce can sit, covered and off the heat, for up to 2 hours. Warm over low heat before proceeding with the recipe.)

5. Return the water in the pot to a boil, if necessary. Add the pasta and cook for 2 minutes less than the low end of the package instructions. Use a mesh spider to transfer the pasta directly to the skillet, then increase the heat to high. Add 1 cup of the pasta cooking water and stir until the sauce thickens and clings to the pasta, 3 to 5 minutes.

6. Transfer the pasta to a serving dish or individual bowls, drizzle with oil, sprinkle with the feta and pangrattato, and serve.

MERGUEZ TIP: To remove the merguez casings, run a paring knife down one side of each link to cut a slit in the casing, then remove the meat mixture, discarding the casing.

FETA TIP: Always try to buy whole Greek, Bulgarian, or French feta in brine (which looks like it's in cloudy water), as opposed to the stuff that's vacuum-sealed and/or precrumbled. It's more expensive but so much more flavorful, and you can keep it for a while—once opened, it will last at least a month as long as it's fully submerged in the brine. (I keep mine for much longer, but the internet says one month and I don't want to get sued because someone who read this book died in their pursuit of deliciousness. So you can make your own decisions.)

SPAGHETTI ALL'ASSASSINA (ASSASSIN'S SPAGHETTI)

SERVES 4 · TOTAL TIME: 50 MINUTES

Spaghetti all'assassina is a relatively new entry into the pasta canon, and one that continues to evolve to this day. It's made by simmering spaghetti in spicy tomato sauce until the pasta is al dente and the sauce is mostly absorbed or evaporated and about as thick as tomato paste. Then you keep frying it until the pasta turns golden brown and crispy in some parts and charred and crunchy in others. (For the story of this dish's creation, and my visit to Al Sorso Preferito, the restaurant in Bari where it was invented, see "In Search of the Assassin's Spaghetti" on page 90.)

I tried the spaghetti all'assassina at Al Sorso Preferito, but to be honest, it wasn't my favorite in Bari. That distinction goes to Ghiotto Panzerotto, where owner Beppe Girone and his chefs give it more crunch and spice, and coax more of a range of nutty, toasty flavors from the pasta itself. I also found that Ghiotto nailed the less obvious but still crucial part of spaghetti all'assassina—cooking the tomato sauce down to the point that its flavors are super concentrated and it becomes sticky and sweet, perfectly complementing the dish's crunch and spice. (That's their assassina pictured on the opposite page.)

When I got home, I set out to re-create Ghiotto's assassina in my own kitchen. Beppe told me they do not preboil the pasta—they put it in the pan raw and add the tomato sauce. (More on that debate on page 90.) I tried that multiple times but determined that it's not the best method for most home cooks. It only works if you have a huge, restaurant-size pan that's wide enough to lay the spaghetti completely flat, so it's submerged in sauce. Otherwise, you have to keep moving the raw spaghetti to get it coated in enough sauce to soften it, and that process breaks a lot of the dry pasta. In the end, I think this version is extremely close to the one I had at Ghiotto, and after much trial and error, I'm frankly skeptical that starting with raw or partially cooked spaghetti really affects the finished product.

A few more key thoughts . . .

While my doubts about the merits of spaghetti are well established (see page 151), this is a dish where it is the perfect shape. If you used a flatter pasta, you'd throw off your ratios—too much of it would be in contact with the pan and you'd have all crunchiness, no chewiness. If you used a thicker spaghetti (spaghettoni), you'd go wrong in the other direction—you'd have too much chewy interior in relation to exterior crisp. And the stickiness of the assassina sauce holds the spaghetti together to make it far more forkable than it normally is.

I'll add that for all the arguments over this dish among the Barese, there is one thing everyone agrees on: Don't use fancy spaghetti. The flatter surface of Teflon-extruded pasta crisps up better. Beppe told me he uses De Cecco spaghetti for his assassina, so I do too!

(continued)

Finally, once the dish is cooked, do not leave it in the pan or serve it in one large bowl because the steam will destroy the crisp you worked so hard to create. Serve it individually and eat it right away. And while it's not traditional, I think a sprinkle of grated cheese at the end is a very nice addition. When I sent my friend Antonello in Bari a video of my spaghetti all'assassina with broccoli rabe, he wrote back, "Wow! You're a master after visiting Bari!" When I told him I added Pecorino Romano on top, he wrote, "Okay, but please don't tell any Barese!"

You can decide for yourself.

1 tablespoon kosher salt

One 24- to 25-ounce jar marinara sauce (see note)

¼ cup tomato paste

5 to 10 jarred whole pepperoncini peppers, finely chopped (see note)

1 pound spaghetti (see headnote)

6 tablespoons extra-virgin olive oil

Finely grated Parmesan, for serving (not traditional but I like it)

1. Bring 2½ quarts of water and the salt to a boil in a large pot.

2. In a large nonstick skillet, combine the marinara, tomato paste, and pepperoncini. Add 1½ cups of water to the empty marinara jar, close it tightly, and shake it to release the residual sauce, then add it to the skillet. Stir well and set the skillet over medium heat.

3. Add the pasta to the boiling water (it may not be fully submerged at first) and cook, stirring gently, until just pliable enough that some pieces form an "S" shape, about 3 minutes. Use tongs to transfer the pasta directly to the sauce in the skillet, then use a rubber spatula to gently spread out and press down the pasta until it is fully submerged. (If necessary, add pasta cooking water 2 tablespoons at a time until the pasta is just submerged.) Bring to a simmer and cook undisturbed for 10 minutes, pressing down to resubmerge the pasta and adding more pasta water if needed.

4. Drizzle 4 tablespoons of the oil over the pasta, then use the tongs (see tip) and spatula to gently turn it over in sections. When all the pasta has been flipped, use the spatula to press it into a flat, even layer, increase the heat to high, and cook undisturbed for 5 minutes. Next, use the tongs and spatula to rotate the pasta, moving the lighter sections to the bottom and the crispy bits to the top. Press into an even layer and cook undisturbed for 2 to 3 minutes. Repeat this process several times, rotating the pan periodically, until about a quarter of the pasta is blackened, a quarter is deeply browned, and half is dark red. (This should take 15 to 18 minutes after the initial 5 minutes on high heat. If you want it crunchier, cook it longer.) Add the remaining 2 tablespoons of oil and toss to combine.

5. Immediately transfer the pasta to individual bowls, top with Parmesan, and serve.

TOMATO SAUCE NOTE: As I say in the section on jarred tomato sauces (page 30), in most dishes you can use whatever kind of jarred tomato sauce you like—marinara is smoother with a purer tomato flavor, while tomato and basil tends to be chunkier with more of the traditional Italian seasonings. However, for spaghetti all'assassina, you don't want chunks because they will burn (and not in a good way, as in the rest of the dish). Use marinara. Its thinner consistency allows it to reduce evenly, cooking down to a sticky concoction of savory, concentrated tomato goodness.

PEPPERONCINI NOTE: In Bari they use dried chili pepper flakes that are not only spicy but also tangy and fruity. The red pepper flakes in most American supermarkets just don't have the same flavor. I found that jarred whole pepperoncini, finely chopped, better replicate the flavor I experienced at Ghiotto and Al Sorso Preferito. You can vary the quantity depending on how spicy you want it, just note that I use regular whole pepperoncini (which are light green), not the ones labeled "extra hot." When I make this for my kids I leave out the pepperoncini, but if I list that ingredient as optional, I'll be banned from Bari for good. You can also sprinkle chopped pepperoncini on top of individual portions at the end—it doesn't infuse quite as well this way, but it's a solid compromise if some in your group like spice and others don't.

TIP: Make sure to use silicone-tipped tongs for this recipe so you don't scratch your nonstick pan. If you own a splatter guard (which I don't), this is probably a great place to use it!

IN SEARCH OF THE ASSASSIN'S SPAGHETTI

I t's rare that you can pinpoint the time and place a pasta dish was invented—most of pasta history is the stuff of legend and folklore. But in the early 1960s, in the southern Italian region of Puglia, in the coastal city of Bari, at a restaurant called Al Sorso Preferito, spaghetti all'assassina—"assassin's spaghetti"—was born.

In August 2022, I go to Al Sorso Preferito, where I meet the eighty-year-old chef Pietro Lonigro, one of the inventors of the dish.

Chef Pietro tells me it happened by accident—and it didn't exactly start with him. He began working at the restaurant at age fourteen, running errands and learning to cook from the restaurant's then owner, Vincenzo Francavilla. Chef Vincenzo often cooked a standard dish of spaghetti with tomatoes and dried chili peppers. But one time, it burned a bit on the bottom. Usually they would have thrown the pasta out, but instead the chefs ate it. And they were surprised to find that they actually *liked* those crunchy burnt bits, using one of my favorite Italian words to describe them—*croccante*, meaning "crunchy." The word even sounds crunchy.

They started serving this crunchy new pasta to customers, who asked them to punch it up: more crunch, more spice, even a little more char. (By the way, the name comes from the dish's spice—it was called spaghetti all'assassina even before the accidental burning. In my visit I found it to be hot by Italian standards but barely medium to my palate overall. My version allows you to vary the spice to your liking.) Chef Pietro says that when he eventually bought the restaurant in 1974, he kept riffing on the dish. He added the technique of rotating the pasta in the pan to char

At Al Sorso Preferito in Bari, I met chef Pietro Lonigro, one of the inventors of spaghetti all'assassina.

more of it, which also had the effect of further reducing the sauce into a sticky tomato paste. Eventually he settled on the spaghetti all'assassina he serves today.

For decades, the dish remained a little-known Barese specialty, served in only a few restaurants in Bari. About a decade ago, the secret started to get out, thanks to a guy named Massimo Dell'Erba—a physicist by day and passionate eater and home cook by night. In 2013, Massimo organized a dinner with a few friends at a local restaurant. Even though spaghetti all'assassina was not on the menu at this particular spot, he begged them to make it, and they did. "It was an amazing evening," he told me when we met at Al Sorso Preferito.

The next morning, inspired, Massimo created a Facebook group and named it Accademia dell'Assassina— Academy of the Assassin. Their mission was to taste the dish at all the restaurants in Bari that served it, with a rigorous

scoring system that rated each version on crunch, spice, and char. They published their results online.

Within months, the Facebook group had hundreds of members, each with a different opinion about who in Bari makes the best spaghetti all'assassina, how crunchy and spicy it should be, and perhaps most contentious of all: whether the spaghetti should be raw or partially boiled before it's fried in the pan with the sauce. Chef Pietro insists on briefly boiling the pasta first because he says otherwise it burns too much in the pan. Others prefer the increased char and crunch that they say comes from skipping the boiling.

When Massimo leads me into the kitchen at Al Sorso Preferito to talk to Chef Pietro and watch the chefs there make the dish, all of these issues continue to provoke strong debate (in Italian) between Massimo, Pietro, and the other chefs. At one point I turn to my friend Antonello, my guide for the day, and ask what they're arguing about. "They're fighting about everything!" he replies. (I guess in Italian pasta culture, even the guy who INVENTED a dish can be accused of doing it wrong. You can hear all of this, as well as my own trials and tribulations re-creating the dish at home for my recipe, in *The Sporkful* podcast series about the making of this cookbook.)

Today, thanks to the influence of social media and the work of Massimo's academy, which he started as a joke, "there is not a restaurant in Bari that doesn't make the assassina," he tells me. "A lot of them have invented their version," including a popular variation made with broccoli rabe instead of tomato sauce, and another done with stracciatella cheese, the tender, spreadable insides of a ball of burrata.

So spaghetti all'assassina is a perfect example of how, even in Italian cuisine, people continue to come up with new ideas. Because that's what people in kitchens do.

*Spaghetti all'Assassina con Cime di Rapa
(with Broccoli Rabe; page 94)*

*Spaghetti all'Assassina
(page 86)*

SPAGHETTI ALL'ASSASSINA CON CIME DI RAPA (WITH BROCCOLI RABE)

SERVES 4 • TOTAL TIME: 50 TO 55 MINUTES • DEVELOPED WITH REBECCAH MARSTERS

Spaghetti all'assassina with broccoli rabe is a newer variation on this dish, proving as I've stated elsewhere that despite its sometimes well-deserved reputation for opposing any tampering with tradition, Italian pasta culture continues to evolve, and new ideas keep gaining acceptance. (Maybe in thirty years people in Bari will be putting grated cheese on their assassina, as I do!) In this case it helps that the addition of broccoli rabe is a familiar choice in the region, which is also the home of the pasta shape orecchiette (little ears), traditionally served with sausage and, you guessed it, broccoli rabe.

2 tablespoons plus 1¼ teaspoons kosher salt

1 bunch broccoli rabe (about 1 pound), ends trimmed, cut into thirds crosswise

5 to 10 jarred whole pepperoncini peppers, stemmed (see note on page 89)

8 tablespoons (½ cup) extra-virgin olive oil, plus more for serving

3 anchovy fillets

3 garlic cloves, minced

1 pound spaghetti (see headnote on page 86)

Finely grated Pecorino Romano, for serving (not traditional but I like it)

Freshly ground black pepper, for serving

1. Bring 4 quarts of water and 2 tablespoons of the salt to a boil in a large pot. In a large bowl, combine about 4 cups of ice and 6 cups of cold water. Add the broccoli rabe to the boiling water, making sure it's completely submerged, and cook until the stems are fork-tender and bright green, about 3 minutes. Use tongs or a mesh spider to transfer the rabe to the ice bath and let sit for at least 2 minutes; keep the water in the pot at a boil.

2. Transfer the rabe to a blender (it's okay if some water gets in there, but try to leave the ice in the bowl), add 1 cup of the hot cooking water, the pepperoncini, and the remaining 1¼ teaspoons of salt, and puree until completely smooth, about 45 seconds; uncover and set aside.

3. Heat 2 tablespoons of the oil in a large nonstick skillet over medium heat until shimmering. Add the anchovies and garlic and cook, stirring and smashing the anchovies, until the garlic is golden around the edges, 1 to 3 minutes. Add the rabe puree to the pan, scraping out the blender jar, then immediately add the pasta to the boiling water and cook, stirring gently, until just pliable enough that some pieces form an "S" shape, about 3 minutes. Use tongs (see tip on page 89) to transfer the pasta directly to the sauce in the skillet, then use a rubber spatula to gently spread out and press down the pasta until it is fully submerged. (If necessary, add pasta cooking water 2 tablespoons at a time until the pasta is just submerged.) Bring to a simmer and cook undisturbed for 10 minutes, pressing down to resubmerge the pasta and adding more pasta water if needed.

4. Drizzle 4 tablespoons of the oil over the top of the pasta, then use the tongs and spatula to gently turn it over in sections. When all the pasta has been flipped, use the spatula to press it into a flat, even layer, increase the heat to high, and cook undisturbed for 5 minutes. Next, use the tongs and spatula to rotate the pasta, moving the lighter sections to the bottom and the crispy bits to the top. Press into an even layer and cook undisturbed for 2 to 3 minutes. Repeat this process several times, rotating the pan periodically, until about a quarter of the pasta is blackened and a quarter is deeply browned. (This should take 10 to 16 minutes after the initial 5 minutes on high heat.) Add the remaining 2 tablespoons of oil and toss to combine.

5. Immediately transfer the pasta to individual bowls, drizzle with more oil, sprinkle with Pecorino and black pepper, and serve.

PAN-SEARED MUSHROOM QUATTROTINI WITH FURIKAKE PANGRATTATO

SERVES 4 TO 6 • TOTAL TIME: 1 HOUR 15 MINUTES • DEVELOPED WITH JAMES PARK

Mushrooms are the steak of the Vegetable Kingdom, and the only thing better than a pasta dish full of some kind of mushrooms is a pasta dish full of many kinds of mushrooms, each contributing different flavors and textures. We add to that a combination of salty oyster sauce, slightly acidic ketchup, earthy miso paste, and sugar to create a mildly sweet, very flavorful sauce, then toss it with the steak of the Pasta Kingdom— quattrotini. All that being said, the highlight of this dish may be the furikake pangrattato, which adds crisp and an extra punch of umami to the dish.

Furikake Pangrattato (page 26)

2 tablespoons kosher salt

¼ cup ketchup

¼ cup oyster sauce

¼ cup white or yellow miso

3 tablespoons unseasoned rice wine vinegar

2 tablespoons sugar

10 tablespoons extra-virgin olive oil

2 pounds assorted mushrooms, such as shiitake, creminis (a.k.a. baby bella), and oyster, cleaned, stemmed, if necessary, and cut or torn into bite-size pieces (see tip)

4 garlic cloves, minced

1 pound quattrotini (or vesuvio, orecchiette, or medium shells, see note)

Freshly ground black pepper, for serving

1. Make the pangrattato and set aside.

2. Bring 4 quarts of water and the salt to a boil in a large pot.

3. In a medium bowl, whisk together the ketchup, oyster sauce, miso, vinegar, and sugar until evenly combined; set aside.

4. Heat 3 tablespoons of the oil in a large, high-sided skillet over medium-high heat until shimmering. Add one-third of the mushrooms, spread them into an even layer, and cook undisturbed until deeply browned on the bottom, about 5 minutes. Continue to cook, stirring and redistributing the mushrooms every 2 minutes, until most are deeply browned all over, 6 to 10 minutes. Transfer the mushrooms to a

(continued)

plate; repeat with the remaining mushrooms, cooking in two more batches and adding another 3 tablespoons of oil per batch (the second and third batches may cook quicker than the first).

5. After cooking the third batch of mushrooms, reduce the heat to medium-low, add the remaining 1 tablespoon of oil and the garlic, and cook, stirring, until golden, 1 to 2 minutes. Add half of the mushrooms and half of the ketchup mixture and stir to combine. Remove the pan from the heat. (At this point the sauce can sit, covered, for up to 3 hours. Warm it over low heat before proceeding with the recipe.)

6. Add the pasta to the boiling water and cook for 2 minutes less than the low end of the package instructions. Use a mesh spider to transfer the pasta directly to the skillet. Place the skillet over medium heat, add ½ cup of the pasta cooking water, the remaining mushrooms, and the remaining ketchup mixture, and cook until the pasta is evenly coated, 3 to 5 minutes, stirring and scraping the bottom of the pan. (The sauce should be syrupy but not gloopy. If it seems too thick, add more pasta water 2 tablespoons at a time until the sauce loosens but still clings to the pasta.)

7. Transfer the pasta to a serving dish or individual bowls, sprinkle with the pangrattato and black pepper, and serve.

TIP: If you use shiitake mushrooms, remove and discard the stems and slice or tear the caps. For creminis, trim the stems but keep them intact, then cut the mushrooms into ¼-inch slices. If you use oyster mushrooms, tear them into pieces with your hands.

NOTE: Quattrotini is so big and sauceable that when I switched this dish to use it instead of orecchiette, as originally planned, we had to fully double the amount of sauce the recipe calls for, even though in both cases we were using 1 pound of pasta. So if you use orecchiette or shells, you can cut the ketchup, oyster sauce, miso, vinegar, and sugar quantities in half, or just set half of the sauce aside and add more to the pasta at the end until it's coated to your liking. If you have some sauce left over, it's fantastic on roasted broccoli.

ZUCCHINI AND FETA PASTA WITH ZA'ATAR PANGRATTATO

SERVES 4 TO 6 • TOTAL TIME: 50 MINUTES • DEVELOPED WITH ASHA LOUPY

The technique for this pasta is inspired by the famed spaghetti alla Nerano, in which sliced zucchini is fried until tender and lightly golden, then a portion of that zucchini is mashed or blended with cheese, butter, and a splash of pasta water to create a creamy, emulsified sauce. Here, we're skipping the shallow fry and just using a generous amount of extra-virgin olive oil to cook the zucchini, which is flavored with garlic, chili flakes for a whisper of heat, and both lemon zest and lemon juice to balance the richness of the caramelized squash. Feta added at the end brings a salty, briny kick to the party, while a generous smattering of za'atar pangrattato lends crunch and aromatic herbaceousness.

    We combine it all with fusilli lunghi bucati. Not to be confused with short fusilli, which is a garbage shape, this is a long, coiled, hollow tube, which legend has it was invented by Neapolitan housewives, who'd wrap bucatini around knitting needles to make tight corkscrews of pasta. While it is sauceable and toothsinkable, it's actually not great in the forkability department—it can be hard to twirl and some strands may break—but it's so fun to look at, I couldn't resist including it.

Za'atar Pangrattato (page 27)

2 tablespoons plus 2 teaspoons kosher salt

½ cup extra-virgin olive oil

2 pounds small zucchini (6 to 8 zucchini), sliced into ¼-inch rounds

4 garlic cloves, thinly sliced

½ to 1 teaspoon red pepper flakes (depending on desired spiciness), plus more for serving

1 pound fusilli lunghi bucati (a.k.a. fusilli col buco and canule; or use bucatini, cavatappi, or fusilloni)

2 teaspoons finely grated lemon zest, plus 1 tablespoon freshly squeezed lemon juice

3 tablespoons cold unsalted butter, cut into 4 pieces

4 ounces feta cheese, coarsely crumbled (1 cup; see feta tip on page 85)

Flaky sea salt, for serving (optional but highly recommended)

1. Make the pangrattato and set aside.

2. Bring 4 quarts of water and 2 tablespoons of the salt to a boil in a large pot.

3. Heat the oil in a Dutch oven (or second large pot) over medium-high heat until shimmering but not smoking. Add the zucchini and cook undisturbed until the slices on the bottom are browned on one side, 5 to 7 minutes. Sprinkle with

(continued)

1 teaspoon of the salt, stir gently, and continue to cook, stirring often, until most of the zucchini is softened and slightly translucent and about a third is well browned, 8 to 12 minutes.

4. Use a slotted spoon to transfer one-third of the zucchini to a blender (or immersion blender) and set aside. Move the remaining zucchini to one side of the pot, add the garlic and red pepper flakes to the empty space, and cook until the garlic starts to color, about 1 minute. Stir, then remove the pot from the heat. (At this point the mixture can sit, covered, for up to 2 hours.)

5. Add the pasta to the boiling water and cook for 1 minute less than the low end of the package instructions. Reserve 2 cups of the pasta cooking water, then drain the pasta. Immediately return the pasta to the empty pot, cover, and set aside. Add 1 cup of the pasta water, the lemon zest and juice, and the remaining 1 teaspoon of salt to the blender with the zucchini. Start blending on low, gradually increasing the speed to high. With the blender running, add the butter and blend until smooth, 30 to 45 seconds.

6. Return the pot with the sliced zucchini to medium heat and cook until it's beginning to sizzle, about 1 minute. Add the pureed zucchini mixture and the pasta and toss until the sauce clings to the pasta, 1 to 3 minutes. (If the sauce seems too thick, add more pasta water 2 tablespoons at a time until it's the consistency of heavy cream and pools slightly in the bottom of the pot.) Remove the pot from the heat and gently stir in the feta, leaving the big crumbles intact.

7. Transfer the pasta to a serving dish or individual bowls, sprinkle with some pangrattato and flaky sea salt, if desired, and serve with additional red pepper flakes and more pangrattato.

CHILI CRISP TAHINI PASTA WITH FRIED SHALLOTS

SERVES 4 TO 6 • TOTAL TIME: 45 MINUTES • DEVELOPED WITH JAMES PARK

The combination of spicy, savory chili crisp and nutty tahini makes an incredibly delicious, satisfying sauce, but we take it to the next level with the addition of oniony crunch in the form of fried shallots. And here you see cascatelli's many properties on full display—the sauce sinks into the canyon between the ruffles, which I call the Sauce Trough, and all the shape's edges and ruffle tips grab bits of chili crisp and fried shallot. You won't have trouble getting all the components of this dish together in one bite!

For more on chili crisp, see Cacio e Pepe e Chili Crisp (page 69). As noted there, we call for Lao Gan Ma brand, one of the original and best-known varieties, but you can use whatever kind of chili crisp you like. Just note that they vary in spice levels, so taste before you add the full amount.

2 tablespoons kosher salt

⅓ cup tahini (see note)

3 tablespoons Lao Gan Ma chili crisp, plus more for serving (see above)

2 tablespoons apple cider vinegar (or rice or white wine vinegar)

2 tablespoons soy sauce

1 pound cascatelli (or reginetti, casarecce, gemelli, or radiatore)

½ cup extra-virgin olive oil

4 large shallots, sliced into very thin rings

4 garlic cloves, minced

½ teaspoon freshly ground black pepper

1. Bring 4 quarts of water and the salt to a boil in a large pot.

2. Line a plate with a double layer of paper towels. Set a fine-mesh strainer over a medium heatproof bowl.

3. In a 2-cup liquid measuring cup, combine the tahini, chili crisp, vinegar, and soy sauce and whisk until fully combined.

4. Add the pasta to the boiling water and cook for 2 minutes less than the low end of the package instructions. Reserve 2 cups of the pasta cooking water, then drain the pasta. Immediately return the pasta to the pot, cover, and set aside.

5. Whisking constantly, pour ½ cup of the hot pasta water into the tahini mixture and whisk until completely smooth; set aside.

(continued)

6. Heat the oil in a large, high-sided skillet over medium heat until shimmering. Add the shallots and cook, stirring occasionally and breaking up the rings, until deeply browned and crispy, 12 to 15 minutes. Carefully strain the shallots and oil into the prepared bowl, reserving the skillet, then transfer the shallots to the prepared plate and spread them into an even layer (see tip).

7. Return 3 tablespoons of the shallot oil to the skillet, add the garlic, and cook over medium heat, stirring, until golden, 1 to 2 minutes. Add the tahini mixture and cook, stirring, until fragrant and thickened, about 2 minutes. Add the pasta to the skillet along with ¾ cup of the pasta water, 1 tablespoon of the reserved shallot oil, and the pepper and toss until the pasta is evenly coated, 2 to 4 minutes. (The sauce should cling to the pasta but still pool slightly at the bottom of the pan. If it seems too thick, add more pasta water 2 tablespoons at a time.) Remove the pan from the heat and stir in half of the fried shallots.

8. Transfer the pasta to a serving dish or individual bowls, top with the remaining fried shallots, and serve immediately with chili crisp. (This dish will thicken quickly. If you have some left in the pan and you go back for seconds, I suggest you put the pan back over medium heat for a minute or two and mix in a splash of pasta water to loosen it back up.)

NOTE: I like Soom or Villa Jerada brand tahini, both of which have incredible flavor and are silky smooth, so they're easier to work with. Because the oil is usually separated when you open a new jar of tahini, my mom likes to transfer all the contents to a bigger container, emulsify it with an immersion blender, then return it to the jar, where it stays emulsified for months. She also likes to store tahini on its side because she says that makes it easier to mix. (Letting it come to room temperature before you work with it also helps.) My mom has put a lot of thought into tahini storage and handling, which I respect. You can also use smooth, unsweetened peanut butter in place of tahini in this recipe.

TIP: Store any leftover shallot oil in an airtight container at room temperature and use it for fried eggs, sauces, dressings—anywhere you'd use olive oil!

SHRIMP SCAMPI WITH LEMON-HERB PANGRATTATO

SERVES 4 TO 6 • TOTAL TIME: 1 HOUR 10 MINUTES • DEVELOPED WITH LINDA PASHMAN

When cascatelli first came out, many people asked me what to make with it. I was a bit busy at the time, so I asked my mom to come up with some options. Two of her best creations—this scampi and the mushroom ragù on page 190—are in this book. For this one she took inspiration from a Colu Henry recipe for linguine with shrimp and lemon-pistachio bread crumbs. I'll let her explain why she chose scampi for cascatelli:

> When I saw the first batch of cascatelli, the shape reminded me of shrimp. I pictured how nicely shrimp would curl into the cascatelli. I also thought this was a great opportunity to see how cascatelli works in a recipe written for a long, thin pasta. It worked beautifully—you just need to make adjustments to produce more sauce, because cascatelli holds so much sauce. It is a delicious combination. In fact, shrimp and cascatelli were made for each other!

The addition of the lemon-herb pangrattato provides the sensation of crispy fried shrimp without the heaviness, and makes this stand out from other scampi recipes. This one passed my Can I Stop Eating It Test with flying colors!

1½ pounds jumbo (21/25) shrimp, peeled, deveined, and tails removed (shells reserved, see note)

1 cup chicken stock

Lemon-Herb Pangrattato (page 28)

1 teaspoon plus 2 tablespoons kosher salt

3 tablespoons extra-virgin olive oil, plus more for serving

4 garlic cloves, thinly sliced

¼ to ½ teaspoon red pepper flakes (depending on desired spiciness)

½ cup dry white wine

1 teaspoon freshly ground black pepper

4 tablespoons (½ stick) cold unsalted butter, cut into 4 pieces

1 pound cascatelli (or mafalde, sagne a pezzi, or campanelle)

½ cup chopped fresh parsley

2 tablespoons freshly squeezed lemon juice

1. In a small saucepan, combine the shrimp shells, if using, and stock and bring to a boil over medium-high heat. Reduce the heat to low, cover, and simmer for 20 minutes.

2. Meanwhile, make the pangrattato and set aside.

(continued)

3. Strain the shrimp broth and set aside, discarding the shells (you should have about ⅓ cup of broth). Pat the shrimp dry, then combine them in a bowl with 1 teaspoon of the salt and toss until evenly coated.

4. Bring 4 quarts of water and the remaining 2 tablespoons of salt to a boil in a large pot.

5. Heat 2 tablespoons of the oil in a large, high-sided skillet over medium heat until shimmering. Add the shrimp, spread them into an even layer, and cook until pink and opaque on both sides, 3 to 5 minutes, flipping halfway through. Remove the pan from the heat and transfer the shrimp to a plate.

6. Add the remaining 1 tablespoon of oil to the pan and return it to medium heat. Add the garlic and red pepper flakes and cook, stirring, until the garlic is golden around the edges, 2 to 3 minutes. Add the wine, reserved shrimp stock, and black pepper, bring to a simmer, and cook, stirring occasionally and scraping up any browned bits from the bottom of the pan, until reduced by half, 4 to 6 minutes. Whisking constantly, add the butter 1 tablespoon at a time, waiting for each tablespoon to melt before adding the next; remove the pan from the heat.

7. Add the pasta to the boiling water and cook for 2 minutes less than the low end of the package instructions. Use a mesh spider to transfer the pasta directly to the skillet. Return the skillet to medium heat. Add ¾ cup of the pasta cooking water and bring to a simmer. Add the shrimp along with any accumulated juices and cook, stirring and tossing, until the shrimp are firm and pink throughout and the sauce is glossy but still pools at the bottom of the pan, 4 to 6 minutes. Remove the pan from the heat and stir in the parsley and lemon juice.

8. Transfer the pasta to a serving dish or individual bowls, drizzle with more oil, sprinkle with the pangrattato, and serve.

NOTE: 1½ pounds of shrimp gives you a dish that's chock-full of shrimp, which is how I like it. But you could reduce the quantity to 1 pound and still have a nice amount. Using the shells in the sauce is crucial, because it infuses the entire dish with delicious shrimp flavor. Try to find shrimp marked "easy peel" or "simple peel," which are easy to work with and come deveined.

ZING: FLAVOR BOMBS, NOT BELLY BOMBS

4

"MOM, WHERE DO RECIPES COME FROM?"

The most common question I got from friends as I was working on this book was, "How do you actually come up with the recipes?" As I've said, you can hear more about the whole project in *The Sporkful* podcast series about the making of this book, but the Cavatelli with Roasted Artichokes and Preserved Lemon (page 112) in particular provides a window into the process, so I'm going to tell you its origin story . . .

In February 2022, I got my hands on as many classic Italian pasta cookbooks as I could find and looked through them for dishes that might provide inspiration. One such book was *Sauces & Shapes: Pasta the Italian Way* by Oretta Zanini De Vita and Maureen Fant, who are also the author and translator, respectively, of the seminal *Encyclopedia of Pasta*.

They have a recipe for a pasta dish with artichoke and lemon, which immediately grabbed my attention because I love artichokes, I love lemon, and I had never had a pasta dish with them before. Their recipe uses fresh artichokes, but I immediately knew I would use canned, because it's so much easier. I consulted with recipe developers Katie Leaird and Asha Loupy, who share my love of preserved lemon, a North African staple that packs a punch of salty, tart, savory flavor, and we came up with the idea of using that in place of the traditional fresh lemon. Katie started testing versions of what would become our Cavatelli with Roasted Artichokes and Preserved Lemon.

After cooking the dish four times to fine-tune her recipe, she sent it to me so I could try it. Katie had hit on the idea of coating artichoke quarters in cornstarch and shallow frying them to make them golden and crispy. I cooked the dish (Test No. 5 overall) and said, "THIS IS AMAZING I LOVE IT, NO NOTES!"

Okay, I had some notes, but they were small. After some tweaks the recipe was sent ahead to Rebeccah Marsters, our recipe editor, who did the final test on every recipe. She had a few more small suggestions, we made the changes, and in May 2022 it was moved into the folder of Finished Recipes.

The dish was so good that I couldn't wait until the book came out to share it with friends. That summer I made it for a barbecue, and people loved it. But I spent the meal furrowing my brow.

There were two issues, and they were related: First, cooking this dish in the July heat, when I'm less inclined to want fried foods, made me worry that frying the artichokes would be a turnoff to some people, both for health reasons and because it can be messy. And the fried crisp that should make those downsides worthwhile turned out not to last long—when the dish sat even a short time, the excess moisture inherent in canned vegetables softened the fried artichokes' exteriors. The second problem? I wanted more artichokes.

At that time the recipe called for two cans of artichokes, which you could fry all together. Adding a third can would mean frying in batches, which would make the recipe take longer and compound my reservations about the frying.

Then one day during one of our weekly *Sporkful* team check-ins, which often begin with conversations about what we're all cooking and eating, producer Andres O'Hara said, "Did you know you can buy jarred artichokes in oil and just dump them onto a sheet pan and roast them and they're delicious?"

I did not know that. But it gave me an idea. If we switched to roasting the artichokes, we could up the recipe to three cans, everything would fit on one sheet pan, and it would resolve my concerns about frying.

I consulted with Katie and Rebeccah, and we agreed to move the recipe back to the folder of Recipes in Progress.

Katie came to my house and we tried the new method together—if you're keeping track, this was Test No. 8. I wanted to stick with canned artichokes (not jarred), which come in water and not oil, because they're easier to find. So we had to work out how best to prepare them—how much you need to pat them dry, how much oil you need to add, how long they need to roast for.

As Katie and I tried different approaches, Janie wandered in and out of the kitchen. When it was finally time to eat, she was struck by how long we were spending on one recipe.

"It seems like so much work," she told us as she ate the pasta, not appearing to notice whether it was any good at all, let alone whether any of the changes we'd made had improved it. "Do you really want to do this cookbook? There's just a lot of recipes already out there."

I pointed out to Janie that this sounded a lot like her skepticism about my quest to invent a new pasta shape, which was preceded by her doubts about me starting my own podcast back in 2010. She started chuckling.

"You're right—I've doubted everything you've done," she said, her face turning red with laughter. "I guess I don't have faith in you."

I chose to take this as a positive. All my other projects that Janie had doubted turned out great! At this point in our lives, I see her skepticism as the ultimate sign that I'm on the right track.

And Katie says that based on her experience as a recipe developer, eight tests isn't even that many. She once tested a recipe a hundred times!

"The value in a cookbook over getting free recipes on the internet—which I'm not trying to knock because I write those too—is knowing that these recipes have really been vetted and that a lot of different sets of hands have made them," she said. "Before you put anything in print like that, I think there is a call to embrace repetition, because that's where you find the ways to streamline. That's where you find

the really balanced flavors or the little thing that's going to make a difference. So, no, I don't think nine times is a lot. I mean, I'd be happy to keep going on this."

Good thing, because that's what we did.

While Janie didn't have feedback on our work that day, I had concerns about the preserved lemon. There was both too much and not enough. We were calling for a whole lemon, half of which was finely chopped and mixed into the dish, and half of which was thinly sliced and laid on top at the end. Those finishing slices looked beautiful, but if you got one in your mouth, it was a lot. As much as I love preserved lemon, it's a very strong flavor and there is such a thing as too much. On the other hand, if I got a bite without one of those slices, I wanted more of it. I suggested we reduce to three-quarters of a preserved lemon in total and chop and mix in all of it, which would mean more of it mixed into the dish, but no more slices on top.

In the following weeks, Katie cooked the recipe twice more to nail down the details. Then I cooked it again (Test No. 11). In September, Rebeccah did her final test (No. 12) and confirmed that she thought it worked.

We were ready to move it back into the Finished Recipes folder. But I couldn't bear the thought of finalizing this recipe, which we had worked so hard on, which I love so much, without being absolutely certain myself that we had it right.

So that is why, in October 2022, eight months and thirty-one cans of artichokes after I found that recipe for that artichoke and lemon dish, I cooked this dish again (Test No. 13). It was perfect.

And that's how we ended up with this recipe. It's one of my five Sleeper Hits of the cookbook, which is partly why I wanted to share the epic tale of its creation. If you found this story incredibly boring, that'll teach you not to ask a cookbook author how they come up with their recipes! Maybe the reason they never tell you is that it's not actually that interesting! But I like nerding out on process, so here we are.

CAVATELLI WITH ROASTED ARTICHOKES AND PRESERVED LEMON

SERVES 4 TO 6 • TOTAL TIME: 40 MINUTES • DEVELOPED WITH KATIE LEAIRD

The journey to arrive at this recipe was monthslong. If you want a real window into the recipe development process, see "Mom, Where Do Recipes Come From?" on page 110.

All I will tell you here is that this is one of my five Sleeper Hits of the cookbook (see page 5) for a reason.

The cheese in this dish dissolves into the sauce, and my daughter Emily, who only believes there's cheese in pasta if she can see it, said, "This pasta doesn't have any cheese on it, so I was like, 'Oh my God, I need cheese on it.' Because you know, cheese is the best. But I still had to taste it and it actually tastes really, really good."

"The pasta shape cavatelli, it goes really well with the flavor," said my other daughter, Becky. "The lemon preserves or whatever you call it sticks to the pasta shape. So I like it because then you get some of it in every bite. I like the flavor, I think it's more interesting than plain pasta."

Try it yourself and find out why this is one dish I'll be making for years to come!

While this dish will lose its sauciness if it sits, the flavor remains outstanding, so it does function well as a pasta salad made in advance, especially if you're using fresh cavatelli, which is very durable. If it's been sitting for an hour or two, just add a drizzle of olive oil and toss before serving.

2 tablespoons kosher salt

Three 14-ounce cans quartered artichoke hearts, drained and patted dry (see note)

7 tablespoons extra-virgin olive oil

1 pound cavatelli (see note; or use casarecce, strozzapreti, gemelli, or gnocchi)

3 garlic cloves, thinly sliced

¼ cup finely chopped preserved lemon (about ¾ medium lemon; see tip)

2 tablespoons drained capers, roughly chopped

½ teaspoon freshly ground black pepper

½ cup chopped fresh parsley

½ cup (2 ounces) finely grated Pecorino Romano

1. Place an oven rack in the lower-middle position and heat the oven to 450°F. Bring 4 quarts of water and the salt to a boil in a large pot. On a rimmed sheet pan, use your hands to gently toss the artichokes with 3 tablespoons of the oil until evenly coated, then spread into a single layer, cut side down. Transfer to the oven and roast until deeply browned on the bottom, 18 to 22 minutes, rotating the pan halfway through.

(continued)

2. Add the pasta to the boiling water and cook for 2 minutes less than the low end of the package instructions.

3. Meanwhile, heat the remaining 4 tablespoons (¼ cup) of oil in a large, high-sided skillet over medium heat. Add the garlic and cook, stirring constantly, until fragrant and just starting to brown, about 1 minute; remove the pan from the heat.

4. Use a mesh spider to transfer the pasta directly to the skillet and return to medium heat. Add 1½ cups of the pasta cooking water, the preserved lemon, capers, pepper, and three-quarters of the roasted artichokes (choose the lighter-colored artichokes to stir in, reserving the more browned ones for topping). Cook, tossing and stirring to combine, until the sauce thickens and clings to the pasta but still pools slightly in the pan, 3 to 5 minutes.

5. Remove the pan from the heat and stir in the parsley and Pecorino. Transfer the pasta to a serving dish or individual bowls, top with the remaining artichokes, and serve.

ARTICHOKES NOTE: Thoroughly drying the artichokes is key to getting some good color on them—use a double layer of paper towels to gently but firmly pat them dry, then discard the towels and repeat. Or roll them up in a clean kitchen towel and press them dry.

PASTA NOTE: We developed this recipe with big, rustic, fresh cavatelli, found in the refrigerator or freezer section of some supermarkets and many Italian specialty stores. (Rustichella d'Abruzzo also makes a great dried one, although if you get the 8.8-ounce package, you'll need two.) If you can't find cavatelli that are at least 1 inch long, don't bother with the little dried ones—just substitute one of the options suggested.

PRESERVED LEMON TIP: Preserved lemons are a punchy powerhouse—their salted citrus brings not only layered lemon flavor and tang but also a special salinity that kosher salt alone cannot compete with. Plus once you have a jar, you can use them in a range of recipes in this book, including Mezze Maniche with Harissa Lamb and Mint-Parsley Gremolata (page 173) and Crispy Gnocchi Salad with Preserved Lemon–Tomato Dressing (page 217). Look for whole packaged preserved lemons in the cheese section, or jarred ones in the international or "Global Flavors" aisle of larger grocery stores or specialty shops. I used Les Moulins Mahjoub brand from Whole Foods. You can also make your own; it's very easy and there are instructions online. When adding to a recipe, use every part but the seeds!

SWORDFISH WITH SALSA VERDE SAGNE A PEZZI

SERVES 4 TO 6 • TOTAL TIME: 45 MINUTES • DEVELOPED WITH ASHA LOUPY

Swordfish is one of my favorite fish in the world, but it can be stressful to make at home. The window between "cooked through and juicy" and "overcooked and dry" is alarmingly small, and this fish can be expensive, so if you overcook it, it's doubly depressing. (Apparently this issue isn't exclusive to home cooks—I ordered swordfish in two restaurants in Italy and it was the only food I had there that was consistently disappointing.)

But the cooking method in this recipe will deliver succulent, flavorful fish every time, even if you've never cooked swordfish before. That's why it's one of my Sleeper Hits of the cookbook (see page 5). I knew it was a winner when Janie raved, "This is like something you'd get at a restaurant!"

I'm pairing it with a shape called sagne a pezzi, which means "short broken pieces of lasagna." You know how Cap'n Crunch makes Crunch Berries, his regular cereal with round berry cereal pieces mixed in? He also has a version that's just the crunch berries, and they make it seem like it was an accident at the factory and call it OOPS! All Berries. I like to think of this pasta shape as "OOPS! All Ruffles," because it's like the ruffles of lasagna without much of the flat part. It's perfect with a high chunk-factor, low-viscosity sauce like this because all those tight ruffles hold even a thin sauce, and its meaty center can stand up to the heartiest piece of fish. As far as I know, Rustichella d'Abruzzo is the only company that makes sagne a pezzi, but you can also use Sfoglini's reginetti, another excellent version of this shape, just with a different name.

Lemon-Herb Pangrattato (page 28; optional)

2 tablespoons plus 2½ teaspoons kosher salt

2 garlic cloves, roughly chopped

2 cups chopped fresh parsley

3 tablespoons finely chopped chives

2 tablespoons drained capers

1 tablespoon finely chopped fresh marjoram or oregano (optional)

3 anchovy fillets, roughly chopped

2 teaspoons finely grated lemon zest, plus 2 tablespoons freshly squeezed lemon juice

½ to 1 teaspoon red pepper flakes (depending on desired spiciness)

½ cup plus 2 tablespoons extra-virgin olive oil

1¼ to 1½ pounds swordfish, skinned and cut into 1-inch cubes (see tip)

½ teaspoon freshly ground black pepper

1 pound sagne a pezzi pasta (or reginetti or cascatelli)

1. Make the pangrattato, if using, and set aside.

2. Bring 4 quarts of water and 2 tablespoons of the salt to a boil in a large pot.

(continued)

3. Use a mortar and pestle to pound the garlic and 1¼ teaspoons of the salt to a fine paste (see tip). Add ⅔ cup of the parsley and pound into a coarse paste; repeat with the remaining parsley, adding it in two more batches. Add the chives, capers, marjoram (if using), anchovies, lemon zest, and red pepper flakes and pound into a coarse, rustic paste. Stir in the lemon juice and the ½ cup of oil and transfer to a shallow serving bowl. (Alternatively, pulse the garlic, salt, and herbs in a food processor, drizzle in the oil with the motor running, then add the capers, anchovies, lemon zest and juice, and red pepper flakes and pulse to combine.)

4. Season the fish all over with the remaining 1¼ teaspoons of salt and the black pepper. Heat the remaining 2 tablespoons of oil in a large skillet over medium-high heat until shimmering. Add the fish to the pan in a single layer and cook, stirring occasionally and keeping a close eye on its color, until light golden on at least one side and the flesh just flakes when pierced with a fork, 4 to 8 minutes. (The precise cooking time will vary depending on a variety of factors so focus on the cues to know when the fish is done.) Transfer the swordfish and any oil in the pan to the dish with the sauce, toss to coat, and let sit for 10 minutes. (This allows the fish to finish cooking without drying out.)

5. Meanwhile, add the pasta to the boiling water and cook until just al dente (the low end of the package instructions). Drain, shaking off the excess water, and immediately transfer to the bowl with the fish. Toss to coat the pasta in the sauce.

6. Serve directly out of the bowl or transfer to individual bowls and serve with the pangrattato, if using.

SWORDFISH TIP: Use a sharp chef's knife or boning knife to remove the skin from the fish, or better yet, have your fishmonger do it. Meaty swordfish has a thick, reddish bloodline that runs through it—it's not bad for you and I love it, but it can taste a bit fishy. If your piece contains some of the bloodline, you can choose to slice it out while you're cutting up the fish.

MORTAR AND PESTLE TIP: Like pesto, this rustic herb sauce really benefits from being made with a mortar and pestle. Pounding the herbs releases their natural oils and creates a luscious sauce. That said, if you don't have a mortar and pestle, you can make it in a food processor. Also, it's fantastic on any meaty white fish—I put it on broiled halibut and it was a home run.

Pappardelle with Arugula and Olives (page 118)

Swordfish with Salsa Verde Sagne a Pezzi (page 115)

PAPPARDELLE WITH ARUGULA AND OLIVES

SERVES 4 TO 6 • TOTAL TIME: 35 MINUTES • DEVELOPED WITH KATIE LEAIRD

If you're looking for a recipe that delivers maximum flavor with minimal effort, look no further. (See photo on previous page.) The only tricky element comes in the serving and eating.

This is a sauce with a high chunk factor and low to medium viscosity, so there's a danger some chunks will fall to the bottom of the mixing bowl or serving platter as you transfer the pasta (the dreaded Brazil nut effect—read more on page 154). In this dish, that may leave some eaters with all the olives and arugula and others with none. Be sure to use a large serving spoon and fork, and scoop from the bottom, to portion good ratios for all.

Now it's time to eat it. Pairing the sauce with a shape like pappardelle, which is flat and smooth and thus not especially sauceable, may seem at first like a mistake. But pappardelle is unique in the Long Shape Kingdom because it's the only pasta of its kind that shouldn't be twirled on the fork. It's so wide that twirling it covers the tines completely, rendering them incapable of picking up anything more. The best way to eat pappardelle is to first pull together a couple of strands of pasta into a small nest on the plate, then pick up and/or stab a few choice morsels of sauce, then use the exposed tines of the fork to stab the pasta nest through the heart. Not only will the pappardelle be especially toothsinkable when piled like this, but stabbing it last creates a cap on the end of your fork that holds other sauce components in place on the utensil. Finish by sweeping the bite through any residual sauce on the plate, lift, and enjoy.

2 tablespoons plus ¼ teaspoon kosher salt

1½ cups pitted green olives, preferably Castelvetrano

1 garlic clove, chopped

½ cup extra-virgin olive oil, plus more for serving

2 teaspoons finely grated lemon zest, plus 2 tablespoons freshly squeezed lemon juice

¾ teaspoon freshly ground black pepper

5 ounces (about 5 cups) baby arugula

1 pound (or two 8.8-ounce packages) pappardelle (or tagliatelle or fettuccine)

Shaved Parmesan, for serving (optional)

1. Bring 4 quarts of water and 2 tablespoons of the salt to a boil in a large pot.

2. Thinly slice ½ cup of the olives and set aside. Place the remaining 1 cup of olives and the garlic in the bowl of a food processor (or immersion blender) and pulse until coarsely chopped, 6 to 8 pulses, scraping down the sides of the bowl halfway through. Transfer the mixture to a large heatproof bowl and stir in the oil, lemon zest, pepper, and remaining ¼ teaspoon of salt. Fold in the arugula and let sit while cooking the pasta. (If making ahead, don't add the arugula until you start cooking the pasta; cover the olive mixture and set aside for up to 3 hours before proceeding with the recipe.)

3. Add the pasta to the boiling water and cook until just al dente (the low end of the package instructions). Transfer ⅓ cup of the pasta cooking water to the bowl with the arugula mixture, then drain the pasta, shaking off the excess water, and immediately add it to the bowl. Add the lemon juice and toss until the pasta is well coated and the arugula is wilted.

4. Transfer the pasta to a serving dish or individual bowls, top with the reserved sliced olives and shaved Parmesan (if desired), drizzle with more oil, and serve.

CRESTE DI GALLO WITH FAVA BEANS AND DANDELION GREENS

SERVES 4 TO 6 • TOTAL TIME: 1 HOUR 20 MINUTES • DEVELOPED WITH KATIE LEAIRD

Fava e cicoria is a classic dish from Puglia made of creamy pureed fava beans with hearty wilted chicory on top—chicory in this case referring to a family of bitter, often foraged greens. It's a wonderful contrast in textures and flavors, but it's not typically a pasta dish—it's more often eaten as an appetizer, side dish, or light lunch, sometimes with bread for dipping.

Fava e cicoria is an example of cucina povera—the food of poverty, or poor people's food, which has come to define the Puglia region.

"It's being resourceful. It's using ingredients that might be considered subprime," says Katie Leaird. She spent time interning in restaurants in Puglia right after culinary school, and the ingenuity of cucina povera has been a big part of her ethos ever since.

"Chicory is a great example," Katie tells me. "It could be considered a weed, but it's got this delicious, bitter, not quite spicy, but very earthy flavor to it. And it's a staple" in Puglia. (For our recipe we call for an easier-to-find bitter green that could also be considered a weed—dandelion greens.)

When I was in Lecce, in the southern tip of Puglia, cooking teacher Silvestro Silvestori told me that in the late 1700s, peasants in the region started foraging greens as a form of protest against a system of sharecropping instituted by the upper class. "It's sort of a middle finger to the nobles, because they can't control foraged greens," he says.

When I told him that we were going to riff on fava e cicoria and make it a pasta dish, he responded, "I don't have a problem with that. I don't wanna be involved in it." His work is about keeping tradition alive. "Some kid with a neck tattoo from New Jersey who thinks he's gonna improve whatever—that's not how I see food," he said. (For the record, while I am from New Jersey, I do not have a neck tattoo.) So we decided not to name this dish after fava e cicoria, but we still used it as our inspiration.

When I asked Katie how she felt about turning it into a pasta dish, she said, "Please do not tell any of my grandma friends in Puglia. It might actually cause heart failure. Nonna Yolanda, I am sorry. The crazy American is at it again."

I'm pairing this sauce with creste di gallo, which means "rooster's combs," although it reminds me more of a stegosaurus. Sometimes confused with cascatelli, this shape is a far superior alternative to elbow macaroni because of its inclusion of a spine of ruffles.

(continued)

8 tablespoons (½ cup) extra-virgin olive oil, plus more for serving

12 ounces dandelion greens (1 large or 2 small bunches), stemmed and sliced into ¼-inch ribbons (see note)

3 garlic cloves, minced

2½ teaspoons plus 2 tablespoons kosher salt

2 cups (11 ounces) shelled and blanched dried fava beans, rinsed (see note)

2 teaspoons finely grated lemon zest, plus 2 tablespoons freshly squeezed lemon juice

1 pound cresto di gallo (or campanelle, torchio, or medium shells)

1. Heat 2 tablespoons of the oil in a large, high-sided skillet over medium-high heat. Add the greens, garlic, and ½ teaspoon of the salt and cook, stirring often, until the greens are softened and just starting to brown around the edges, 5 to 7 minutes. Transfer to a plate and set aside, reserving the skillet.

2. Add 6 cups of water, the beans, and 2 teaspoons of the salt to the skillet and bring to a boil over medium-high heat. Reduce the heat to medium-low, cover, and simmer until the beans are completely tender and beginning to fall apart, 45 to 60 minutes, adjusting the heat as necessary to maintain a medium simmer.

3. While the beans are cooking, bring 4 quarts of water and the remaining 2 tablespoons of salt to a boil in a large pot.

4. When the beans are done, remove the pan from the heat. Using the back of a spoon, mash about half of the beans. Stir in the remaining 6 tablespoons of oil and the lemon zest, cover, and set aside.

5. Add the pasta to the boiling water and cook for 3 minutes less than the low end of the package instructions. Use a mesh spider to transfer the pasta directly to the skillet and return the heat to medium-high, reserving the pasta cooking water. Return the greens and garlic to the skillet and stir until the sauce is warmed through and evenly coats the pasta, 1 to 3 minutes. (The sauce should coat the pasta but still pool at the bottom of the pan; it will continue to thicken as it sits. If it seems too thick at any point, add reserved pasta water 1 tablespoon at a time to loosen it.) Remove the pan from the heat and stir in the lemon juice.

6. Transfer the pasta to a serving dish or individual bowls, drizzle very generously with more oil, and serve immediately.

GREENS NOTE: If you can't find dandelion greens, you can use another bitter leafy green like kale or Swiss chard, although when I started working on this recipe, I was surprised to see that dandelion greens were in several of my local supermarkets—I had just never looked for them before. (They're the same dandelion leaves you see growing in your grass, and are usually in bunches near the kale.) To prep the greens, cut off and discard the bottom few inches of the stem that protrudes beyond the leaf. If the stems are thick and tough, strip the leaves off and discard the whole stem; if the stems seem thin and tender, leave them in and cut them with the leaves. To slice the greens, stack the stemmed leaves and roll them into a tight cylinder, then slice crosswise to create ¼-inch ribbons.

FAVA BEANS NOTE: This recipe was developed with Bob's Red Mill dried fava beans, labeled "Shelled Blanched Fava Beans," which are readily available online if you don't see them in the dried bean aisle of your local grocery store. Do not use Middle Eastern brown fava beans, which are wonderful in many things but won't have the right flavor here.

NAPA CABBAGE KIMCHI

PROBIOTIC · VEGAN · GLUTEN-FREE · RAW · NO ADDED SUGAR

VOLCANO KIMCHI

SMALL BATCH

16 oz

Kimchi Carbonara

Kimchi alla Gricia
(page 131)

KIMCHI CARBONARA

SERVES 4 TO 6 • TOTAL TIME: 40 MINUTES • DEVELOPED WITH IRENE YOO

When I looked for collaborators for this book, I wanted to work with people who would be comfortable bringing together elements of different cuisines. When I came across Irene Yoo's recipe for kimchi carbonara, I knew she'd be perfect.

Irene grew up in Southern California, spending childhood summers in Seoul. She ate a lot of Korean food cooked by her mom in California, her grandma in Korea, and street vendors around Seoul.

When she left home at eighteen, she moved to Philadelphia.

"I discovered Italian food, because there are so many amazing Italian restaurants there," Irene told me. "The first thing that I ate that really opened my eyes was risotto. And I was like, 'This is amazing. I've never experienced anything like this before.' It kind of reminded me of Korean juk, which is a rice porridge. I was like, 'I need to learn how to make this,' and I went home and made it over and over again until I could do it with my eyes closed."

Then Irene discovered carbonara, the classic Italian pasta dish made with guanciale (cured pork jowl, similar to bacon but less smoky), eggs, cheese, and black pepper.

"[It] was one of those BYO restaurants in Philly, one of those family restaurants," Irene says. "And I remember it was so simple but so creamy: that thick al dente pasta, with the really fatty pork and just the creaminess that comes from the eggs. And I love eggs. Growing up, I had only really known about fettuccine Alfredo or tomato sauce, so the fact that there were other types of pasta was really mind-blowing. And something like carbonara, which was so simple in its ingredients, but so transcendent in terms of its flavors, was really amazing. I had spent eighteen years eating only Korean food and I still loved Korean food, but I was really excited to eat other things."

Irene quickly became excited to cook them, too, which she did for years.

"I got to a point where I realized I was really homesick for my own cultural food and Korean food in general. So that's when I started to sort of meld the two."

While working at Food Network in New York, Irene started hosting pop-up dinners under the umbrella of Yooeating, which she billed as Korean American comfort food. Yooeating would become a YouTube channel, and in 2020 she posted her first video: kimchi carbonara.

"It's not just that you add kimchi to carbonara and your day's done. The concept behind it is cooking the kimchi in a way that you would with kimchi fried rice or even kimchi jjigae. Kimchi is a wonderful ingredient. I think it's really underrated when cooked. Frying kimchi in butter or bacon fat just takes it to a whole other level."

(continued)

I completely agree. Cooking the kimchi mellows its spice, and adding it to carbonara brings an acidity that this rich dish didn't know it needed. Irene and I made some tweaks to her original recipe, but the core concept remains the same, and it remains incredible.

So that's the story of kimchi carbonara. To read about the surprising history of traditional carbonara, see "Carbonara, Italy's Hot New Pasta Trend" on page 128.

A couple more notes . . .

This is a great way to use up older kimchi, which continues to ferment in your fridge and may eventually be more fermented than you like. Cooking it softens that flavor.

And yes, I decided to go with spaghetti for the carbonara and gricia, which follows. These are such classic dishes that it just feels right, and this is one instance where spaghetti works well—it's a thin, fairly clingy sauce and the chunks are easily stabbed.

2 tablespoons kosher salt

4 large eggs

1 cup (4 ounces) store-bought grated Pecorino Romano or Parmesan, plus more for serving (see tip)

1 teaspoon freshly ground black pepper, plus cracked peppercorns for serving (see tip on page 70)

8 ounces guanciale (see note)

1 tablespoon extra-virgin olive oil

2 cups napa cabbage kimchi, drained and chopped into 1-inch pieces

1 pound spaghetti (or spaghettoni, bucatini, or rigatoni)

1. Bring 4 quarts of water and the salt to a boil in a large pot.

2. In a large heatproof bowl, whisk the eggs, Pecorino, and ground pepper until smooth and consistent; set aside.

3. Line a plate with a double layer of paper towels. Slice the guanciale ¼ inch thick (about the thickness of thick-cut bacon), then into 1- by ½-inch rectangles, and add them to a large, high-sided skillet along with the oil. Spread the guanciale into a single layer, set the pan over medium-low heat, and cook, stirring occasionally, until the fat has rendered and the guanciale is deeply browned in spots, 8 to 12 minutes. Use a slotted spoon to transfer the guanciale to the prepared plate.

4. Pour the rendered fat into a heatproof bowl or liquid measuring cup, using a spatula to scrape out the pan. Return 3 tablespoons of the rendered fat to the skillet, discarding any excess or reserving it for another use, and place the skillet over medium-high heat. Add the kimchi and cook, stirring occasionally and scraping the bottom of the pan, until the moisture has evaporated and the kimchi starts to caramelize around the edges, 6 to 8 minutes; remove the pan from the heat.

5. Add the pasta to the boiling water and cook for 1 minute less than the low end of the package instructions. Use tongs to transfer the pasta directly to the skillet and return the heat to medium-high. Add the guanciale and cook, stirring constantly, until heated through and the pasta is evenly coated with the kimchi mixture, 1 to 2 minutes.

6. Immediately transfer the pasta to the bowl with the egg mixture. Add ½ cup of the pasta cooking water and use a rubber spatula to rapidly toss everything together until the pasta is well coated, the cheese is dissolved, and the sauce is smooth and glossy. (There should be extra sauce pooling in the bowl at first, but it should all cling to the pasta after 1 to 2 minutes of stirring. If the sauce looks too thick after 1 minute, add more pasta water 1 tablespoon at a time until smooth and creamy.)

7. Transfer the pasta to a serving dish or individual bowls, sprinkle generously with more Pecorino and the cracked peppercorns, and serve.

TIP: Pecorino is the traditional cheese for carbonara and gricia, but Parmesan will work and it's easier to find. Try to get cheese that's grated as finely as possible, so it will dissolve into the egg mixture more readily. For more, see page 10.

NOTE: If you can't find guanciale, substitute pancetta or bacon. American bacon will have a much smokier flavor than the Italian meats but will still be delicious. Make sure to cut the meat as directed—smaller pieces will cook much faster. Depending on the variety and brand of cured meat you use, it may vary considerably in fat content. If your meat is very lean and you end up without enough fat, add more olive oil to make up the difference.

CARBONARA, ITALY'S HOT NEW PASTA TREND

In Italian food culture, great emphasis is placed on continuing the old ways of doing things (even if Italians themselves often can't agree on which of the old ways is correct). This focus on preserving traditional methods is part of the romanticism that surrounds the cuisine and the reason why the food at a shack on the beach in Italy is better than the food at most restaurants in America.

When I showed cascatelli to the owner of a B&B outside Naples where I was staying, he stared at it like it was a moon rock, then said, "But . . . it's American."

So the stereotype that Italians oppose any deviation from tradition, and any idea from beyond their borders, is not unearned. Still, in my travels there, my biggest takeaway was that it's an oversimplification. In fact, I came to believe that Italians themselves don't give their cuisine enough credit for its continued evolution.

While I was in Rome, I met Katie Parla, an American cookbook author who moved there twenty years ago. She's been giving food tours and researching and writing about Italian cuisine ever since. Over lunch at the trattoria Piatto Romano, Katie shared a single fact that shocked me:

Pasta didn't become a core part of Italian food identity until the early 1900s.

Katie explained that some Italian regional cuisines always relied on pasta as a staple. But in other regions, she said, "They might have eaten pasta on a holiday if the duke or the noble in that town provided flour. It wasn't a daily thing."

A variety of factors came together over a century to spread pasta across Italy, and to fuel pasta innovation:

- Mid to late 1800s: The northern and southern regions of Italy are unified into one country, which leads to more regional intermixing.

- Early 1900s: Italy's fascist government sees pasta as a way to unite the people behind a new pasta-centric Italian identity, and to feed the masses cheaply as the population booms. Pasta factories are built in regions where there were none before.

- Mid-1900s: Italians move in droves from the countryside to the cities. As it usually does, all this migration leads to cultural mash-ups and culinary innovation.

Over pasta at another trattoria, Armando al Pantheon, Katie explained that when this migration to cities started, there was already a dish called pasta alla gricia common in some rural areas—"the OG shepherd's pasta" in Katie's words—made with Pecorino and guanciale. (She says black pepper, now part of the recipe, would likely have been too precious a spice for the average shepherd.) As rural Italians moved to cities in the mid-1900s, gricia came to Rome. Over time eggs were added, and carbonara was born. (Others added tomatoes instead, creating another dish that would become iconic—amatriciana.)

So carbonara is a pretty new addition to the pasta canon, but that's not the most shocking thing about it. According to Italian food historian Luca Cesari, author of *A Brief History of Pasta,* carbonara is actually "an American dish born in Italy." In other words, it was made possible by the American presence in Italy during World War II. As the *Financial Times* explained in a March 2023 piece:

> The story that most experts agree on is that an Italian chef, Renato Gualandi, first made it in 1944 at a dinner in Riccione for the U.S. army with guests including [British statesman] Harold Macmillan. "The Americans had fabulous bacon, very good cream, some cheese and powdered egg yolks," Gualandi later recalled.
>
> For Italians born after boom years, carbonara has an unalterable set of ingredients: pork jowl, Roman pecorino cheese, eggs, and pepper. But early recipes are surprisingly varied. The oldest was printed in Chicago in 1952 and featured Italian bacon, not pork jowl. Italian recipes from around the same time include everything from gruyère (1954, in the magazine La Cucina Italiana) to "prosciutto, and thinly sliced sautéed mushrooms" (1958, Rome's Tre Scalini restaurant). Pork jowl didn't come to replace bacon until as recently as the 1990s.

And Americans are far from the first non-Italians to have influenced Italian pasta history. One example is orecchiette, the "little ears" pasta shape from Bari. Some historians believe it's actually from France and came to southern Italy during the thirteenth century with the Angevins. (The French influence extends beyond pasta. Ciabatta, which you'd think is a centuries-old Italian bread, was actually invented in the 1980s, inspired by the popularity of baguettes.) And there would be no pasta in Italy at all if Muslims from North Africa hadn't brought durum wheat across the Mediterranean in the first place.

So not only is Italian pasta history much more fluid than I thought, it's also not exclusively Italian. Despite this fact, I suspect when folks around Rome took the dish many people knew as gricia and started making carbonara, there were some who cried, "HOW CAN YOU ADD EGGS TO GRICIA?! THAT'S NOT THE WAY IT'S DONE! YOU RUINED THE GRICIA!!!"

Today, I'm sure many of the children and grandchildren of those Italians can't imagine this dish *without* the eggs—to them, carbonara is an obvious combination and a timeless classic.

But if you told them someone was adding kimchi to it, some of them might say, "HOW CAN YOU ADD KIMCHI TO CARBONARA?! THAT'S NOT THE WAY IT'S DONE! YOU RUINED THE CARBONARA!!!"

Then again, I think some of them would be intrigued by the idea. Because as Katie Parla showed me when we ate at Cesare al Casaletto (yet another Roman trattoria—I really made the most of my time with her), Italian food continues to evolve today. Instead of serving cacio e pepe with a long pasta, which is traditional, chef Leonardo Pia makes it with deep-fried gnocchi. It's incredible, and Leonardo's light touch with his breaded lamb chop (see photo on next page) and the paper-thin crust of his Roman pizza tell me he's not just throwing things together for shock value.

Toward the end of the meal he pulled up a chair, and with Katie translating, we talked about changes over time in Italian cuisine. Leonardo told me it doesn't come out of nowhere. "You're in the kitchen every day, the ingredients are right there. So just combining them in a new way is actually not a huge paradigm shift," he said, echoing what Khushbu Shah told me about South Asians in diaspora cooking pasta dishes (page 54). Leonardo continued, "It's just a natural evolution of understanding an ingredient and seeing how it works with another seasonal element."

Cooking, he says, depends on context. "If you're in America and you're making pasta, you would pull from the ingredients that are close to you. Maybe you are getting cheese from Wisconsin and Mexican-origin chile peppers." That statement may be even truer than Leonardo realizes—roughly speaking that's how the Tex-Mex staple green spaghetti, which inspired the dish on page 48, was born!

So Italian cuisine doesn't change at the pace of some others, and that's part of its charm. But like every cuisine, thanks to new ideas from inside and out, it does evolve, and combinations that seemed outlandish at first become canon in time.

The spaghetti alla gricia at Armando al Pantheon

Katie Parla at Piatto Romano

Taking a rare break from eating pasta (but not from recording) with Katie Parla at Piatto Romano

The lightly breaded lamb chops made by chef Leonardo Pia at Cesare al Casaletto

KIMCHI ALLA GRICIA

SERVES 4 TO 6 • TOTAL TIME: 45 MINUTES • DEVELOPED WITH IRENE YOO

Gricia has been called the mother of Italy's traditional pastas because it's the primary source material for the classic dishes carbonara and amatriciana. (For more, see page 128.)

Of all the incredible meals around Rome that food writer Katie Parla and I shared, the most memorable was at Armando al Pantheon. Their spaghetti alla gricia, which they make with a little white wine (not traditional!), was the most incredible pasta dish I had in Italy, and no, I did not suggest that they try it with a different shape. It was simple and perfect and I wouldn't change a thing about it. (See photo on opposite page.)

But when I got home, I thought to myself, *I wonder how it would taste with kimchi.* I already knew kimchi worked in carbonara—how would it work in gricia, carbonara's mother dish?

So I used Irene's kimchi cooking technique from the carbonara, tweaked the ratios of pasta water and rendered fat, and added a bit of white wine like they do at Armando's. Turns out kimchi in gricia is equally incredible, but different. In carbonara it's about how the kimchi cuts through the richness of the eggs. In gricia it's more about how the kimchi plays with the guanciale, contrasting both its fattiness and its meatiness, providing a light crunch and acidity that makes the combo almost reminiscent of a funked-up BLT.

Try both kimchi pastas and see if you can pick a favorite!

1 tablespoon kosher salt

8 ounces guanciale (see note on page 127)

1 tablespoon extra-virgin olive oil

2 cups napa cabbage kimchi, drained and chopped into 1-inch pieces

¼ cup dry white wine

1 pound spaghetti

1 teaspoon freshly ground black pepper, plus cracked peppercorns for serving (see tip on page 70)

1 cup (4 ounces) store-bought grated Pecorino Romano or Parmesan, plus more for serving (see tip on page 127)

1. Bring 4 quarts of water and the salt to a boil in a large pot.

2. Line a plate with a double layer of paper towels. Slice the guanciale ¼ inch thick (about the thickness of thick-cut bacon), then into 1- by ½-inch rectangles, and add them to a large, high-sided skillet along with the oil. Spread the guanciale into a single layer, set the pan over medium-low heat, and cook, stirring occasionally, until the fat has rendered and the guanciale is deeply browned in spots, 8 to 12 minutes. Use a slotted spoon to transfer the guanciale to the prepared plate.

(continued)

3. Pour the rendered fat into a heatproof bowl or liquid measuring cup, using a spatula to scrape out the pan. Return 3 tablespoons of the rendered fat to the skillet, reserving any excess, and place the skillet over medium-high heat. Add the kimchi and cook, stirring occasionally and scraping the bottom of the pan, until the moisture has evaporated and the kimchi starts to caramelize around the edges, 6 to 8 minutes. Add the wine and simmer, scraping up any browned bits from the bottom of the pan, until evaporated, 1 to 3 minutes; remove the pan from the heat.

4. Add the pasta to the boiling water and cook for 2 minutes less than the low end of the package instructions. Use tongs to transfer the pasta directly to the skillet and return the heat to medium-high. Add 1 cup of the pasta cooking water, 1 tablespoon of the guanciale fat (or 1 tablespoon of olive oil if you don't have enough fat), discarding any excess, and the ground pepper and cook, stirring constantly, until the pasta is coated with the sauce but sauce still pools in the bottom of the pan, 2 to 4 minutes. Stir in the guanciale and Pecorino and cook, stirring, until the cheese is melted and all the ingredients are evenly distributed, about 1 minute. (If the sauce seems too thick, add more pasta water 1 tablespoon at a time until smooth and creamy.)

5. Transfer the pasta to a serving dish or individual bowls, sprinkle with more Pecorino and the cracked peppercorns, and serve.

SHAKSHUKA AND SHELLS

SERVES 2 OR 3 (OR 4 TO 6, SEE NOTE) • TOTAL TIME: 50 MINUTES • DEVELOPED WITH ASHA LOUPY

Shakshuka, a dish of eggs poached in tomato sauce that's found across North Africa and the Middle East, is one of my favorite things to make for my family for weekend brunches and lunches. Sharing a meal is always nice, but there's something especially communal about having everyone help themselves right from the pan you cooked the food in. Typically I serve it with grilled crusty bread, but then I thought, why not make it into a pasta dish?

I like my shakshuka with cherry tomatoes and no bell peppers, and I'll tell you why. There have been great advances in cherry tomato cultivation in recent years, and you can now get incredibly sweet, plump ones in most supermarkets all year round. So this is a tomato dish that you don't have to wait for tomato season to enjoy.

As for bell peppers, to me, you put those in a sauce and that's all you taste. The stars of my preferred shakshuka are tomatoes, eggs, and herbaceous za'atar. Everyone else is a supporting player—cumin seeds add earthy fragrance, lemons and feta add acidity and tang. I leave out the traditional spiciness so everyone in my family enjoys it, and serve it with sriracha on the side for those who want it. So we don't need bell peppers trying to hog the spotlight. This production already has plenty of star power!

⅓ cup extra-virgin olive oil

¾ teaspoon cumin seeds (optional)

1 white or yellow onion, finely diced

2½ teaspoons plus 1 tablespoon kosher salt, plus more for the eggs

3 tablespoons tomato paste

4 garlic cloves, minced

6 cups (30 ounces) cherry tomatoes

3 teaspoons za'atar

8 ounces (about 3 cups) lumache pasta (or cestini or medium shells; see note)

4 to 6 large eggs

4 ounces feta cheese, coarsely crumbled (1 cup; see feta tip on page 85)

½ cup roughly chopped fresh parsley or cilantro

Lemon wedges, for serving

Sriracha or other hot sauce, for serving

1. Heat the oil in a large, high-sided skillet over medium heat until shimmering. Add the cumin seeds, if using, and cook until darkened a shade, 30 to 45 seconds. Add the onion and 1 teaspoon of the salt and cook, stirring occasionally, until the onion is softened and golden around the edges, 9 to 13 minutes, adjusting the heat if the onion starts to darken too quickly.

(continued)

2. Meanwhile, bring 2 quarts of water and 1 tablespoon of the salt to a boil in a pot.

3. Reduce the heat under the skillet to medium-low, add the tomato paste and garlic, and cook, stirring often, until the tomato paste has darkened to a brick red, 1 to 3 minutes. Add the tomatoes and the remaining 1½ teaspoons of salt. Stir to coat the tomatoes in the oil, cover, and cook, stirring occasionally, until the tomatoes start to burst, about 10 minutes. Using the back of a spoon or potato masher, gently press the tomatoes to break them open and release their juices. Stir in 2 teaspoons of the za'atar and cover.

4. Add the pasta to the boiling water (remember, it's only half the package, unless you mean to use it all!) and cook for 3 minutes less than the low end of the package instructions. Use a mesh spider to transfer the pasta directly to the skillet and increase the heat to medium-high. Stir in ¾ cup of the pasta cooking water and bring to a simmer, scraping up any browned bits from the bottom of the pan.

5. Using the bottom of a ladle or spoon, do your best to make a well in the pasta-tomato mixture and immediately crack an egg into the sauce. Repeat with the remaining eggs, spacing them evenly apart around the pan. Season each egg with a pinch of salt and sprinkle with the remaining 1 teaspoon of za'atar. Scatter the feta over the pasta (not so much over the eggs), then cover the pan and cook until the egg whites just start to turn opaque, 1 to 2 minutes. Remove the pan from the heat and let sit, covered, until the egg whites are set, 4 to 8 minutes. (This will result in runny yolks; for firmer yolks, leave the pan on the heat for 2 to 4 minutes before removing it and letting it sit.)

6. Sprinkle with the parsley and serve with lemon wedges and sriracha.

SERVINGS AND PASTA NOTE: This recipe is designed to create a saucy, spoonable shakshuka, using 8 ounces (a half pound) of pasta and 2 eggs per person. If you want more servings, you can easily use a full pound of pasta and as many eggs as you can fit on the surface in a single layer—that's what I do when making this for my family. Just remember to also double the amount of water and salt that you use to boil the pasta. You can add more pasta water to increase the volume of the sauce as desired. If you use the full pound of pasta, it'll be less saucy, more hearty, and still delicious in its own way!

VEGAN DIRTY ORZO (WITH MEAT OPTION)

SERVES 4 TO 6 • TOTAL TIME: 1 HOUR • DEVELOPED WITH DARNELL REED

This play on classic Louisiana dirty rice is made with orzo and was developed and tested using a plant-based ground meat alternative. (Technically that's an option for any dish in this book that calls for ground meat, but Darnell and I made this one vegan by default. That said, you're welcome to use ground beef or pork.) We also replace the traditional minced chicken liver with mushrooms. But we don't skimp on the Creole seasoning, and of course the holy trinity of onions, bell peppers, and celery plays a key role. To me, though, this dish's secret weapon is a healthy dose of whole-grain mustard. It doesn't take over—it just gives the dish a deep savoriness that you can't quite place and can't stop eating.

1⅓ cups vegetable stock or chicken stock, plus more as needed

1 slice white sandwich bread, crusts removed, torn into 1-inch pieces

1½ tablespoons plus ¾ teaspoon kosher salt

1 small green bell pepper, seeded and finely chopped

3 ounces (about 1 cup) shiitake mushrooms, cleaned, stemmed, and minced

2 shallots or 1 small yellow onion, minced

1 celery stalk, finely chopped

¼ cup finely chopped fresh parsley

3 garlic cloves, minced

2 teaspoons Creole seasoning, plus more for serving

1½ teaspoons minced fresh thyme leaves (optional)

¾ teaspoon freshly ground black pepper

1 pound ground meat alternative (or ground beef or pork)

2 tablespoons canola or other neutral oil, like soybean or vegetable

3 tablespoons whole-grain mustard

1 pound orzo

Crystal or other vinegar-based hot sauce, for serving

1. In a medium bowl, combine the stock and bread, pressing down to fully submerge the bread. Let sit until completely saturated, 10 to 15 minutes.

2. Meanwhile, bring 2½ quarts of water and 1½ tablespoons of the salt to a boil in a pot.

3. In a large bowl, combine the bell pepper, mushrooms, shallots, celery, 2 tablespoons of the parsley, the garlic, Creole seasoning, thyme (if using), black pepper, and remaining ¾ teaspoon of salt. Squeeze out the bread, reserving the stock, and crumble it into the vegetable mixture. Add 3 tablespoons of the reserved stock and mix until evenly combined. Add the ground meat and use your hands to mix until just combined (do not overmix). Transfer the remaining stock to a liquid measuring cup and, if necessary, add or pour off enough to measure 1 cup.

4. Heat the oil in a large, high-sided skillet over medium-high heat. Add the meat mixture and cook, stirring frequently and breaking it up with a wooden spoon, until the moisture has evaporated and the meat starts to form a layer on the bottom of the pan, 8 to 12 minutes. Add the reserved stock and the mustard, bring to a simmer, scraping up the browned bits from the bottom of the pan, and cook, stirring occasionally, until thickened but still saucy, 6 to 8 minutes. Cover and remove the pan from the heat.

5. Add the pasta to the boiling water and cook until just al dente (the low end of the package instructions). Drain in a fine-mesh strainer, shaking off the excess water. Immediately add the pasta to the skillet and stir until thoroughly combined with the meat mixture.

6. Transfer the pasta to a serving bowl or individual bowls, sprinkle with the remaining 2 tablespoons of parsley, and serve with more Creole seasoning and hot sauce.

LINGUINE WITH MISO CLAM SAUCE

SERVES 4 TO 6 • TOTAL TIME: 1 HOUR 10 MINUTES (40 MINUTES' ACTIVE TIME) • DEVELOPED WITH IRENE YOO

Linguine with clam sauce has a fantastic ratio of impressiveness to degree of difficulty. It feels like the kind of thing you'd only make on New Year's Eve or for a dinner party for old friends, but in reality, with a bit of forethought, you can whip it up on a Tuesday night just because you deserve it. Miso adds umami savoriness to the brininess of this classic dish and makes it even more foolproof.

The traditional pairing of this sauce with linguine has a lot of wisdom to it. Many people think linguine is just a narrower fettuccine, but if you look closely at its cross section, you'll see it's ovular, not flat. This makes it an ideal shape for slurping, because it's easier for your lips to form a seal around it. Coating it in a thin, oily sauce like this one provides lubrication for slurping and maximizes linguine's unique properties.

That being said, slurping always comes with the risk of a mess.

"Slurping noodles can be highly dangerous," David Hu, professor of mechanical engineering at Georgia Tech and an expert in fluid mechanics, warned in an episode of *The Sporkful*. "It really is more . . . advanced."

As Professor Hu explained, slurping exerts a great deal of force on noodles. As you slurp, the part of the noodle outside your mouth gets shorter, which means it gets lighter, which means it starts moving faster and faster, whipping back and forth as it hurtles toward your lips, spraying oily sauce in all directions.

"When you have high speeds applied to flexible objects, they start generating what we call 'instabilities,'" says Professor Hu. "You could create a mealtime disaster."

He says you can try to slurp slowly, or use shorter noodles, to reduce instability. But Professor Hu would rather take his chances: "It's only fun when you can actually endanger yourself."

So chow down, daredevils!

---

30 littleneck clams (2½ to 3 pounds; see note)

4 tablespoons kosher salt

½ cup dry white wine

¼ cup white or yellow miso

4 tablespoons (½ stick) unsalted butter

1½ cups (7½ ounces) cherry tomatoes, halved

4 garlic cloves, minced

½ teaspoon freshly ground black pepper

1 pound linguine (or spaghetti, fettuccine, or mafalde)

½ cup chopped fresh parsley

2 tablespoons freshly squeezed lemon juice

Crusty bread, for serving (optional)

(continued)

1. Place the clams in a large bowl and cover them with cold water. Stir the clams around a few times to loosen any sand and grit, then drain. Add fresh water to the bowl, covering the clams by at least 1 inch. Add 3 tablespoons of the salt, stir gently, and refrigerate for at least 30 minutes and up to 3 hours; drain.

2. Bring 4 quarts of water and the remaining 1 tablespoon of salt to a boil in a large pot.

3. In a small bowl or liquid measuring cup, whisk the wine and miso until no lumps remain; set aside.

4. Melt the butter in a large, high-sided skillet over medium heat. Add the tomatoes and cook, stirring occasionally, until they are just starting to soften, 2 to 4 minutes. Add the garlic and cook, stirring, until fragrant, 1 to 2 minutes. Add the wine-miso mixture and the pepper, increase the heat to medium-high, and bring to a simmer. Add the drained clams, cover, and cook until most of the clams have opened up at least partially, 7 to 9 minutes. Uncover and cook, stirring occasionally, until all the clams are fully opened, 5 to 10 minutes. (If any clams remain closed at this point, remove and discard them. See the note for more details). Remove the pan from the heat.

5. Add the pasta to the boiling water and cook for 1 minute less than the low end of the package instructions. Use a slotted spoon or mesh spider to remove the clams from the sauce and transfer them to a bowl, then use tongs to transfer the pasta directly to the skillet. Return to medium heat and stir until the sauce just coats the pasta but is still very brothy, 1 to 3 minutes. Remove the pan from the heat and stir in ¼ cup of the parsley and the lemon juice.

6. Transfer the pasta to a serving platter or individual bowls, top with the clams and any accumulated juices, and sprinkle with the remaining ¼ cup of parsley. Serve with crusty bread, if desired.

NOTE: When you buy clams, they should smell like seawater, not fishy, and the shells should be tightly closed. If any shells are open, tap them firmly; if they don't close after that, discard those clams. If you aren't cooking them immediately, store them in the fridge in netted bags or open-top containers, not in sealed bags. The soaking in step 1 helps clean the clams and get rid of grit. When you cook the clams, they should all open up at least ¼ inch—any that don't should be discarded. (If most of your clams aren't opening, they may just need to cook a little longer, especially if they were on ice or very cold when you started.)

LARB-ISH CASCATELLI

SERVES 4 TO 6 • TOTAL TIME: 45 MINUTES • DEVELOPED WITH JAMES PARK

This recipe is inspired by the one dish I always order at a Thai restaurant—the savory, spicy ground meat dish larb. You place the meat in a lettuce leaf, add a squeeze of lime, and enjoy. Because it involves ground meat, I wondered whether it could be adapted into a pasta sauce with similar flavors. I brought this idea to James, we did some brainstorming, and after he ran some tests and refined the concept, he texted me that it was "one of the best pasta dishes I've made IN MY LIFE. It was AMAZINGGGGG. I shocked myself."

Our larb-ish pasta recipe uses hot oil to bloom the fragrant, spicy Thai chili flakes, then adds plenty of lime juice, fish sauce, and nutty toasted rice powder to bring together the signature flavors of larb. Cascatelli is a perfect pairing as it holds on to the bits of meat, even in a sauce with low viscosity. Try it today and you'll shock yourself too!

Some fun facts about larb . . .

It originated in Laos and migrated to Thailand. In America it's more associated with Thai cuisine because of the proliferation of Thai restaurants in the U.S., which is largely due to a Thai government-sponsored program in the 2000s meant to bring more Thai restaurants to the States.

While it's spelled *larb* on most menus, the *r* is not pronounced. As my friends at the packaged food company Omsom explain, "Larb [is] pronounced 'lab' with a short *a* sound, as in *l-a-a-p*, with the tone falling during the vowel sound. The *b* in *larb* actually sounds more like a *p*, with the final consonant unvoiced." So it's not "laRRRb."

In some places you may see it spelled *laab*, *lahp*, or *laap*, all of which would be more phonetically accurate.

1 teaspoon plus ¼ cup canola or other neutral oil

¼ cup uncooked glutinous or jasmine rice (or other white rice; see note)

2 tablespoons kosher salt

3 medium shallots, sliced into very thin rings

½ cup roughly chopped fresh cilantro leaves and tender stems

½ cup roughly chopped fresh mint leaves

2 scallions, sliced

1 to 3 tablespoons Thai chili flakes (see note)

2 tablespoons brown sugar

¼ cup fish sauce

¼ cup freshly squeezed lime juice, plus lime wedges for serving

1 pound ground pork, turkey, or chicken

1 pound cascatelli pasta (or radiatore or creste di gallo)

(continued)

Toasted rice powder is available online or in Asian grocery stores, where it may be called khao khua (Thai) or bột thính gạo or thính (Vietnamese). If you want to buy it prepackaged, substitute 3 tablespoons of the ground and toasted powder for the rice and 1 teaspoon of the oil and skip step 1.

THAI CHILI FLAKES NOTE: Thai chili flakes are available online and at many Asian markets and some supermarkets. I bought mine from my favorite local Thai restaurant, Thai USA, where they make them in-house. Larb is supposed to be hot, but of course "hot" is different for different people. Unless your "hot" is very hot, I recommend sticking with 1 tablespoon. Also, while you won't get the same flavor, you can substitute gochugaru or ground Sichuan peppercorns in a pinch.

1. Heat 1 teaspoon of the oil in a large skillet over medium heat. Add the rice and toast, stirring and shaking the pan often, until deep golden brown, 4 to 6 minutes. Transfer to a spice grinder, reserving the skillet, and pulse until powdery. (The rice can also be pounded in a mortar and pestle, but it will take some time and elbow grease to achieve the right texture; it can be a little uneven, but you don't want large pieces or whole grains of rice.)

2. Bring 4 quarts of water and the salt to a boil in a large pot.

3. In a large heatproof bowl, combine the shallots, ¼ cup of the cilantro, ¼ cup of the mint, the scallions, chili flakes, and sugar. Heat the remaining ¼ cup of oil in the reserved skillet over high heat until just starting to smoke (this may take several minutes depending on your stovetop; you want the oil extremely hot). Carefully pour the hot oil over the shallot-herb mixture (it should sizzle), reserving the skillet. Add the fish sauce and lime juice to the bowl and stir until the sugar is dissolved.

4. Add the pork and ¼ cup of water to the reserved skillet and cook over medium-high heat, stirring occasionally and breaking up the meat, until cooked through but not browned, 6 to 8 minutes. (If the meat begins to color, add more water to the skillet 2 tablespoons at a time to prevent browning.) Use a slotted spoon to transfer the meat to the bowl with the shallot-herb mixture, discarding any liquid in the pan. Add the remaining ¼ cup each of cilantro and mint and stir to combine. (If making ahead, wait to add the remainder of the cilantro and mint until you start cooking the pasta; cover the meat mixture and set aside for up to 1 hour before proceeding with the recipe.)

5. Add the pasta to the boiling water and cook until just al dente (the low end of the package instructions). Drain, shaking off the excess water, and return to the pot. Add the meat mixture to the pasta, scraping out the bowl, along with three-quarters of the rice powder. Toss to combine.

6. Transfer to a serving dish or individual bowls, sprinkle with the remaining rice powder, and serve with lime wedges.

BUSIATE WITH ROASTED TOMATO BUTTER AND GIM

SERVES 4 TO 6 • TOTAL TIME: 1 HOUR 15 MINUTES • DEVELOPED WITH ASHA LOUPY

Silky, sumptuous, and packed with umami, this sauce tastes so layered you won't believe it has so few ingredients. (I often find myself eating it straight out of the blender.) The base umami flavor comes from cherry tomatoes, which are roasted in butter and garlic to concentrate their sunny sweetness. Doenjang, or Korean fermented soybean paste, adds funky, layered salinity, while toasted sesame oil brings a sweet nuttiness that tempts you back bite after bite. Tomatoes are naturally glutamate-rich, but a little bit of MSG amps up their inherent flavor, transforming them into the best versions of themselves. (See more about MSG on page 171.) The last layers of umami come from the garnishes: a hefty amount of crumbled gim, or roasted seaweed snacks, and store-bought roasted sesame seeds.

4 cups (20 ounces) cherry tomatoes

8 tablespoons (1 stick) unsalted butter, cut into cubes

4 garlic cloves, peeled

2 teaspoons toasted sesame oil

1 teaspoon plus 2 tablespoons kosher salt

2 tablespoons doenjang (or white or yellow miso)

¼ teaspoon MSG (optional)

1 pound busiate (a.k.a. cannolicchi; or use fusilloni, vesuvio, gemelli, or cavatappi)

One 0.17-ounce package salted, roasted seaweed snacks, crushed

2 tablespoons packaged roasted sesame seeds (see tip on page 44)

1. Heat the oven to 400°F. Combine the tomatoes, butter, garlic, sesame oil, and 1 teaspoon of the salt in a 9- by 13-inch baking dish. Place in the oven until the butter melts, 5 to 7 minutes. Stir to coat the tomatoes in the butter, return to the oven, and roast until the tomatoes start to wrinkle and turn golden in spots, 30 to 35 minutes.

2. A few minutes before the tomatoes are done, bring 4 quarts of water and the remaining 2 tablespoons of salt to a boil in a large pot.

3. Remove the tomatoes from the oven, stir in the doenjang and MSG, if using, and let cool for 5 minutes.

4. Transfer the tomato-butter mixture to a blender, scraping out the dish. Start to blend on low, gradually increasing the speed to high, and blend until smooth, 30 to 45 seconds. Transfer to a large, high-sided skillet and set aside. (At this point the sauce can be covered and refrigerated for up to 2 days. Warm over low heat before proceeding with the recipe.)

5. Add the pasta to the boiling water and cook for 2 minutes less than the low end of the package instructions. A few minutes before the pasta is done, bring the sauce to a simmer over medium heat. Use a mesh spider to transfer the pasta directly to the skillet, increase the heat to medium-high, and stir in ½ cup of the pasta cooking water. Cook, stirring constantly, until the sauce clings to the pasta but still pools at the bottom of the pan, 3 to 5 minutes. (If the sauce seems too thick and gloopy, add more pasta water 2 tablespoons at a time until the sauce loosens to the consistency of heavy cream.)

6. Transfer the pasta to a serving dish or individual bowls, sprinkle with the seaweed and sesame seeds, and serve immediately.

GNOCCHI WITH BACON AND SAUERKRAUT

SERVES 4 • TOTAL TIME: 35 MINUTES

My in-laws, Alice and Gene Fossner, were born and raised in communist Czechoslovakia. They escaped during the Prague Spring in 1968 and eventually made it to America. When Janie and I started dating I was introduced to a range of Slovak dishes, most of which involve meat with one or more carbs, often with cabbage. It's not the most colorful cuisine you'll find, but after a cold day outside, there's nothing better—especially when paired with a nice pilsner.

The best-known carb in Slovak cuisine is halušky—boiled dumplings made with a potato dough that are similar to gnocchi and found in some form across much of central and eastern Europe. Halušky with cured pork and sauerkraut is one of the most classic ways to have it. Na zdravie!

2 tablespoons kosher salt

6 ounces thick-cut bacon (about 5 slices), cut into ½-inch pieces

1 medium yellow onion, sliced ¼ inch thick

16 ounces (about 1½ cups) sauerkraut, drained

One 16- to 18-ounce package potato gnocchi

2 tablespoons unsalted butter

1. Bring 4 quarts of water and the salt to a boil in a large pot.

2. Meanwhile, cook the bacon in a large, high-sided skillet over medium heat, stirring occasionally, until the fat has rendered and the bacon is browned, 5 to 8 minutes. Add the onion and cook, stirring often, until softened and somewhat translucent, 4 to 6 minutes. Add the sauerkraut and cook, stirring, until just starting to soften, 2 to 4 minutes; remove the pan from the heat. (At this point the sauce can sit, covered, for up to 2 hours. Warm over low heat before proceeding with the recipe.)

3. Add the gnocchi to the boiling water and cook according to the package instructions. Use a mesh spider to transfer the gnocchi directly to the skillet along with 2 tablespoons of the pasta cooking water and the butter. Toss until the butter is melted and everything is evenly combined, scraping up any browned bits from the bottom of the pan.

4. Transfer the pasta to a serving dish or individual bowls and serve, preferably with the beer of your choice.

CARAMELIZED ENDIVE AND RADICCHIO WITH SAVORY BAGNA CAUDA

SERVES 4 • TOTAL TIME: 45 MINUTES • DEVELOPED WITH ASHA LOUPY

Bagna cauda (meaning "hot bath" in Italian) is a classic Piedmontese dip of olive oil, butter, garlic, and anchovies served warm with both raw and cooked vegetables for dipping. This dish transforms bagna cauda into a pasta sauce along with pieces of deeply caramelized endive and radicchio, which soften enough that you can leave their cores in. While searing the veggies tames their bitterness a touch, there's still enough to counterbalance the fragrant garlic, nutty anchovies, and richness of both the olive oil and butter. Plus, a little lemon zest, lemon juice, and parsley add a bit of brightness.

2 tablespoons plus 1½ teaspoons kosher salt

12 tablespoons (¾ cup) extra-virgin olive oil

1 large head radicchio (8 to 10 ounces), sliced vertically into 4 rounds

3 Belgian endive, halved lengthwise

4 tablespoons (½ stick) unsalted butter

15 to 18 anchovy fillets (see tip)

10 garlic cloves, minced

½ cup roughly chopped fresh parsley, plus more for serving

2 teaspoons finely grated lemon zest, plus 2 tablespoons freshly squeezed lemon juice

1 pound rigatoni

Shaved or coarsely shredded Parmesan, for serving (see note)

Red pepper flakes, for serving (optional)

1. Bring 4 quarts of water and 2 tablespoons of the salt to a boil in a large pot.

2. Heat 2 tablespoons of the oil in a large, high-sided skillet over medium-high heat until just beginning to smoke. Add the radicchio, cut side down, sprinkle with ¾ teaspoon of the salt, and cook until the bottoms are dark brown and deeply caramelized, 2 to 4 minutes. Flip and cook until the second side is well browned (it may go quicker than the first); transfer to a plate. Add 2 more tablespoons of the oil to the pan and return to medium-high heat. Add the endive, cut side down, sprinkle with the remaining ¾ teaspoon of salt, and cook until deeply golden on the bottom, 3 to 5 minutes. Transfer to the plate with the radicchio; reserve the skillet and let the endive cool for at least 5 minutes. When cool enough to handle, cut the radicchio and endive into large bite-size pieces.

3. Add the remaining 8 tablespoons (½ cup) of oil, the butter, anchovies, and garlic to the skillet. Place over medium heat and cook until the garlic is golden, 5 to 8 minutes, stirring often and breaking up the anchovies with a spoon. Remove the pan from the heat and stir in the parsley and lemon zest and juice; cover.

4. Add the pasta to the boiling water and cook for 2 minutes less than the low end of the package instructions. Use a mesh spider to transfer the pasta directly to the skillet and return the heat to medium-high. Add ½ cup of the pasta cooking water and cook, stirring often, until the sauce lightly coats the pasta, 2 to 4 minutes. Add the radicchio and endive and cook until just heated through.

5. Transfer the pasta to a serving dish or individual bowls, sprinkle with parsley, top with Parmesan and red pepper flakes, if desired, and serve.

TIP: I know this sounds like a lot of anchovies but trust me: they dissolve into the sauce and make it incredibly savory. Some of the folks who tried this dish wanted MORE anchovies!

NOTE: For this dish we encourage you to seek out a block of high-quality Parmigiano-Reggiano and use a vegetable peeler to shave it or the large holes of a box grater to coarsely shred it. The bigger pieces of cheese provide textural variety (a.k.a. dynamic contrast), and because they don't dissolve into the sauce, they make certain bites sharper and cheesier. That being said, standard grated Parmesan will also work!

WE INTERRUPT THIS COOKBOOK FOR A SERIES OF RANTS

ON THE SCOURGE OF MEDIOCRE PASTA SHAPES (OR, WHY SPAGHETTI SUCKS)

Long ago I established the three criteria I use to judge all pasta shapes. In case you're new to my work (or didn't read the introduction), I'll restate them here:

FORKABILITY: how easy it is to get the pasta on your fork and keep it there

SAUCEABILITY: how well sauce adheres to the pasta

TOOTHSINKABILITY: how satisfying it is to bite into the pasta

At the start of episode one of *The Sporkful* podcast series "Mission: ImPASTAble," about the creation of my pasta shape, I made a controversial statement: SPAGHETTI SUCKS.

I stand by this statement.

Of course, if you invite me to your house and serve me spaghetti, I'll be happy to eat it. Pasta is always good, even when it's bad. What I really meant is that spaghetti sucks when you consider how dominant it is in the pasta world. It's the most commonly eaten shape, to the point that some people use the word "spaghetti" to refer to all pasta, the way southerners call all sodas "Coke."

Spaghetti does not deserve its position atop the Pasta Pantheon.

I recognize there's a lot of nostalgia and romanticism attached to it, and it has its place—with a thin, oily sauce it can be very nice. But its optimal uses are limited. Getting spaghetti on a fork is maddening. When you twirl it, you risk splattering sauce everywhere, and no matter how hard you try, you usually end up with a bite that's either too big or too small, and almost definitely has perilous danglers. If you actually succeed in getting a well-proportioned, well-composed bite on the end of your fork, you must maintain complete focus as you transport it to your mouth. Tilt the fork downward for a split second and your bite unravels. No forkability.

Put meat sauce on spaghetti and you'll find that after you've eaten all the pasta, your plate looks like a volcanic swamp. Yes there is some pleasure in mopping up extra sauce with bread, but that maneuver should be reserved for a few errant streaks. If you've finished your pasta and half the sauce is still on your plate, that is not a feature, it's a bug. Spaghetti is not sauceable.

Finally, spaghetti is round, which means it has a low surface-area-to-volume ratio, which means it has very little relative exterior to contact your teeth when you bite it, which means it's not especially toothsinkable. I will say that if it's cooked just right and the stars align and you get a great bite of it on the fork, it can be pretty satisfying. So toothsinkability is the one area where spaghetti has some merit.

Still, in almost all cases I'd rather have spaghettoni, a thicker, more toothsinkable spaghetti that's sometimes just labeled as "thick spaghetti." Or for a more interesting variation, try spaghetti alla chitarra, which is long strands that are squared instead of cylindrical, made by pressing a flat sheet of pasta through a device that looks like the strings of a guitar (*chitarra* means "guitar"). Around Rome this shape is called tonnarelli and made with egg dough. There's also pici, which is even thicker than spaghettoni and also traditionally handmade, giving it subtle twists instead of being perfectly straight.

So please, break your limp, boring spaghetti chains and be free!

THE WORST PASTA SHAPES

ANGEL HAIR—Much too thin, it goes from raw to mush as soon as you drop it in water. Also, it's a terrible name. Health codes everywhere are specifically designed to keep hair out of your food. Do you really think an angel's hair would be so much more delicious than anyone else's?

FUSILLI/ROTINI—I'm referring here to the spiral pasta that goes by both names, and in either case is too sauceable (yes, that's a thing). It has so much surface area that it is overwhelmed by sauce and falls apart in your mouth. (There's a similar shape sometimes called fusilli that's like if a short piece of spaghetti was wrapped around a knitting needle, so it's more like a spring or old-timey telephone cord. That one still tends toward flimsiness, but it's better, and I like its long, hollow cousin, fusilli lunghi bucati, with the Zucchini and Feta Pasta with Za'atar Pangrattato on page 99.)

BOW TIES (FARFALLE)—The wings of the bow ties are flaccid while the center knot is still raw, and nothing sticks to this shape. It's like it was designed not to hold sauce. I'm okay with using a spoon for some pasta dishes, but not when it's because of the inferiority of the shape.

ELBOW MACARONI—So small, so mushy, so useless. Sorry, kids.

WAGON WHEELS—Like bow ties, these are an inherently flawed gimmick. The hub is raw while the wheel is soft. And everyone knows it! When Benedetto Cavalieri, whose eponymous company invented wagon wheels in the 1930s, was told that the shape cooks unevenly, he responded, "But of course that's the whole point of it—so you end up with different textures on the plate." As a lover of dynamic contrast, I appreciate that—in theory. But with all due respect, Mr. Cavalieri, from one pasta shape inventor to another, the textural contrast in wagon wheels is too extreme. (Cascatelli contains chewier and softer sections, but it still comes out cooked throughout. That this facet of it works as well as it does was pure luck.) I spent fifteen dollars on a box of Benedetto Cavalieri wagon wheels, just to see if a high-quality version of the shape, made by its inventor, would be better. It was like eating pasta mixed with uncooked rice.

PENNE AND ZITI—These shapes are the worst kinds of tubes. For more, see "On the Unfulfilled Promise and Underrated Virtues of Tubes."

ON THE UNFULFILLED PROMISE AND UNDERRATED VIRTUES OF TUBES

Tubes were one of the first pasta shape innovations, an early step forward after solid shapes like spaghetti. Of course the idea with these is that the tube holds sauce, but only if you thoroughly toss the pasta with the sauce before serving it, to get the sauce inside those cavities. (Bucatini, which is like spaghetti but hollow down the center, is the only common tube that fails to live up to this promise. Despite the Pastagentsia's insistence that it's a better version of spaghetti because of its sauce retention capabilities, its opening is in fact too narrow to gather sauce. Bucatini is superior to spaghetti for a different reason, which I will get to.)

Point being, most tubes hold sauce pretty well. So to distinguish the good ones from the bad ones, we must look at their other characteristics—in particular, the toothsinkability produced by different types of tubes.

Toothsinkability can come from chewiness, which is mostly a function of the thickness of the pasta. But it can also come from springiness, which in the case of a tube is more a function of the tube pushing back against your teeth, seeking to return to its natural, tubular state. (Let us not forget Newton's Third Law of Pasta: For every bite action there is an equal and opposite tube reaction.)

Both chewiness and springiness are wonderful sources of toothsinkability and contribute to the glorious diversity of the pasta-eating experience, but they're created in different ways.

When you bite down on a tube with a very wide diameter, like rigatoni, it goes flat in your mouth. It's not very springy, but when flat, it essentially

becomes two layers of pasta on top of each other, a double-decker of deliciousness, which is very chewy and toothsinkable. (This is why, for my money, rigatoni is the best commonly available short shape.)

An extremely narrow tube like bucatini reacts quite differently to the bite. It's not big enough to flatten into two thick layers, but because it's so narrow, the walls are more compact and stronger. They don't give way so easily when exposed to bite force. In fact, they spring back, and this springiness is what makes bucatini superior to spaghetti.

Which brings me to the most commonly eaten tubes with a medium diameter—penne and ziti. These recalcitrant devils are the worst of all tube worlds. They're not wide enough to flatten into a thick and satisfying bite like rigatoni, and not narrow enough to spring back against bite force like bucatini. Just about the only thing they're springy enough to do is spring off your fork as you're trying to get them to your mouth.

ON GREAT SHAPES, PAIRING WITH SAUCES, AND THE LIMITS OF TRADITION

No shape works perfectly with every conceivable preparation, and I don't think it would be possible to invent one. On the other hand, I think the idea that every sauce has one perfect shape is overrated and more tied to tradition and culture than the actual eating experience. There are some shapes that were developed to work with certain local ingredients and dishes, while other classic Italian combos are more a function of the common foods of a region being brought together with the common shapes of the region. In both cases there's usually good logic to the pairing, but it doesn't mean that's the ONLY one that works.

I believe any great pasta shape should work well with 75 percent of the preparations out there. That was my goal for cascatelli, and I think it achieves that. (I wouldn't recommend it with thin, oily sauces that don't contain big chunks.) In the time since cascatelli came out, I've become even more obsessed with obscure pasta shapes. Every month or two I order another shipment of different ones online. Janie rolls her eyes as the bags and boxes pile up in the pantry. As much as I love cascatelli and my newer shapes, vesuvio and quattrotini, life's too short to limit yourself to only a few pasta shapes!

When deciding what shapes pair with a sauce, I consider two key properties of the sauce:

VISCOSITY: a fancy word for how thick and sticky the sauce is

CHUNK FACTOR: a combination of both how many chunks there are in the sauce and how big they are

Here are different types of sauces, how to pair them, and examples of each from this book . . .

HIGH VISCOSITY, LOW CHUNK FACTOR: These sauces are the easiest to pair with shapes. Their thickness means they'll stick to almost anything, and you don't have to worry about finding places to hold chunks. The only shapes that won't work are very small and/ or thin ones, which will likely be overwhelmed by the sauce.

Examples: *Casarecce alla Vodka with Tomato Achaar (page 51), Shells with Miso Butter and Scallions (page 42), Thai Curry Quattrotini Mac 'n' Cheese (page 58), Creste di Gallo with Fava Beans and Dandelion Greens (page 120)*

LOW VISCOSITY, HIGH CHUNK FACTOR: Without a thick sauce to bind all those chunks to the pasta, you need to think carefully about how you're going to get all the components of the dish into your mouth at once. If the chunks are big, then you want hearty, forkable short shapes, so you can stab around the plate to compose bites that combine pasta and chunks. If the chunks are small or mixed, use shapes with nooks and crannies. Cascatelli really shines here because once bits and pieces get into the space between its ruffles, which I call the Sauce Trough, they don't escape. Ruffles in general are great for grabbing small bits, so I love mafalde and campanelle, as well as the spiral shape of fusilloni, a larger (and far better) version of fusilli. Shells also cradle little chunks beautifully.

All that being said, when you have low viscosity and chunks of different sizes, a big key to success is not in the shape pairing but in how you serve and eat the finished dish. With varying chunk sizes, smaller pieces will fall to the bottom of the skillet, mixing bowl, or serving platter as you transfer the pasta. This phenomenon is known to scientists as granular convection, or the Brazil nut effect, because in a bowl of mixed nuts, as the nuts are jostled, small ones sink to the bottom and big ones like Brazil nuts rise. (I'm serious, this is actual science—google it.) So use a serving spoon to get bits that may have sunk to the bottom, and consider eating these types of dishes with a spoon to open up more pasta shape options, like orecchiette and ditalini, which are small but mighty.

Examples: *Cajun Crawfish Carbonara with Cascatelli (page 175), Conchiglie with Corn, Avocado, and Fried (or Grilled) Halloumi (page 206), Raw Heirloom Puttanesca with Fish Sauce and Calabrian Chili (page 204), Lemony Tuna with Olives, Capers, Green Beans, and Parsley (page 201)*

HIGH VISCOSITY, HIGH CHUNK FACTOR: Again, with higher viscosities, the sauce does a lot of the work for you. But when you add a bunch of chunks, you need a shape that gives them somewhere to nestle. Tubes work nicely here, but be sure at least some of the chunks are smaller than the diameter of your tubes so the chunks will fit inside, and be sure to mix the tubes well with the sauce before serving. (Tubes don't fill themselves!) Long, flat shapes are also excellent with these types of sauces, but you have to be deft with your fork. If using fettuccine, get the pasta on the fork first in a way that leaves the tines exposed, then stab and swab around the plate to compose an optimal bite. With pappardelle I prefer a different approach: first, collect chunks on the fork, then stab the pappardelle, then swab the bite through residual sauce before enjoying.

Examples: *Keema Bolognese (page 160), Mapo Tofu Cascatelli (page 165), Mezze Maniche with Harissa Lamb and Mint-Parsley Gremolata (page 173), Green Fettuccine with Chorizo Verde (page 48)*

LOW VISCOSITY, LOW CHUNK FACTOR: Thin, simple sauces go best with thin(ish) simple shapes. So fine, you can use spaghetti. But you're still better off with spaghettoni. Unless the dish is soupy, in which case I recommend pairing with a small shape like shells, ditalini, or orecchiette, and eating with a spoon.

Examples: *Spaghettoni alla Tadka (page 63), Mac 'n' Dal (page 45), Fregola Sarda with Calamari and Saffron Broth (page 193), Raw Heirloom Puttanesca with Fish Sauce and Calabrian Chili (page 204)*

In closing, there's more than one right pasta for every dish. As long as you pick shapes that are generally forkable, sauceable, and toothsinkable, you really can't go wrong. But if you put a little more thought into your pairings, you'll have the most optimal eating experience!

DECODING PASTA SHAPE NAMES

RIGATE MEANS "RIDGED."

Penne rigate is penne with ridges on the outside. I can't for the life of me understand why someone would want a smooth (lisce) version of a shape when they could have it rigate. Ridges provide a playful texture in your mouth, and they increase surface area, which boosts sauceability.

-ONI > -INI

The *-oni* suffix on a pasta shape's name means it's bigger (and generally thicker), which usually means more toothsinkable. The *-ini* suffix means a shape is smaller and/or thinner. So don't buy spaghetti, and stay far away from spaghett<u>ini</u>, which is basically angel hair in disguise. Buy spaghett<u>oni</u>, which some brands just call "thick spaghetti." Don't buy fusilli, buy fusill<u>oni</u>. (While fusilli is one of the worst shapes, fusilloni is one of my favorites.)

STROZZAPRETI IS THE BEST PASTA SHAPE NAME.

Most pasta shapes are named after the Italian word for the thing they resemble. *Spaghetti* means "thin strings," like twine. *Fettuccine* means "ribbons." *Penne* means "pens," as in quill pens, because of their pointy ends. *Orecchiette* are "little ears" and *radiatore* are "radiators." The shape we in America tend to call bow ties is farfalle, which actually means "butterflies." I wanted my pasta shape to fit into this tradition so I named it cascatelli, after waterfalls, because as *Sporkful* senior producer Emma Morgenstern noted, when you hold it vertically, it looks like flowing water.

I love this system of pasta shape naming, but perhaps because it's so ubiquitous, my favorite name is one that breaks the mold. *Strozzapreti* (pronounced stroh-tzuh-PREH-tee) means "priest strangler," a name that dates to the 1500s and refers to gluttonous clergymen who, as legend has it, would eat so much of it they'd choke. It's not just a great name, though—it's also an excellent shape, a flat rectangle of pasta, a few inches long, that's twisted several times to form a rope-like stick with folds, and a sauceable interior channel. It's genius in its simplicity and proof that tubes aren't the only way to hold sauce.

STEWS, ROUXES, AND RAGÙS: THICK AND HEARTY, WARM AND TOASTY

5

KEEMA BOLOGNESE

SERVES 6 TO 8 • TOTAL TIME: 3 HOURS (1½ HOURS' ACTIVE TIME) • DEVELOPED WITH ASHA LOUPY

After I made this recipe, I left some with my neighbor Jess to try. Later that evening she texted me, "That dish was so good I feel like I need a cigarette now." Getting that same reaction from your friends and family will require some time, but the process is straightforward and the end result is well worth it.

If you eat a lot of Indian food, then you probably already know keema as a classic dish of spiced ground meat. The details can vary from region to region and home to home, but because it always has ground meat, it's a prime candidate to be mashed up with Bolognese, the traditional Italian tomato-based sauce that combines ground meat, wine, milk, and more.

When recipe developer Asha Loupy pitched the concept of keema Bolognese, I was immediately on board. As it turns out, this dish has special significance for her.

"I started cooking when I was about four years old," she told me. Asha was born in Kolkata, India, and adopted at ten weeks old by a white single mom of French descent in Sacramento, where Asha grew up. As a child, she spent Saturday mornings watching PBS cooking shows instead of cartoons, and wrote her own cookbook, including a recipe for something called "chicken mix up." And she and her mom cooked a lot of keema.

When Asha was twelve, her mom asked, "Do you want to go to Girl Scout camp this year, or do you want to take weekend classes at the California Culinary Academy in San Francisco?"

I think you can guess which she picked.

"I was a twelve-year-old with adults—these weren't children's cooking classes," she says. "And none of the adults wanted to be my partner. I ended up doing a lot of stuff by myself."

After college Asha got a job at Market Hall Foods, a Bay Area shop that features a range of specialty items. Eventually she started writing recipes for the shop's website and newsletter to showcase their products. And wouldn't you know it, one of their featured products is PASTA.

Not just any pasta. Market Hall Foods and their sister company, Manicaretti, are America's leading importers of Rustichella d'Abruzzo pasta, which as I've said is one of my very favorite brands in the world. Even before I connected with Asha, I had ordered from Market Hall's website many times. Meeting her for me was like Charlie meeting Willy Wonka.

Over her time there, the store began offering a wider range of items. "We started bringing in sambal and looking for people that were outside of just the 'European equals specialty foods,'" she says.

(continued)

In 2021 Asha left Market Hall and began developing recipes for Diaspora Co., a company founded by Sana Javeri Kadri that imports high-quality, fair-trade, single-origin spices from farmers in South Asia (and a great place to order spices you need for many recipes in this book, including this one!). At Diaspora Co., Asha often mixes the traditional with the more experimental, as in her recipe for pani puri two ways—one with a more classic potato-chickpea filling, the other a more off-the-cuff mango-avocado filling.

"Connecting with a lot of South Asian cooking and having that become part of my job, but also having it be a way for me to connect to a different part of myself, has been really rewarding, and it has been something that I don't think I had as much of growing up," Asha told me.

"I want to push beyond what people traditionally see pasta as, because in households across America, pasta is utilized in so many different ways beyond just the Italian ways that you see in magazines and in food media."

Keema Bolognese is a perfect example.

Asha says keema remains a personal favorite of hers as an adult, and for this recipe she combines it with some of the techniques used in a Bolognese. There's a soffritto—Italian for "gently fried"—but instead of carrots, onions, and celery, it's carrots, onions, and hot peppers. You'll add an array of spices as the vegetables cook down and caramelize over time, to build the layers of flavor that make this dish so satisfying. Milk is a classic ingredient in Italian Bolognese, and here it tames the gaminess of the lamb and creates a luscious, silky texture.

Originally we were going to make the yogurt at the end optional, but when I tasted it, I said, "This is such a good addition, it's not optional—it's mandatory."

Asha, recipe editor Rebeccah Marsters, and I had several conversations about the length of the ingredient list, which is a concern for any recipe developer. On one hand you want as many people as possible to make a dish, so you want to remove potential barriers. On the other hand you want it to taste as amazing as possible, and you want to be true to the source inspiration.

"I tweaked the spices and felt like I got them to a really good place, and all of the things felt very necessary to me," says Asha. "There are some recipes that are going to have a longer ingredient list, and they're going to take a little bit longer. But the end result is so well worth it that you'll be eating it out of the pan while you're doing dishes."

I completely agree. Just make sure you have some cigarettes handy.

¼ cup extra-virgin olive oil, plus more for serving

4 tablespoons (½ stick) unsalted butter

4 whole cloves

2 green cardamom pods, lightly crushed with the side of a knife (it's okay if some seeds fall out)

¾ teaspoon cumin seeds

2 yellow onions, diced

1 large carrot, peeled and diced

1 poblano pepper, seeded and diced

2 Indian long peppers or 1 serrano chile, diced

2 teaspoons plus 2 tablespoons kosher salt

8 ounces ground beef (80/20, see note)

8 ounces ground lamb (see note)

2 tablespoons tomato paste

4 garlic cloves, minced

1 tablespoon minced fresh ginger (see tip)

1 teaspoon brown sugar

2 teaspoons ground coriander

1½ teaspoons ground cumin

1½ teaspoons Kashmiri chili powder (or hot paprika)

½ teaspoon ground turmeric

One 14-ounce can whole peeled tomatoes, crushed with your hands

1 cup whole milk

1 cup frozen peas

1 teaspoon garam masala

1 pound (or two 8.8-ounce packages) egg pappardelle (or egg fettuccine)

¼ cup roughly chopped fresh cilantro leaves and tender stems, plus more for serving

2 tablespoons chopped fresh mint leaves

Plain whole-milk Greek yogurt, for serving

1. In a Dutch oven (or large pot, if you also have a second large pot for the pasta), heat the oil and butter over medium heat. When the butter has melted, add the cloves, cardamom, and cumin seeds and cook, stirring, until fragrant, about 1 minute. Add the onions, carrot, poblano, long peppers, and 1 teaspoon of the salt and cook, stirring occasionally, until the peppers and onions are softened and browned, 20 to 25 minutes.

2. Meanwhile, combine the beef, lamb, 1 cup of water, and 1 teaspoon of the salt in a bowl and mix with your hands until the water is fully incorporated; set aside.

3. Stir the tomato paste, garlic, ginger, and sugar into the vegetables and cook until the tomato paste darkens to a brick red, about 3 minutes. Add the coriander and ground cumin and cook, stirring, for 30 seconds, then add the chili powder and turmeric and cook until fragrant, about 30 seconds. Add the tomatoes and their juices, increase the heat to medium-high, and cook until the mixture is very thick and sizzles when stirred, 4 to 6 minutes.

(continued)

4. Add the meat mixture to the pot and cook, stirring often, until no longer pink, 3 to 5 minutes. Stir in the milk and bring to a simmer. Reduce the heat to low and cook, partially covered, until the sauce has thickened and reduced by a third, about 1½ hours, stirring occasionally. (Check the sauce periodically; if the bottom of the pot starts to look too dark and smell a bit scorched, add water ¼ cup at a time to loosen the sauce and scrape up the browned bits. If making ahead, cool, cover, and refrigerate for up to 2 days or freeze for up to 1 month. Thaw if frozen, then warm over low heat before adding the peas and garam masala and proceeding with the recipe.)

5. Bring 4 quarts of water and the remaining 2 tablespoons of salt to a boil in a large pot.

6. Stir the peas and garam masala into the sauce, cover, and remove from the heat. Add the pasta to the boiling water and cook for 2 minutes less than the low end of the package instructions. Use tongs to transfer the pasta directly to the pot with the sauce and return the heat to medium. Add ½ cup of the pasta cooking water and cook, stirring constantly, until the meat mixture clings to the pasta but is still saucy, 2 to 4 minutes. (If the sauce seems too thick, add more pasta water 2 tablespoons at a time until it loosens and just coats the pasta.) Remove the pot from the heat and stir in the cilantro and mint.

7. Transfer the pasta to a serving dish or individual bowls, dollop with yogurt, drizzle with additional oil, sprinkle with more cilantro, and serve.

BEEF AND LAMB NOTE: If you don't want to use lamb or can't find it, just use 1 pound of 80/20 ground beef. Mixing water into ground meat is a technique used in some keema recipes to create a more homogeneous texture. If you haven't done it, note that as the meat sits in the water it will take on an unfamiliar look. I find this step helps create a sauce that holds together and clings well to the pasta, so you don't end up with a bunch of meat crumbs on your plate at the end of the meal.

TIP: If you use ginger in a tube, increase it to 1½ tablespoons. If you buy fresh ginger, note that the leftovers can be kept in plastic wrap in the freezer for months.

MAPO TOFU CASCATELLI

SERVES 4 TO 6 • TOTAL TIME: 40 MINUTES • DEVELOPED WITH ANDREA NGUYEN

This is my absolute favorite way to eat cascatelli. The chewy bits of meat and chewiest parts of the pasta combine for incredibly toothsinkable bites, and the high viscosity of the sauce combined with cascatelli's patented Sauce Trough ensure that every bite arrives at your mouth fully loaded. Add to that the deep, soul-satisfying spice that comes from Sichuan peppercorns and doubanjiang and you have texture and flavor that'll bring a tear to your eye.

If you have any doubts about my devotion to this recipe, you need only thumb through the photos at the start of each chapter, which show me increasingly enraptured as I work my way through a pot of it.

This recipe is important for another reason.

Its original version, a mapo tofu spaghetti created by the esteemed cookbook author (and my friend) Andrea Nguyen, played a pivotal role in pushing me to expand my own ideas of what could and should go on pasta, long before I had the idea for this cookbook. Andrea looked at the Sichuan dish mapo tofu, traditionally made with cubed tofu and ground pork, and saw a pasta sauce. Her stroke of genius: she purees the silken tofu instead of cubing it, to create a sauce that's thick and creamy and clings beautifully to pasta but that doesn't use dairy. My only quibble with her approach is that she used spaghetti. We worked together to adapt the recipe for cascatelli, and I'm very excited to share it with you here!

If you're like me and often have to cook for people with a range of spice thresholds, I have a tip for you . . .

This recipe calls for 8 ounces (½ pound) of ground meat, so buy a full pound and divide it. Take the half that doesn't go in this dish, brown it in a pan with some salt, and add half a jar of tomato sauce to make a basic meat sauce. (To add other flavors, see the Jarred Tomato Sauce Decision Tree on page 30.) Janie and Becky love the mapo tofu flavor but not all the heat, so they actually mix the two sauces to get that taste with less spice. Emily has the meat sauce. I have mapo tofu. Everyone's happy!

This dish comes together quickly once you start cooking, so be sure to have everything prepped in advance.

2 tablespoons kosher salt

One 16-ounce package silken tofu

2 teaspoons Sichuan peppercorns (see note)

3 tablespoons canola or other neutral oil

8 ounces ground pork (or 80/20 ground beef or other ground meat)

3 tablespoons doubanjiang (see note)

2 garlic cloves, minced

2 teaspoons minced fresh ginger (or 1 tablespoon tubed ginger)

1 tablespoon soy sauce

1½ teaspoons sugar

1½ tablespoons cornstarch

1 pound cascatelli pasta (or quattrotini, vesuvio, or rigatoni)

3 scallions, thinly sliced, white and green parts separated

(continued)

DOUBANJIANG AND SICHUAN PEPPERCORN NOTES:

Doubanjiang, sometimes written as *toban djan* or *tobanjan*, is a Sichuan fermented broad bean chili paste. Try to find one from Pixian. This dish is spicy by nature, but to soften the heat you can reduce the amount of doubanjiang to 2 tablespoons or even 1 tablespoon. Both that and Sichuan peppercorns can be found at Asian markets, H Mart, some other large grocery stores, and online at the Mala Market and elsewhere. If you don't have a mortar and pestle or spice grinder to grind the peppercorns, just put them on a cutting board and grind them with the bottom of a pan or pot.

1. Bring 4 quarts of water and the salt to a boil in a large pot.

2. Drain the excess water from the tofu, transfer to a blender (or use an immersion blender or food processor), and puree until smooth, about 30 seconds; set aside.

3. Toast the peppercorns in a large saucepan over medium heat until fragrant and slightly darkened, about 3 minutes. Let cool slightly, then coarsely grind in a mortar and pestle or spice grinder; reserve the pan.

4. Add the oil to the pan and heat over medium-high heat until shimmering. Add the meat and cook, stirring and breaking it up with a wooden spoon, until no pink remains, 2 to 4 minutes. Add the doubanjiang, garlic, and ginger and cook, stirring constantly, until dark reddish brown, about 2 minutes. Stir in the soy sauce, sugar, and reserved tofu, scraping out the blender jar, and bring to a simmer. Reduce the heat to medium-low, cover the pan, leaving the lid slightly ajar, and cook for 5 minutes, stirring occasionally and scraping the corners of the pan. (Orange oil will appear on the surface.)

5. Meanwhile, combine the cornstarch with 2 tablespoons of water in a bowl.

6. Add the cornstarch mixture to the sauce and simmer for 1 minute. Remove the pan from the heat and stir in half of the peppercorns; let sit while cooking the pasta to allow the flavor to deepen. (At this point the sauce can be cooled, covered, and refrigerated for up to 3 days.)

7. Add the pasta to the boiling water and cook for 2 minutes less than the low end of the package instructions. Reserve 2 cups of the pasta cooking water, then drain the pasta. Scrape the sauce into the empty pasta pot, add 1 cup of the reserved pasta water, and bring to a boil over medium-high heat. Add the pasta to the sauce along with the scallion whites and stir until the pasta is well coated but the sauce still pools slightly at the bottom of the pot, 1 to 3 minutes. (If the sauce seems too thick, add more pasta water 2 tablespoons at a time until the sauce loosens but still clings to the pasta.)

8. Transfer the pasta to a serving dish or individual bowls, sprinkle with the scallion greens and remaining peppercorns, and serve.

STEWS, ROUXES, AND RAGÙS: THICK AND HEARTY, WARM AND TOASTY **167**

MEXICAN WEDDING SOUP WITH CHIPOTLE TURKEY ALBÓNDIGAS

SERVES 6 TO 8 • TOTAL TIME: 1 HOUR 30 MINUTES • DEVELOPED WITH ASHA LOUPY

A mash-up of Italian wedding soup and Mexican sopa de conchas, this comforting soup starts with a tomatoey foundation that's combined with chicken stock to create a bright, homey landing pad for toasted pasta, carrots, and mini turkey albóndigas (meatballs) flavored with smoky chipotles in adobo, lime zest, cumin, coriander, dried oregano, and cilantro. While this dish is great year-round, it's especially good in the late summer and early fall when the evenings are growing cooler but the tomatoes are still full of bright, sunshiny flavor. In the end, though, it's the garnishes that really make this soup fun: Top with any combination of pickled onions, sliced avocado, crumbled cotija, and thinly sliced serrano chiles. Choose your own adventure!

To make ahead: The meatballs can be rolled and baked in advance, cooled, and refrigerated for up to 2 days or frozen for up to 3 months. The soup base can be made through the end of step 5, cooled, covered, and refrigerated for up to 2 days, and the cooled, toasted pasta can be kept in an airtight container at room temperature. When ready to serve, bring the soup base to a boil and proceed with the recipe at step 6.

2½ cups chopped fresh cilantro leaves and tender stems (or substitute parsley)

½ cup panko bread crumbs

1 large egg, lightly beaten

1 to 3 chipotles in adobo, finely chopped, plus 1 to 2 tablespoons adobo sauce (see note)

4 teaspoons finely grated lime zest and 2 tablespoons freshly squeezed lime juice, plus lime wedges for serving

3½ teaspoons kosher salt

2 teaspoons ground cumin

1½ teaspoons garlic powder

1 teaspoon ground coriander

1 pound ground turkey

1½ pounds plum or Early Girl tomatoes (5 to 7 tomatoes), cored and quartered

2 medium white onions, peeled and halved

4 garlic cloves, peeled

1 teaspoon dried oregano

¼ teaspoon MSG (optional; see page 171)

4 tablespoons (¼ cup) canola or other neutral oil

8 ounces (about 1¾ cups) ditalini (a.k.a. tubetti)

3 medium carrots, peeled and diced

8 cups (64 ounces) chicken stock

10 to 11 ounces (about 10 cups) baby spinach

Crumbled cotija cheese, for serving (see note)

Sliced avocado, pickled red onion (see tip), and thinly sliced serrano pepper, for serving (optional)

(continued)

CHIPOTLES NOTE: Chipotle peppers in adobo sauce are widely available; they come in cans and are produced by Goya, among other brands. You can vary the quantities depending on how spicy you want it. The lowest quantities will make the spice level mild to medium. If you taste it at the end and want it spicier, add adobo sauce to the broth 1 tablespoon at a time or to individual servings ½ teaspoon at a time until you're happy with it.

COTIJA TIP: As noted elsewhere, while cotija cheese is preferable here and pretty easy to find, you can use Pecorino Romano in a pinch.

PICKLED ONION TIP: To make pickled onions, combine thinly sliced red onion with salt and either vinegar or lime juice and let sit for at least 30 minutes, then use or refrigerate for a few days.

1. In a large bowl, combine 1 cup of the cilantro, the panko, egg, chipotles and adobo sauce, lime zest, 2 teaspoons of the salt, the cumin, garlic powder, and coriander and mix well. Add the turkey and use your hands to mix until just combined (do not overmix). Cover and refrigerate for 30 minutes.

2. Meanwhile, combine the tomatoes, 2 cups of water, 1 onion half, the garlic, oregano, and MSG, if using, in a blender and blend until smooth, about 30 seconds. Dice the remaining 1½ onions and set them aside.

3. Heat the oven to 425°F.

4. With lightly oiled hands and working with about a walnut-size piece at a time, roll the meat mixture between your palms to form meatballs and transfer them to a rimmed sheet pan. (You should have about 36 balls.) Bake until firm to the touch, 8 to 10 minutes.

5. Heat 2 tablespoons of the oil in a Dutch oven or large, heavy-bottomed pot over medium heat until shimmering. Add the ditalini (remember, it's only half the package!), stir to coat in the oil, and toast, stirring often, until deep golden, 4 to 6 minutes; transfer to a bowl. Add the remaining 2 tablespoons of oil to the pot and increase the heat to medium-high. Add the diced onions and carrots and cook, stirring occasionally, until the onions start to turn golden around the edges, 10 to 15 minutes. Stir in the pureed tomato mixture, stock, and remaining 1½ teaspoons of salt. Cover, increase the heat to high, and bring to a boil.

6. Add the pasta and meatballs to the boiling soup, reduce the heat to medium, and simmer, uncovered, stirring occasionally to make sure the pasta doesn't stick to the bottom of the pot, until the pasta is just al dente (the low end of the package instructions). Remove the pot from the heat and stir in the spinach, remaining 1½ cups of cilantro, and the lime juice.

7. Ladle the soup into bowls and sprinkle with cotija. Serve with avocado, pickled onions, and serranos, if desired. (The pasta tends to sink to the bottom, so when serving, use a soup spoon to fish some of it out to be sure each person gets a roughly even distribution of ingredients.)

A WORD ABOUT MSG

MSG, or monosodium glutamate, is a staple in my pantry and a quick and convenient flavor enhancer for soups, stews, and sauces. Where I call for it in this book it is optional, but I personally would never skip it. It's so good!

What exactly is MSG?

Well, glutamate is an amino acid that exists naturally in a range of foods—part of the savory, umami flavor in tomatoes, Parmesan cheese, mushrooms, and more. It's in human breast milk, and it's inside your brain right now. (At least it should be! It plays a key role in learning and memory.)

To make glutamate into a shelf-stable seasoning that you can add to food, it's bound with sodium to make MSG. The result is a crystal powder that can sit in your pantry next to the salt and pepper. That's it.

The glutamate in MSG is chemically identical to the glutamate in your body right now. And as my friend Kenji López-Alt explains in his excellent book *The Wok*, whether or not you realize it, you've probably eaten MSG very recently because it's in many packaged foods, although it may go by other names. (Autolyzed yeast extract and hydrolyzed soy protein are MSG precursors that combine with the salt in a food to form MSG, a process that takes place either in the food or in your mouth.)

Years ago the term "Chinese restaurant syndrome" came to describe a set of symptoms some people felt after eating Chinese restaurant food—headaches, dizziness, stuffy nose. Many people blamed those symptoms on MSG. In recent years there's been pushback against this perception, which was tied up in racist tropes about "sneaky" Asian people adding "mysterious" ingredients to their food.

MSG has been the subject of a number of scientific studies going back decades, and here is what experts have found:

The FDA considers MSG safe for human consumption. There is no evidence that it causes major long-term health issues when consumed in normal amounts. A 1970 study that showed serious issues involved injecting massive quantities of MSG into infant mice. But as Dr. Aaron Carroll, a pediatrician and professor of pediatrics at Indiana University School of Medicine, told me on *The Sporkful* when we covered this issue years ago, "No one is suggesting that human beings should inject huge amounts of MSG under their skin!"

I don't want huge amounts of duck fat injected under my skin, but if you offer me some fries cooked in it, I'll gladly go to town on them.

As for the milder, short-term symptoms some people say they experience? A key 2000 study from the *Journal of Allergy and Clinical Immunology* that focused specifically on people who self-identify as having an MSG sensitivity found that there are people who have a legitimate reaction to MSG, but most people who *think* they have that sensitivity in fact do not.

So what's happening to those people? They may be reacting to other ingredients they don't realize they're eating. In some cases it's probably psychosomatic. The question is complicated by anecdotal evidence that certain people may have a mild reaction to MSG sometimes and not others. It's possible eating it on an empty stomach is a factor. More research is needed.

So in my view, MSG is kind of like onions. My sister-in-law has a sensitivity to onions, so she tries not to eat them. If she gets some onions in her food, she may have an unpleasant reaction, but it's not so serious. I love onions, but occasionally, when I eat a very onion-heavy dish, they don't agree with me. That doesn't stop me from loving them. And furthermore, just because some of us have this issue sometimes doesn't mean onions are generally unsafe or unhealthy. For some people chocolate is a migraine trigger. Are you going to stop eating chocolate now?

If a person tells you they have an issue with MSG, you should believe them, because it may be true, and even if it's psychosomatic, they still feel those symptoms, so you shouldn't invalidate their experience. That said, if you have any kind of platform in the food world and people look to you as any kind of expert, it's irresponsible and incorrect to suggest that MSG is some kind of public health concern. And if you're a corporation, putting a big "NO MSG" seal on the label of your products only adds to the misperception that MSG must be avoided.

MEZZE MANICHE WITH HARISSA LAMB AND MINT-PARSLEY GREMOLATA

SERVES 4 TO 6 • TOTAL TIME: 5 HOURS (1 HOUR ACTIVE TIME) • DEVELOPED WITH ASHA LOUPY

This recipe takes a long time, but the technique itself is simple, making it the perfect way to impress a crowd. You'll end up with fall-off-the-bone tender lamb bursting with spice and flavor, thanks in large part to harissa, a fragrant jarred chili sauce originally from Tunisia but used in many dishes throughout North Africa and the Middle East. Best of all, you can tell your friends you spent five hours cooking this for them, when really most of the time the pot was just sitting in the oven. And this recipe is easily doubled for a larger group.

I love stewed meat dishes like this with mezze maniche, which means "short sleeves"—it's essentially a slightly shorter rigatoni. If you like the extra-thick, extra-long tubes called paccheri, that's also a good option here. Paccheri has incredible toothsinkability, but it's often too big to fit in my mouth, so I end up cutting it in half, which effectively makes it mezze maniche except without the benefit of ridges.

One more thing: Do not skip the fresh, herbaceous gremolata—its brightness contrasts perfectly with the meaty sauce and takes this dish way beyond a typical ragù.

LAMB SAUCE

1 large or 2 medium lamb shanks (1½ to 2 pounds)

3 teaspoons kosher salt

4 tablespoons (¼ cup) extra-virgin olive oil

2 medium carrots, peeled and finely diced

1 yellow onion, finely diced

1 fennel bulb, cored and finely diced

4 garlic cloves, minced

One 28-ounce can whole tomatoes

⅓ cup jarred harissa sauce (see note)

1 cinnamon stick

3 tablespoons finely chopped preserved lemon (about ½ medium lemon, see tip on page 114)

GREMOLATA AND PASTA

1 whole lemon

2 garlic cloves, roughly chopped

1 cup lightly packed flat-leaf parsley leaves

½ cup lightly packed mint leaves

2 tablespoons kosher salt

1 pound mezze maniche pasta (or rigatoni, paccheri, calamarata, or quattrotini)

1. For the lamb sauce: Heat the oven to 325°F. Season the lamb all over with 2 teaspoons of the salt. Heat 2 tablespoons of the oil in a Dutch oven over medium-high heat until shimmering. Add the lamb and cook, turning often, until well browned on all sides, 10 to 15 minutes (see tip); transfer to a plate.

(continued)

2. Reduce the heat to medium and add the remaining 2 tablespoons of oil, the carrots, onion, fennel, and remaining 1 teaspoon of salt to the pot. Cook, stirring frequently, until the moisture has evaporated and the onions start to turn golden around the edges, 10 to 15 minutes. Add the garlic and cook, stirring, until fragrant, about 1 minute. Stir in the tomatoes and their juices, the harissa, and cinnamon stick and use a wooden spoon to break up the tomatoes into smaller chunks and scrape up any browned bits from the bottom of the pot. Add 3 cups of water, increase the heat to medium-high, and bring the mixture to a simmer. Return the lamb to the pot, spooning the sauce over the meat, then partially cover the pot (leave about 1 inch open) and transfer to the oven. Cook until the lamb is very tender and can easily be pulled from the bone, 3½ to 4 hours, stirring the sauce and flipping the lamb halfway through.

3. For the gremolata and pasta: Use a vegetable peeler to remove the zest from the lemon in strips, avoiding the bitter white pith; save the lemon flesh for another use. Stack the strips of zest, thinly slice lengthwise into matchsticks, then slice crosswise into a fine dice. Pile the garlic on top of the zest, followed by the parsley and mint, and finely chop everything together; transfer to a bowl, cover, and set aside.

4. Transfer the lamb to a cutting board and let rest. Remove and discard the cinnamon stick and stir the preserved lemon into the sauce.

5. Meanwhile, bring 4 quarts of water and the salt to a boil in a large pot.

6. When the lamb is cool enough to handle, use your fingers or 2 forks to remove the meat from the bone and shred into bite-size pieces, discarding the fat and gristle as you go; discard the bones. Stir the meat into the sauce, cover, and place over low heat. (At this point the sauce can be cooled and refrigerated for up to 3 days or frozen for up to 2 months. Bring the sauce to room temperature and warm over low heat before proceeding with the recipe.)

7. Add the pasta to the boiling water and cook for 2 minutes less than the low end of the package instructions. Use a mesh spider to transfer the pasta directly to the sauce in the pot. Increase the heat to medium-high. Add ¾ cup of the pasta cooking water and cook, stirring and tossing, until the sauce is uniformly thick and coats the pasta, about 3 minutes. (If the sauce seems too thick, add more pasta water 2 tablespoons at a time until the sauce loosens but still clings to the pasta.)

8. Transfer the pasta to a serving dish or individual bowls, sprinkle generously with the gremolata, and serve.

CAJUN CRAWFISH CARBONARA WITH CASCATELLI

SERVES 4 TO 6 • TOTAL TIME: 45 MINUTES • DEVELOPED WITH DARNELL REED

After cascatelli's viral moment passed, I began reaching out to restaurants in the hope that some would feature it on their menus. A friend connected me with Darnell Reed, a James Beard Award semifinalist who's the chef/owner of Luella's Southern Kitchen in Chicago.

Darnell spent many years in hotel restaurants around the city, working his way up from dishwasher to executive chef. He was always known for his southern dishes—chicken and waffles, shrimp and grits—so as executive chef, he decided to make a special southern menu at the hotel restaurant for the summer. But the hotel chain's corporate office wasn't so sure about it—so they sent a manager for a taste test.

"Honestly, I was a little bit offended," Darnell says, "because when we were making Peruvian, you didn't do this. But now that I'm making southern . . ."

But when the food and beverage director tried Darnell's menu, he was floored by it. He asked who Darnell's inspiration was. "I'm like, 'I never thought about that,'" Darnell says. "'But I would have to say that it's my great-grandmother, because she's the one who used to cook all of this food that I cooked for you guys.'"

(continued)

Recipe testing and audio recording with chef Darnell Reed in his restaurant, where I made sure to get the sound of the sizzle

Corporate agreed that Darnell could go ahead with his new southern menu. But right when it was about to launch, the hotel brought in a new general manager who outright refused to serve a southern menu. The implication was that this food didn't belong at a fancy downtown Chicago hotel.

"I got exhausted with the idea that I have to continue to fight to put these items on the menu," Darnell told me. So after eighteen years with the company, he left.

In late 2014 he opened Luella's Southern Kitchen, named for his great-grandmother who inspired him.

Fast-forward to today and Luella's is a Chicagoland destination, with a second location at Soldier Field, home of the Chicago Bears. Darnell is a two-time James Beard Award semifinalist, and he's launched Luella's Southern Popcorn (order online—they ship!).

So I sent Darnell some cascatelli samples, and I was honored when he decided to serve it. I told him to prepare it however he thought it would be best.

"When I tasted the cascatelli, I was like, 'It's gonna hold my carbonara sauce perfectly,'" Darnell says. "I just felt like the textures that were going on, it would work." But he wanted to put his stamp on it. "I'm like, 'I know how to make a carbonara, I'm going to figure out a way to make it southern.' And I think almost anything you add crawfish to, you just made it southern."

Crawfish, also known as crayfish, are freshwater crustaceans that look like tiny lobsters but taste slightly sweeter. They're found both in Cajun cooking and a range of Asian dishes (which is why Viet-Cajun crawfish has become popular in Houston and across much of Texas and Louisiana's Gulf Coasts).

In the fall of 2021, Luella's Southern Kitchen became the first restaurant in America to feature cascatelli on its menu, and this was the dish. In June 2022, I went to Chicago to eat it at Luella's, and it was everything I dreamed it would be. Darnell's use of extra egg yolks elevates an already luscious dish to true decadence. Now this dream can be your reality too. Grab some Crystal hot sauce and Cheerwine and enjoy!

1 tablespoon kosher salt

3 large eggs plus 2 yolks

¾ cup (3 ounces) store-bought grated Parmesan (see tip on page 8)

¾ cup (3 ounces) store-bought grated Pecorino Romano (see tip on page 10)

1 teaspoon freshly ground black pepper, plus cracked peppercorns for serving (see tip on page 70)

1 teaspoon Creole seasoning

¼ teaspoon red pepper flakes

6 ounces guanciale, diced (see note on page 127)

1 shallot, finely chopped

2 garlic cloves, minced

1 pound cascatelli pasta (or vesuvio or reginetti)

1 pound cooked crawfish tail meat (see note)

⅓ cup finely chopped fresh parsley

Crystal or other vinegar-based hot sauce, for serving

1. Bring 4 quarts of water and the salt to a boil in a large pot.

2. In a large heatproof bowl, whisk the eggs and yolks until smooth and consistent. Add the Parmesan, Pecorino, ground black pepper, Creole seasoning, and red pepper flakes and whisk until homogenous, breaking up clumps of cheese and scraping down the sides of the bowl if necessary; set aside.

3. Add the guanciale to a large, high-sided skillet and set the skillet over medium heat. Cook undisturbed until the guanciale begins to sizzle, 1 to 2 minutes. Stir, reduce the heat to medium-low, and cook until browned, 5 to 7 minutes, stirring occasionally. Remove and discard all but 2 tablespoons of the rendered fat, leaving the guanciale in the pan, then add the shallot and garlic and cook, stirring, until the shallot is softened and the garlic is lightly browned, 1 to 3 minutes; remove the pan from the heat.

4. Add the pasta to the boiling water and cook for 1 minute less than the low end of the package instructions. Use a mesh spider to transfer the pasta directly to the skillet and set the skillet over medium-high heat. Add the crawfish and cook, stirring and tossing, until heated through and evenly distributed, 2 to 4 minutes. Transfer the pasta to the bowl with the egg mixture, scraping out the pan, and use a rubber spatula to rapidly toss everything together until the pasta is well coated, the cheese is dissolved, and the sauce is smooth and glossy. (There should be extra sauce pooling in the bowl at first but it should all cling to the pasta after 1 minute of stirring. If the sauce looks too thick after 1 minute, add pasta cooking water 1 tablespoon at a time until creamy, smooth, and glossy.)

5. Stir in the parsley, then transfer the pasta to a serving dish or individual bowls, sprinkle with cracked peppercorns and hot sauce, and serve.

NOTE: You can find packaged crawfish tails, which come cleaned and cooked, at H Mart, the Texas chain H-E-B, and many other Asian grocers. You can also have them shipped straight from Louisiana, which isn't cheap but is fun for a special occasion. If you get the crawfish frozen, thaw, drain, and pat them dry first. Or you can substitute a pound of cooked jumbo shrimp (21/25 size), patted dry and cut in half.

Shrimp and Andouille
Mac 'n' Cheese (page 180)

Cajun Crawfish Carbonara
with Cascatelli (page 175)

SHRIMP AND ANDOUILLE MAC 'N' CHEESE

SERVES 4 TO 6 • TOTAL TIME: 45 MINUTES • DEVELOPED WITH DARNELL REED

There are two types of people in this world: those who will look at the name of this dish and say, "OMG yes I need that in my belly," and those who will look at the name of this dish and say, "That sounds too rich and heavy for me." Well I am here to tell you that whichever category you fall into, this dish is in fact for you. Never have I eaten such a light yet flavorful mac 'n' cheese. When I was finished I felt like going for a run! I didn't, but I could have.

The key is the emphasis on American cheese, which is the best melting cheese known to humankind and quite possibly our nation's greatest contribution to world culture.

"But American cheese isn't even cheese!" cry some listeners when I mention it on *The Sporkful,* or heaven forbid, during one of my appearances on public radio.

Technically American cheese starts with real cheese, but a few other things are added to it to give it its magical powers—often additional whey (a natural byproduct of cheesemaking), milk proteins, and emulsifying salts. It's science. And this science allows American cheese not only to easily transform into a divinely oozy consistency but also to STAY IN THAT STATE much longer than lesser cheeses, which is why this mac 'n' cheese will still be saucy long after you turn the heat off. You're not antiscience, are you?

Other cheeses rely primarily on their fat content to make them melty, which is why, as a mac 'n' cheese cools, it tends to solidify. That's also why most mac 'n' cheeses, though delicious, are so heavy. But because American cheese gets some of its meltability from other sources beyond fat, we're able to make this dish not only deliciously gooey but also light enough that you can go for a run afterward. Or not.

Thanks, science.

2 tablespoons plus 1 teaspoon kosher salt

1 pound vesuvio (a.k.a. trottole or nodini; or use cascatelli, fusilloni, or rigatoni)

1 pound jumbo (21/25) shrimp, peeled, sdeveined, and tails removed

3 tablespoons unsalted butter

3 tablespoons all-purpose flour

1 teaspoon freshly ground black pepper

¼ teaspoon sweet or hot paprika (or cayenne for even more heat)

2 tablespoons Dijon mustard

4 cups (32 ounces) whole milk

1 bay leaf

8 ounces American cheese, shredded (2 cups; see tip on page 59)

3 ounces (¾ cup) sharp Cheddar, shredded

2 tablespoons canola or other neutral oil

8 ounces andouille sausage, sliced into ¼-inch rounds

Crystal or other vinegar-based hot sauce, for serving (optional)

1. Bring 4 quarts of water and 2 tablespoons of the salt to a boil in a large pot. Add the pasta to the boiling water and cook for 2 minutes less than the low end of the package instructions. Reserve 1 cup of the pasta cooking water, then drain the pasta and immediately return it to the pot; cover and set aside.

2. Pat the shrimp dry, then add to a bowl and toss with the remaining 1 teaspoon of salt until evenly coated; set aside.

3. In a large, heavy-bottomed saucepan, melt the butter over medium heat. Whisk in the flour, pepper, and paprika until no lumps remain, then cook, whisking constantly, for 1 minute. Whisk in the mustard, then very slowly whisk in the milk until smooth. Add the bay leaf, bring to a simmer, and cook, whisking often and scraping the bottom and corners of the pan, until the sauce thickens and holds a line when you drag your finger across the back of the spoon, 3 to 5 minutes. Remove the pan from the heat and add the cheeses one handful at a time, whisking thoroughly to incorporate between each addition, until the sauce is completely smooth. Remove and discard the bay leaf, cover the pan, and set aside.

4. Heat 1 tablespoon of the oil in a large skillet over medium-high heat until shimmering. Add the sausage and cook, stirring often, until browned around the edges, 4 to 6 minutes. Use a slotted spoon to transfer the sausage to the pot with the pasta. Add the remaining 1 tablespoon of oil to the pan, then add the shrimp, spread into an even layer, and cook until just opaque, 1 to 2 minutes, flipping and stirring halfway through. Add ½ cup of the reserved pasta water and bring to a simmer, scraping up any browned bits from the bottom of the pan. Transfer the shrimp to the pot with the pasta, scraping out the skillet. Add the cheese sauce to the pot, set over medium heat, and stir until the shrimp are cooked through and the pasta is evenly coated with the sauce, 2 to 4 minutes. (If necessary, add more pasta water 2 tablespoons at a time until the sauce is creamy and loose but clings to the pasta.)

5. Transfer the pasta to a serving dish or individual bowls and serve with hot sauce, if desired.

TORTELLINI IN KIMCHI PARMESAN BRODO

SERVES 2 TO 4 • TOTAL TIME: 45 MINUTES • DEVELOPED WITH JAMES PARK

A play on Italian tortellini en brodo (tortellini in broth) with a shout-out to kimchi soup, this dish comes together quickly thanks to the use of store-bought tortellini. Add sautéed kimchi, simmered lemon, Parmesan, and bacon for a broth that's bright, tart, salty, and savory down to your bones. This recipe for coziness in a bowl is easily doubled. One bite and you'll see why this is one of my Sleeper Hits of this cookbook (see page 5).

1 tablespoon unsalted butter

2 bacon slices, cut into ½-inch pieces

3 scallions, sliced

1 cup napa cabbage kimchi, coarsely chopped

½ to 1 tablespoon gochugaru (depending on desired spiciness)

4 cups (32 ounces) chicken stock

1 lemon, quartered and seeded

1 Parmesan rind (optional)

1¼ cups (5 ounces) finely grated Parmesan, plus more for serving

½ teaspoon freshly ground black pepper

One 8- to 10-ounce package refrigerated cheese or spinach-and-cheese tortellini

1. Melt the butter in a large pot over medium heat. Add the bacon and cook, stirring occasionally, until the fat has rendered and the bacon begins to brown, 3 to 5 minutes. Reserve about 2 tablespoons of the scallion greens, then add the remaining scallions to the pot and cook, stirring, until fragrant, about 1 minute. Add the kimchi and cook, stirring occasionally, until it begins to soften, 2 to 4 minutes. Stir in the gochugaru and cook for 30 seconds, then add the stock, 2 cups of water, the lemon, and the Parmesan rind, if using. Increase the heat to high and bring to a boil, scraping up any browned bits from the bottom of the pot, then reduce the heat to medium-low and cook for 15 minutes, adjusting the heat as necessary to maintain a medium simmer.

2. Remove and discard the Parmesan rind, if using. Use tongs to squeeze the lemon pieces, extracting as much liquid as possible, then remove and discard. Stirring constantly, add the Parmesan to the broth, followed by the pepper, and continue stirring until the cheese has dissolved into the broth. Simmer for 5 minutes, stirring once or twice, then add the tortellini and cook according to the package instructions.

3. Ladle the broth and tortellini into individual bowls, sprinkle with the reserved scallion greens and more Parmesan, and serve.

THE FAUX MANTI (ARMENIAN SPICED LAMB AND SHELLS)

SERVES 4 TO 6 • TOTAL TIME: 1 HOUR • DEVELOPED WITH ANDREW JANJIGIAN

When I first set out to find collaborators for this cookbook, the respected recipe developer, baking teacher, and writer Andrew Janjigian was one of the first people I called. He said he was too busy to work together on a bunch of recipes, but he did have one idea for a pasta dish that he'd been noodling on for years, waiting for the right place to share it. He decided this cookbook should be that place. So I'll let Andrew set this one up in his own words . . .

Sini manti are miniature canoe-shaped, lamb-filled dumplings, baked until crisp and then served in a tomatoey lamb broth with a large dollop of garlic-laden yogurt and a sprinkle of ground sumac. It's an essential dish to many Armenian families, mine included, and we eat it every year on Christmas Eve. But the dumplings are absurdly time-consuming to make; my aunts used to gather several weekends in a row in the lead-up to the feast in order to make enough of them, only to have them disappear in a flash on the big day.

Which is why it makes sense that you find "mock" manti recipes in many Armenian church cookbooks, substituting shell pasta for the dumpling skins and a liquidy meat gravy meant to re-create both the filling and the broth. Most take a pretty simple approach, cooking ground beef or lamb with chicken broth and tomato paste, but I wanted mine to replicate all of the vibrance and savor of the real thing. The soft texture of the pasta is a far cry from that of the crisp, crunchy dumplings, but the joy of the dish still comes through.

What I love about this dish is that because it shares some similarities with other tomato-based meat sauces, it feels instantly familiar. But the depth of flavor from the sumac and Aleppo pepper and the addition of the garlic yogurt add whole new layers to an experience I thought I knew. Thank you, Andrew, for choosing my book to share your recipe!

(continued)

YOGURT-GARLIC SAUCE (SEE NOTE)

2 garlic cloves, minced

½ teaspoon kosher salt

2 cups (16 ounces) plain whole-milk or 2% Greek yogurt

MEAT SAUCE AND PASTA

1 pound ground lamb (or 80/20 ground beef)

½ teaspoon baking soda

2 tablespoons extra-virgin olive oil

1 medium yellow onion, finely chopped

3 garlic cloves, minced

1 teaspoon plus 2 tablespoons kosher salt

¼ cup chopped fresh parsley leaves and tender stems

¼ cup tomato paste

3 teaspoons Aleppo pepper (see note)

2 teaspoons sweet paprika

1 teaspoon ground allspice

½ teaspoon freshly ground black pepper

2 cups (16 ounces) chicken stock

2 teaspoons ground sumac

1 pound medium shells

1. For the yogurt-garlic sauce: Place the garlic on a cutting board, sprinkle with the salt, and use a fork to mash it into a rough paste. Place the yogurt in a medium bowl and use the fork to stir the garlic paste into the yogurt until evenly combined; cover and set aside.

2. For the meat sauce and pasta: In a medium bowl, combine the lamb, 2 tablespoons of water, and ¼ teaspoon of the baking soda and gently knead until just combined; set aside. Heat the oil in a Dutch oven (or large pot if you also have a second large pot for the pasta) over medium heat until shimmering. Add the onion, garlic, 1 teaspoon of the salt, and the remaining ¼ teaspoon of baking soda and cook, stirring often, until the onion begins to soften and coat the pot, 6 to 8 minutes. Add the lamb mixture and use a wooden spoon to break it up into ¼- to ½-inch pieces. Cook, stirring often, until the meat begins to brown and form a fond (or browned layer) on the bottom of the pot, 12 to 16 minutes; remove the pot from the heat.

3. Move the meat to one side of the pot, then tilt slightly to let the fat drain to the opposite side. Use a spoon to remove and discard all but about 2 tablespoons of the fat (if your lamb is very lean and you have less than 2 tablespoons of fat, make up the difference with olive oil). Add 2 tablespoons of the parsley, the tomato paste, 1 teaspoon of the Aleppo pepper, the paprika, allspice, and black pepper to the pot and return the heat to medium. Cook, stirring, until the tomato paste darkens to a brick red, 2 to 4 minutes. Add the broth and 1 cup of water, increase the heat to high, and bring to a simmer, scraping up any browned bits from the bottom of the pot. Reduce the heat to medium and cook, stirring occasionally, until thickened slightly and the fat has separated from the sauce, 8 to 10 minutes. Cover and remove from the heat. (At this point the sauce can sit for up to 1 hour, be refrigerated for up to 3 days, or frozen for up to 1 month. Warm in a covered pot over low heat before proceeding with the recipe.)

4. Bring 4 quarts of water and the remaining 2 tablespoons of salt to a boil in a large pot. Add the pasta to the boiling water and cook for 2 minutes less than the low end of the package instructions. Use a mesh spider to transfer the pasta directly to the sauce in the pot and return the heat to medium. Add ¼ cup of the pasta cooking water and toss until the sauce is thickened but still brothy, 2 to 4 minutes. (If the sauce seems too thick, add more pasta water ¼ cup at a time to loosen.) Remove the pot from the heat and stir in the remaining 2 tablespoons of parsley.

5. In a small bowl, stir together the remaining 2 teaspoons of Aleppo pepper and the sumac and set aside.

6. Transfer the pasta to individual bowls, dollop 2 tablespoons of the yogurt-garlic sauce on each serving, and sprinkle with ½ teaspoon of the Aleppo-sumac mixture. Serve with the remaining yogurt sauce and Aleppo-sumac mixture.

YOGURT-GARLIC SAUCE NOTE: This will likely yield more yogurt-garlic sauce than you need, but as Andrew told me, "Armenians like a lot of yogurt." You can make half, but then you risk running low, and making three-quarters of it just feels annoying. (I don't want to ask you to use 1½ cloves of garlic.) So if you have extra yogurt-garlic sauce, you can keep it in the fridge for up to a week, and it'll work well on any of the other dishes in this book that call for yogurt, including the Keema Bolognese (page 160) and the Mac 'n' Dal (page 45).

ALEPPO PEPPER NOTE: If you can't find Aleppo pepper, substitute an additional 1 teaspoon of paprika plus ⅛ teaspoon of cayenne pepper in the sauce in step 3. For the finishing Aleppo-sumac mixture in step 5, substitute paprika or gochugaru.

GARLIC-AND-HERB CHEESE AND POTATOES WITH PASTA MISTA

SERVES 4 TO 6 • TOTAL TIME: 1 HOUR • DEVELOPED WITH NATHALIE CHRISTIAN

When one carb just isn't enough, there's the classic Neapolitan comfort dish pasta with potatoes and provola cheese. Once considered cucina povera (peasant cooking), today it's a regional specialty served with pride at upscale trattorias.

Everyone has their own version—some quite soupy and loose; some adding garlic, carrots, and celery to the onion; some with tomatoes and basil; some with smoked cheese. Often this dish is done with a mixture of different pasta shapes (pasta mista), which is always fun, so that's what we're doing (see note). Despite the many variations, it's almost always made in one pot to yield a dish that Italians call *azzeccata*, roughly translated to "gooey, creamy, and homey."

Because provola is very hard to find in the U.S., and because I wanted something with a little more tang, we adapted this classic into the recipe you see here. Cutting the potatoes in different sizes allows some to melt into the starchy pasta water to form the sauce. Beyond that we kept our recipe simple, but you're welcome to add a handful of cherry tomatoes or a coarsely chopped plum tomato a few minutes after adding the onion, allowing the tomatoes to burst and break down a bit before adding the hot liquid and potatoes. You can even finish it with a handful of torn basil if you're feeling fancy.

Note that this dish is best when eaten right away.

1 tablespoon extra-virgin olive oil, plus more for serving

4 ounces pancetta, diced (see note)

1 yellow onion, diced

2 fresh rosemary sprigs

1 pound Yukon Gold or yellow potatoes (2 to 4 potatoes), peeled and cut into ½- to ¾-inch pieces

1 Parmesan rind (optional)

1½ teaspoons kosher salt

1 pound pasta (see note)

One 5.2- to 6-ounce package garlic-and-herb cheese spread, such as Boursin

Finely grated Parmesan or Pecorino Romano, for serving

Cracked black peppercorns, for serving (see tip on page 70)

1. In a medium saucepan, heat 3 quarts of water over medium heat, adjusting the heat as necessary to keep the water steaming but not simmering.

PANCETTA NOTE: We used a package of diced pancetta for this recipe, and we encourage you to do the same. If the packaged pancetta at your grocery store is 6 ounces instead of 4, feel free to use the whole thing.

2. Heat the oil in a large, high-sided skillet or Dutch oven over medium heat until shimmering. Add the pancetta and cook, stirring occasionally, until the fat has rendered and the pancetta is crispy, 4 to 6 minutes. Add the onion and rosemary and cook, stirring often and scraping up any browned bits from the bottom of the pan, until the onion is soft and translucent, 3 to 5 minutes.

3. Add the potatoes, Parmesan rind (if using), and salt to the skillet along with enough of the hot water to just cover the potatoes (about 1½ cups, keeping the remaining water hot). Increase the heat under the skillet to medium-high, bring the mixture to a simmer, and cook, stirring occasionally and adjusting the heat as necessary to maintain a gentle simmer, until the smaller potato pieces are just fork-tender, 8 to 10 minutes.

4. Add the pasta to the skillet, then ladle in enough hot water to cover (3 to 5 cups). Return to a simmer and cook, stirring often and adjusting the heat as necessary to maintain a vigorous simmer, until the pasta is just tender, most of the liquid has been absorbed, and the potatoes are completely tender (with some having disintegrated), 10 to 20 minutes. (The cooking time will depend on how thick your pasta is. Just keep checking and adding more hot water ¼ cup at a time as needed to prevent scorching; you may not use all of the water.)

5. Remove the pan from the heat and remove and discard the rosemary and Parmesan rind, if using. Add the garlic-and-herb cheese spread and stir continuously until completely melted. (If the sauce seems too thick, add more hot water 2 tablespoons at a time, stirring well after each addition, until the sauce is creamy and thin enough to pool a little in the pan. It will tighten up when removed from the heat.)

6. Ladle the pasta into individual bowls, drizzle with more oil, sprinkle with the Parmesan and cracked peppercorns, and serve.

PASTA NOTE: *Pasta mista* translates as "mixed pasta"—it means different shapes cooked together. Traditionally it's a way to use up pasta odds and ends in your pantry, and I encourage you to do just that. In Italy some brands actually sell boxes of two or three different shapes mixed together. It's an excellent way to engineer more textural variety (dynamic contrast) into your pasta-eating experience. Try to bring together shapes with different strengths—tubes plus twists plus ruffles, and so on. Experiment with different combos! Just break any long pasta into smaller pieces and avoid pastas with wildly different cook times. A difference of 1 to 2 minutes is fine; just add them to the pan in stages, ladling in more hot water with each addition. Of course you can also use one whole box of any single short shape. But is that as much fun?

MOM'S MUSHROOM RAGÙ WITH CASCATELLI

SERVES 4 TO 6 • TOTAL TIME: 1 HOUR 30 MINUTES • DEVELOPED WITH LINDA PASHMAN

When cascatelli came out, my mom quickly recognized that a meaty pasta goes perfectly with a meaty vegetable—mushrooms. As with the Shrimp Scampi with Lemon-Herb Pangrattato (page 105), she developed this recipe so I'd have something to send to people who kept asking me, "What should I put on this pasta shape?"

By combining different varieties of mushrooms, each contributing a different taste and texture, you get a dish that's rich in flavor and dynamic contrast. The crème fraîche makes it lightly creamy, while the white wine adds a contrasting zing. Finish it off with the freshness of parsley and lemon zest and this dish hits all the notes, without any meat.

My mom says, "If you need any confirmation as to how delicious this preparation is, I will refer you to my friends, who eagerly took home leftovers. Verdict: Delicious even the day after."

7 tablespoons extra-virgin olive oil, plus more as needed

3 tablespoons unsalted butter

1½ pounds cremini (baby bella) mushrooms, cleaned, trimmed and sliced ¼ inch thick (see tip)

1½ teaspoons plus 2 tablespoons kosher salt

12 ounces mixed wild mushrooms, cleaned, sliced or torn (see tip)

8 ounces shiitake mushrooms, cleaned, stemmed and torn into ½- to 1-inch pieces (see tip)

2 large shallots, roughly chopped

1 leek, roughly chopped (see tip)

3 garlic cloves, minced

1 tablespoon chopped fresh thyme leaves

½ teaspoon freshly ground black pepper

¼ teaspoon red pepper flakes

1 tablespoon tomato paste

¾ cup dry white wine

1½ cups (12 ounces) chicken or vegetable stock

1 pound cascatelli pasta (or quattrotini or rigatoni)

½ cup crème fraîche

½ cup (2 ounces) finely grated Pecorino Romano, plus more for serving

¼ cup chopped fresh parsley

Finely grated lemon zest for serving, plus 2 tablespoons freshly squeezed lemon juice

1. In a large, high-sided skillet, heat 2 tablespoons of the oil and 1 tablespoon of the butter over medium-high heat. When the butter has melted, add half of the cremini mushrooms and cook, stirring occasionally, until the mushroom liquid has evaporated and the mushrooms begin to sizzle and brown, 6 to 9 minutes. Stir in ½ teaspoon of the salt and transfer to a bowl. Repeat with another 2 tablespoons of

(continued)

MUSHROOMS TIP: While the tough stems of shiitake mushrooms should be removed and discarded (or saved for veg stock), trim only a bit off the stem of the cremini mushrooms—they've got great texture and flavor. For the wild mushrooms, we like a mix of oyster and king trumpet. For king trumpets, slice thinly, but the oysters can simply be torn in half if large or left whole if small. H Mart has a fantastic selection of wild mushrooms, and at excellent prices.

LEEK TIP: Make sure to wash the leek well, slicing it lengthwise and rinsing under cold water while separating the layers to dislodge any sand or grit. Use only the tender white and very light green parts of the leek for this recipe, saving the tough green parts for stock.

the oil, 1 tablespoon of the butter, the remaining cremini mushrooms, and another ½ teaspoon of the salt, transferring the cooked mushrooms to the same bowl (the second batch may cook more quickly than the first). Add 2 tablespoons of the oil and the remaining 1 tablespoon of butter to the skillet. When the butter has melted, add the wild and shiitake mushrooms, spread them in an even layer, and cook undisturbed until the mushrooms on the bottom are well browned in spots, 5 to 7 minutes. (If the mushrooms begin to stick to the pan, add more olive oil and stir until they release.) Stir and redistribute the mushrooms, then continue to cook, stirring occasionally, until all the mushrooms are softened and browned, 4 to 6 minutes. Stir in ½ teaspoon of the salt and transfer to a second bowl, reserving the skillet.

2. Bring 4 quarts of water and the remaining 2 tablespoons of salt to a boil in a large pot.

3. Place the reserved skillet over medium heat and add the shallots, leek, and remaining 1 tablespoon of oil. Cook, stirring occasionally, until the shallots and leek are softened and beginning to brown, 3 to 6 minutes. Add the garlic, thyme, black pepper, and red pepper flakes and cook, stirring, until fragrant, about 1 minute. Stir in the tomato paste and cook until darkened to a brick red, 1 to 2 minutes. Add the wine and simmer, scraping up any browned bits from the bottom of the pan, until reduced by half, 1 to 2 minutes. Add the cremini mushrooms, along with any accumulated juices, and the stock. Increase the heat to medium-high, return to a simmer, and cook, stirring occasionally, until the sauce is no longer watery and the spoon leaves a trail in the bottom of the pan when the sauce is stirred, 6 to 8 minutes. Stir in the wild and shiitake mushrooms along with any accumulated juices and remove the pan from the heat. (At this point the sauce can be covered and set aside for up to 2 hours or refrigerated for up to 24 hours. Warm the sauce over low heat before proceeding with the recipe.)

4. Add the pasta to the boiling water and cook for 2 minutes less than the low end of the package instructions. Use a mesh spider to transfer the pasta directly to the skillet and return the heat to medium-high. Add ½ cup of the pasta cooking water and the crème fraîche and cook, stirring and tossing, until the sauce clings to the pasta but still pools slightly in the bottom of the pan when stirred, 3 to 5 minutes. (It will thicken when you add the cheese. If the sauce seems too thick, add more pasta water 2 tablespoons at a time until the sauce loosens but still clings to the pasta.) Remove the pan from the heat and stir in the Pecorino, parsley, and lemon juice.

5. Transfer the pasta to a serving dish or individual bowls, sprinkle with lemon zest, and serve with more Pecorino.

FREGOLA SARDA WITH CALAMARI AND SAFFRON BROTH

SERVES 4 • TOTAL TIME: 50 MINUTES • DEVELOPED WITH ASHA LOUPY

Fregola sarda—a beloved pasta cut of Sardinia, the largest island off the west coast of Italy—is a small, rolled shape similar to Israeli couscous that's toasted, resulting in pebble-size pieces that vary from pale yellow to deep and roasty.

While you often see this pasta paired with clams, I love it with tender tentacles and rings of squid. The sauce is light and brothy, with just enough white wine to give it some oomph and acidity, and our technique for cooking the squid is simple and foolproof, to make sure this temperamental mollusk comes out soft and tender.

1 cup dry white wine

Pinch of saffron

1 pound cleaned squid, tentacles separated and bodies cut into ¼-inch rings (see note)

2 teaspoons plus 1 tablespoon kosher salt

¼ cup extra-virgin olive oil, plus more for serving

1 medium fennel bulb, cored and finely diced, plus optional torn fronds, for serving (see tip)

2 medium shallots, minced

2 tablespoons tomato paste

3 garlic cloves, finely grated

3 cups (24 ounces) fish stock or vegetable stock

8 ounces (about 1⅓ cups) fregola sarda (see note)

2 cups (10 ounces) cherry tomatoes, halved

½ cup finely chopped fresh parsley

2 teaspoons finely grated lemon zest

1. In a small bowl or liquid measuring cup, combine the wine and saffron and set aside. In a medium bowl, toss the squid with 1 teaspoon of the salt until evenly coated.

2. Bring 2½ quarts of water and 1 tablespoon of the salt to a boil in a large saucepan.

3. Heat the oil in a large skillet over medium-high heat until shimmering. Add the fennel, shallots, and remaining 1 teaspoon of salt, reduce the heat to medium, and cook, stirring occasionally, until the vegetables are soft and golden around the edges, 7 to 10 minutes. Add the tomato paste and garlic and cook, stirring, until the tomato paste darkens to a brick red, 2 to 4 minutes. Add the wine-saffron mixture

(continued)

and cook, stirring occasionally, until reduced by a quarter, about 5 minutes. Add the stock and bring to a simmer, then cover and reduce the heat to low.

4. Add the pasta to the boiling water (remember, it's only half the package!) and cook for 2 minutes less than the low end of the package instructions. A few minutes before the pasta is done, return the sauce to medium heat and bring to a simmer. Drain the pasta, shaking off the excess water, and immediately transfer to the skillet with the sauce. Stir in the squid and tomatoes, increase the heat to medium-high, and cook, stirring often, until the squid is milky white and the rings start to curl up around the edges, 3 to 5 minutes. Remove the pan from the heat and stir in the parsley and lemon zest.

5. Transfer to a serving bowl or individual bowls, drizzle with more oil, sprinkle with fennel fronds, if desired, and serve. Eat it with a soup spoon.

SQUID NOTE: Buy squid that's been cleaned—most prepackaged squid comes that way, and they should be able to do it for you at your local fish market. If you get it before it's been cleaned, buy 1½ pounds and assume an extra 10 to 15 minutes for cleaning.

FENNEL TIP: Do your best to dice the fennel into pieces that are about the same size as the fregola sarda. The fennel fronds are the feathery tops of the stalks that look a bit like dill. For more on fennel anatomy and how to core it properly, see page 79.

FREGOLA SARDA NOTE: You can also use Israeli couscous—just toast the couscous in a pan in a bit of olive oil over medium heat until it smells toasty and about a quarter of the pieces are golden brown to well browned. Transfer to a plate and proceed with the recipe.

TTEOKBOKKI BOLOGNESE (KOREAN RICE CAKES IN MEAT SAUCE)

SERVES 4 TO 6 • TOTAL TIME: 35 MINUTES • DEVELOPED WITH IRENE YOO

This is the only dish in this pasta cookbook that doesn't actually include pasta. Tteok are Korean rice cakes—usually the star ingredient in the spicy rice cake dish tteokbokki. Tteok is a great substitute for pasta. It's chewy like gnocchi but more so, and if you panfry it as we do here, it has a delightful exterior crisp that gives way to that deeply satisfying interior.

You can find tteok (often sold as tteokbokki) at H Mart and many other Asian groceries. It can be stored in your freezer for months and prepared in minutes. Tteok can be boiled prior to use but is generally not cooked in salted water like pasta.

To doctor this tomato sauce as you like, see the Jarred Tomato Sauce Decision Tree (page 30).

1 tablespoon canola or other neutral oil

1 pound ground beef (80/20), pork, turkey, or a combination

½ teaspoon kosher salt

One 24- to 25-ounce jar marinara sauce (see above)

1 tablespoon unsalted butter (or olive oil)

1 pound rice cakes (tteok)

½ cup (2 ounces) finely grated Parmesan, plus more for serving

¼ cup chopped fresh parsley (optional)

1. Heat the oil in a large nonstick skillet over medium-high heat until shimmering. Add the beef, sprinkle with the salt, and cook, stirring and breaking up the meat with a wooden spoon, until no longer pink, 5 to 7 minutes. Add the marinara sauce, then add ¾ cup of water to the empty marinara jar, cover, shake, and add to the skillet. Stir to combine, bring to a simmer, and cook until thickened, 5 to 7 minutes, stirring occasionally. Cover and remove from the heat.

2. Melt the butter in a large skillet over medium heat. Add the rice cakes and cook, stirring and tossing often, until uniformly softened and lightly browned, about 5 minutes. Carefully transfer the rice cakes to the sauce in the first skillet (the pan will be very full) and stir until evenly coated. Add the Parmesan and parsley, if using, and stir until the cheese is melted.

3. Transfer to a serving dish or bowls, and serve immediately with more Parmesan.

PASTA SALADS REDEEMED: FRESH AND BRIGHT, HOLD THE MAYO

6

WHY PASTA SALADS NEED REDEEMING

Too often when we hear the term "pasta salad," it refers to a mayo-based slurry, or even worse, overcooked pasta and undercooked veggies coated in an acrid vinaigrette. Pasta salad is the thing people tack on to their party menu when they want a carby side and aren't aware of other options, or that they buy premade in a leaden plastic tub because they realize on the way to your house that they don't have anything to bring.

We can do better.

Think of your favorite greens-based salad. It's probably fresh and bright, acidic and crunchy. Now imagine that same salad but instead of a base of greens, you have a base of pasta. Suddenly it's more substantial and comforting, more satisfying to body and mind, while still working on the same flavor principles.

These are the types of pasta salads you'll find in this chapter.

Truth is, many great pasta dishes function beautifully as pasta salads. To me the best candidates for this reimagining are lighter, more acidic, veg-centric pastas held together with oil and grated Parmesan or Pecorino. High-viscosity sauces that rely on butter, cream, eggs, rendered fat, pureed tomatoes, and/or meltier cheeses feel too thick to fill the role of salad, and are more likely to dry out or tighten up when they sit.

Many of the best candidates for your pasta salad consideration have a high chunk factor (see page 154), because you want pieces to stab, which is part of the experience of eating a salad. That's why, in addition to the recipes in this chapter, dishes like the Cavatelli with Roasted Artichokes and Preserved Lemon on page 112 and the Caramelized Endive and Radicchio with Savory Bagna Cauda on page 148 are excellent pasta salad options. Prepare them a couple of hours in advance and toss with a drizzle of olive oil before serving to freshen them up!

LEMONY TUNA WITH OLIVES, CAPERS, GREEN BEANS, AND PARSLEY

SERVES 4 TO 6 · TOTAL TIME: 40 MINUTES · DEVELOPED WITH ASHA LOUPY

We'll start our pasta salad odyssey with one of my go-to weekday lunches, which I often throw together with leftover pasta from last night's dinner. Everyone needs a good pantry pasta salad in their back pocket for those meals, or for days when it's too hot to cook or you get a last-minute invite—something that delivers on ease, elegance, and flavor. This is that dish for me.

Here we're pairing it with torchiette (little torches), which are similar to my vesuvio shape and work on similar principles, with curving slides that hold bits and pieces. With torchiette, I love the dynamic contrast between the torch's narrower, denser handle and wider flame.

2 tablespoons kosher salt, plus more as needed

1¼ cups roughly chopped fresh flat-leaf parsley

⅔ cup extra-virgin olive oil

1 tablespoon finely grated lemon zest, plus ¼ cup freshly squeezed lemon juice

3 tablespoons finely chopped preserved lemon (about ½ medium lemon), plus 1 tablespoon preserved lemon liquid (see tip on page 114)

2 garlic cloves, roughly chopped

1 teaspoon freshly ground black pepper

1 pound torchiette pasta (a.k.a. torchio; or use vesuvio, cascatelli, or rigatoni)

8 ounces haricots verts (or regular green beans), cut into 1-inch pieces

8 to 12 ounces jarred or canned oil-packed tuna, lightly drained (see note)

⅔ cup pitted green olives, torn in half (use a full cup if you really love olives)

2 tablespoons drained capers, roughly chopped

1. Bring 4 quarts of water and the salt to a boil in a large pot. In a blender, combine ½ cup of the parsley, the oil, lemon zest and juice, preserved lemon and preserved lemon liquid, garlic, and ½ teaspoon of the pepper. Blend until smooth, about 30 seconds, then transfer to a large bowl, scraping out the blender jar.

2. Add the pasta to the boiling water and cook until just al dente (the low end of the package instructions); during the last 3 minutes of cooking, add the green beans to the pot. Drain the pasta and beans, shaking off the excess water, and immediately transfer to the bowl with the dressing. Add the tuna (flaking it into

(continued)

large pieces), olives, capers, ½ cup of the parsley, and the remaining ½ teaspoon of pepper and gently fold until evenly coated. Taste and season with salt, if necessary. Transfer the pasta to a serving dish, sprinkle with the remaining ¼ cup of parsley, and serve warm, room temperature, or cold.

NOTE: When it comes to tuna, this is the time to splurge on the good stuff instead of the flaked tuna packed in water. Look for tuna packed in olive oil—I love Spanish brands Ortiz and La Brújula, the Italian brand Tonnino, and Portuguese brands Santa Catarina and Porthos. If you want to make this dish extra luscious, you can use ventresca, the tender, fatty belly tuna sold by Ortiz and Tonnino. Because these tunas come in all different sizes, and because they can be pricey, I'm giving you a range of quantities that will work. When draining the tuna, you want to get rid of just the excess oil in the tin or jar, letting a little of the flavorful stuff cling to the fish. And whatever you do, don't rinse it!

RAW HEIRLOOM PUTTANESCA WITH FISH SAUCE AND CALABRIAN CHILI

SERVES 2 TO 4 • TOTAL TIME: 30 MINUTES • DEVELOPED WITH ASHA LOUPY

We've arrived at the fifth of my five Sleeper Hits of the cookbook (see page 5). By the metric of Flavor Generated per Minute of Effort, this one is off the charts.

Puttanesca—the beloved pasta dish of Naples—is traditionally a cooked tomato sauce with anchovies, olives, capers, chili flakes, and garlic, tossed with a long pasta like spaghetti. This fresh version uses grated heirloom tomatoes and good extra-virgin olive oil as a base for the sauce, which is layered with a couple of spoonfuls of fish sauce (instead of anchovies), green olives, capers, grated garlic, torn basil, and a kiss of Calabrian chili paste for heat.

I know I said I'm tired of tomato sauces, but uncooked tomato sauces are totally different!

Because tomatoes are the star of this dish, you want to make this at the height of summer when heirloom tomatoes are the best, sweetest versions of themselves. This is also the time to pull out that bottle of your extra-good extra-virgin olive oil, because you will taste the difference.

Instead of spaghetti, I like this with pastina (small pasta shapes), like ditalini, which gives me the ability to scoop everything up with a spoon and enjoy its almost brothy sauce. This is a fantastic meatless main course (except the fish sauce) or summer barbecue side with burgers or steaks, easily doubled and delicious when made ahead. In fact it might be better when made ahead, because ditalini excels at soaking up the intense flavors of the sauce without turning too soft.

1 tablespoon kosher salt, plus more as needed

1½ pounds ripe but firm heirloom tomatoes (see tip)

½ cup extra-virgin olive oil, plus more for serving

1½ tablespoons fish sauce

1 tablespoon Calabrian chili paste (bomba sauce; see note)

1 garlic clove, finely grated

1 cup pitted green olives, thinly sliced (see note)

3 tablespoons drained capers

8 ounces (1¾ cups) ditalini (a.k.a. tubetti; or use orecchiette)

½ cup chopped fresh basil leaves, plus small leaves for serving

1. Bring 2½ quarts of water and the salt to a boil in a large saucepan. Slice ¼ inch off the top of each tomato and remove the tough core (see tip). Place a box grater in a large bowl and use the large holes to shred the cut side of the tomato until the flesh has all been grated off the skin; discard the skins. Add the oil, fish sauce, chili paste, and garlic to the tomatoes and whisk until the oil is evenly incorporated. Stir in the olives and capers and let sit for at least 15 minutes and up to 3 hours.

2. Add the pasta to the boiling water (remember, it's only half the package!) and cook until just al dente (the low end of the package instructions). Drain, shaking off the excess water, and immediately transfer to the bowl with the tomato mixture, stirring to combine. Stir in the basil, then taste and add salt if necessary.

3. Transfer the pasta to a serving bowl or individual bowls, drizzle with more oil, sprinkle with basil leaves, and serve. Eat it with a spoon!

TIP: Use a small paring knife to cut out the cone-shaped core until all the hard, whitish flesh is gone. If your tomatoes have tough brown spots, cut them out too. You want ripe but firm tomatoes for this recipe—the super-ripe, super-soft ones aren't ideal for grating. When you sniff the stem ends, they should smell like a fresh-cut tomato.

CALABRIAN CHILI PASTE NOTE: Calabrian chili paste is also sometimes called bomba sauce or, in the case of the TuttoCalabria brand found at Whole Foods and other specialty stores, Hot Pepper Paté. You can add as much or as little as you like depending on how spicy you want it. I suggest serving more on the side so people can adjust to their liking. Calabrian chili paste is also great on pizza, as a sandwich spread, as an addition to jarred tomato sauce (page 33), and as an ingredient in the Cascatelli with Spicy Broccoli Rabe Pesto on page 214 and the Eggplant Timpano on page 253!

OLIVES NOTE: This dish has a lot of olives, which I really enjoy. To me they're the "meat" of the dish. But if you're not as olive crazy as I am, reduce to ⅔ cup.

*Raw Heirloom Puttanesca
with Fish Sauce and
Calabrian Chili (page 204)*

Conchiglie with Corn, Avocado, and Fried (or Grilled) Halloumi (page 208)

CONCHIGLIE WITH CORN, AVOCADO, AND FRIED (OR GRILLED) HALLOUMI

SERVES 4 TO 6 • TOTAL TIME: 45 MINUTES • DEVELOPED WITH ASHA LOUPY

This pasta salad combines peak summer with peak flavor. We balance the corn's inherent sweetness with a bright and zingy dressing—punctuated by preserved lemon, lemon zest, and lemon juice. Chunks of creamy avocado add richness, while torn basil brings a wallop of herbaceous, bright green flavor and savory cubes of halloumi add even more deliciousness. The corn nestles beautifully in the conchiglie, which is Italian for "shells"—but doesn't it sound more impressive when you say *conchiglie*?

A lot of times you may see halloumi seared in a hot pan, but I love this firm Greek cheese cut into cubes and shallow fried, which turns the outside golden and crispy and the inside plush and bouncy, almost like cheese curds. That being said, grilling the halloumi is also a great option.

½ cup extra-virgin olive oil

2 teaspoons finely grated lemon zest, plus ¼ cup freshly squeezed lemon juice

1 medium shallot, minced

1 teaspoon plus 2 tablespoons kosher salt

2 tablespoons finely chopped preserved lemon (see tip on page 114)

1½ teaspoons Dijon mustard

1 garlic clove, finely grated

1 teaspoon honey

Canola or other neutral oil, for frying

8 ounces halloumi, cut into ½-inch cubes and patted dry (see note)

3 ears corn, shucked (see tip on page 213)

1 pound conchiglie (medium shells), cestini, or torchio pasta

2 large avocados, pitted, peeled, and diced

1½ cups lightly packed fresh basil leaves, roughly torn

1. In a jar with a tight-fitting lid, combine the olive oil, lemon zest and juice, shallot, 1 teaspoon of the salt, the preserved lemon, mustard, garlic, and honey. Seal and shake vigorously until the dressing thickens and emulsifies; set aside.

2. Bring 4 quarts of water and the remaining 2 tablespoons of salt to a boil in a large pot.

3. If grilling the halloumi, follow the instructions in the note instead of this step, then proceed with step 4. Line a plate with a double layer of paper towels. Add enough canola oil to a medium saucepan to measure 1 inch deep and heat the pan over medium-high heat until it registers 325°F on an instant-read thermometer. (You can also throw a bread crumb into the oil—if it immediately starts to sizzle, the oil is ready.) Add half of the halloumi in a single layer and fry, stirring occasionally, until golden brown, 2 to 4 minutes. Use a slotted spoon to transfer to the prepared plate and repeat with the remaining halloumi.

4. Add the corn to the boiling water and cook until tender, 3 to 5 minutes. Use tongs to transfer the corn to a colander and rinse it under cold water until warm to the touch. Return the water to a boil, add the pasta, and cook until just al dente (the low end of the package instructions). Drain, shaking off the excess water, and transfer to a large bowl. Shake the dressing to recombine, then pour over the pasta and toss to coat. (At this point the pasta mixture can sit, covered, for up to 3 hours. If making ahead, wait to peel and dice the avocados until right before serving.)

5. Cut the corn kernels off the cobs, leaving some larger clusters intact, and add them to the bowl with the pasta. Add the avocados and 1¼ cups of the basil and gently toss to combine, taking care not to smash the avocado.

6. Transfer the pasta to a serving dish or individual bowls, top with the halloumi, sprinkle with the remaining ¼ cup of basil, and serve.

NOTE: If you prefer to grill your halloumi, set a grill to medium-low heat and slice the halloumi lengthwise to create ½-inch-thick slabs. Coat the grill grates lightly with olive oil or cooking spray, place the halloumi directly on the grill, and cook until you have golden-brown grill marks on both sides (2 to 4 minutes per side). Remove the halloumi from the grill, cut it into 1-inch squares, and proceed with step 4. If you want to skip cooking cheese entirely, big crumbles of feta are also a very tasty option here.

NO-COOK HEIRLOOM TOMATO SAUCE WITH CURRANTS, CAPERS, AND MARINATED PINE NUTS

SERVES 4 TO 6 • TOTAL TIME: 50 MINUTES • DEVELOPED WITH KATIE LEAIRD

This no-cook sauce builds on a base of summer's finest heirloom tomatoes by adding tart currants, briny capers, and crunchy, seasoned pine nuts. You can use a mix of red and yellow tomatoes to make the dish especially colorful. I love medium shells here because they catch the capers, currants, and pine nuts, creating ready-made salty-sweet-crunchy bites. Small shells won't catch enough bits, and large ones would be unwieldy.

TOMATO SAUCE AND PASTA

1½ pounds ripe heirloom tomatoes, cored (see tip on page 205)

¼ cup drained capers

¼ cup dried currants (see note)

1 tablespoon red wine vinegar

2 teaspoons plus 2 tablespoons kosher salt

¼ teaspoon freshly ground black pepper

1 pound medium shells

¼ cup extra-virgin olive oil, plus more for serving

¼ cup torn fresh basil

MARINATED PINE NUTS

½ cup pine nuts

½ cup chopped fresh basil

2 tablespoons extra-virgin olive oil

1 teaspoon finely grated orange zest

¼ to ½ teaspoon red pepper flakes (depending son desired spiciness)

¼ teaspoon kosher salt

1. For the tomato sauce and pasta: Chop the tomatoes into ¼- to ½-inch pieces and transfer to a colander set in a large bowl. Add the capers, currants, 2 teaspoons of the vinegar, 1½ teaspoons of the salt, and the pepper and stir gently to combine; set aside for at least 20 minutes and up to 1 hour. (Giving it more time allows the currants to plump up and absorb extra flavor.)

2. Meanwhile, for the marinated pine nuts: Toast the pine nuts in a small skillet over low heat until golden brown and fragrant, 4 to 6 minutes, tossing and shaking the pan often. Transfer them to a medium bowl and let cool to room temperature. Add the remaining marinade ingredients to the cooled pine nuts and stir to combine.

3. Bring 4 quarts of water and 2 tablespoons of the salt to a boil in a large pot. Add the pasta to the boiling water and cook for 1 minute less than the low end of the package instructions. (If you have only one colander, at this point you can transfer the drained tomato mixture to a clean bowl, reserving the juices separately, and rinse the colander before draining the pasta.)

4. Drain the pasta, shaking off the excess water, and immediately return it to the pot (off the heat). Add the tomato mixture, 2 tablespoons of the tomato juices (reserving the remainder), the oil, remaining 1 teaspoon of vinegar, and the remaining ½ teaspoon of salt and stir until well combined, about 1 minute. (If the pasta looks dry, add more of the tomato juices 1 tablespoon at a time until the pasta is well coated. At this point the pasta can sit, covered, for up to 3 hours.)

5. Stir in the pine nuts and marinade, then transfer the pasta to a serving dish or individual bowls. Drizzle with more oil, sprinkle with the torn basil, and serve.

NOTE: Dried currants aren't as hard to find as you may think. Many supermarkets sell Sun-Maid brand Zante currants, and most organic markets, including Whole Foods, carry their own dried currants. (Don't use raisins—they're too sweet.)

CAVATELLI WITH CRUNCHY FRESH CORN, TOMATOES, RICOTTA SALATA, AND MOZZARELLA

SERVES 4 TO 6 • TOTAL TIME: 30 MINUTES • DEVELOPED WITH KATIE LEAIRD

There are a lot of summery corn and tomato pasta salads out there, but this one has a few touches that I think make it special. First, the corn is raw. The heat of the pasta cooks it very slightly, but each kernel provides a fresh, sweet, crunchy snap—the perfect textural counterpoint to the chewy cavatelli. Second, we use salty, crumbly ricotta salata, which is nothing like regular ricotta, and which melts into the dish and holds it all together without making it heavy. In pasta as in life, sometimes the smallest change to the status quo can make a huge difference.

4 ears corn, kernels cut from the cobs (about 2½ cups; see tip)

3 cups (15 ounces) cherry tomatoes, halved (see tip)

8 ounces fresh mozzarella, cut into ½-inch cubes

½ cup finely chopped fresh basil leaves, plus small leaves for serving

6 tablespoons extra-virgin olive oil

3 tablespoons drained capers

1 tablespoon red wine vinegar (or white wine vinegar)

1 teaspoon plus 2 tablespoons kosher salt

½ teaspoon freshly ground black pepper

¼ to ½ teaspoon red pepper flakes (depending on desired spiciness)

1 pound cavatelli (see note on page 112; or gemelli, vesuvio, or medium shells)

3 ounces ricotta salata, shredded (¾ cup)

TIPS: Look for ears of corn that feel heavy for their size, and peel back the husk just a bit to check for pests or rot. Regular old cherry tomatoes are fine here, but if you can find Sungold, pear drop, or another small heirloom variety, that's even better.

1. In a large heatproof bowl, stir together the corn, tomatoes, mozzarella, basil, oil, capers, vinegar, 1 teaspoon of the salt, the black pepper, and the red pepper flakes. Let sit for at least 15 minutes and up to 1 hour. (You can set it aside for up to 3 hours, but wait to add the basil with the ricotta salata in that case.)

2. Meanwhile, bring 4 quarts of water and the remaining 2 tablespoons of salt to a boil in a large pot. Add the pasta to the boiling water and cook until just al dente (the low end of the package instructions). Drain, shaking off the excess water, and immediately transfer to the bowl with the tomato-corn mixture. Add the ricotta salata and stir thoroughly until all the ingredients are evenly distributed and warmed through, about 1 minute.

3. Transfer the pasta to a serving dish or individual bowls, sprinkle with basil leaves, and serve. I recommend eating this one with a spoon.

CASCATELLI WITH SPICY BROCCOLI RABE PESTO

SERVES 4 TO 6 • TOTAL TIME: 25 MINUTES • DEVELOPED WITH KATIE LEAIRD

I could easily have put this recipe in the Pestos section, or the Zing chapter, but I'm putting it here with salads to prove my point that lots of pasta dishes can be pasta salads (see page 200 for more on this).

While this dish has a low chunk factor (see page 154), pesto pastas can be easily chunkified—just add cooked shrimp or chicken or grilled veggies or canned tuna, and some extra pesto to coat them. But they don't have to be. When kept simple, they take the place of that ubiquitous bow-tie pasta salad with chopped bell peppers and vinaigrette, which is the Quasimodo of Cookouts, having spent decades haunting barbecues near and far. Let us vanquish that scourge and embrace pesto pasta salads instead!

2 tablespoons plus 1 teaspoon kosher salt

1 bunch broccoli rabe (about 1 pound), bottom 2 inches of the ends trimmed

6 tablespoons extra-virgin olive oil, plus more as needed

1 to 2 tablespoons Calabrian chili paste (bomba sauce; depending on desired spiciness), plus more for serving (see note on page 205)

1 garlic clove, peeled and smashed (see tip)

1 pound cascatelli (or vesuvio, radiatore, or cavatappi)

Finely grated Parmesan, for serving (optional)

1. Bring 4 quarts of water and 2 tablespoons of the salt to a boil in a large pot. In a large bowl, combine about 4 cups of ice and 6 cups of cold water. Add the broccoli rabe to the boiling water, making sure it's completely submerged, and cook until the stems are tender, about 2 minutes. Use tongs to transfer the rabe to the ice bath and let sit for at least 2 minutes; keep the water in the pot at a boil.

2. Transfer the rabe to a strainer and use your hands to squeeze out the excess moisture, then add the rabe to the bowl of a blender or food processor (or immersion blender, see note). Add the oil, chili paste, garlic, and remaining 1 teaspoon of salt and blend until smooth, about 1 minute, scraping down the sides of the bowl with a rubber spatula as necessary. (At this point the pesto can be kept, covered, at room temperature for a few hours before proceeding with the recipe. It can also be transferred to an airtight container and refrigerated for up to 1 week or frozen for up to 2 months.)

(continued)

3. Add the pasta to the boiling water and cook until just al dente (the low end of the package instructions). Reserve 2 cups of the pasta cooking water, then drain the pasta and return it to the pot (off the heat). Add the pesto and ¾ cup of the reserved pasta water and stir until the pasta is well coated. (If necessary, add more pasta water 2 tablespoons at a time until the sauce is creamy but clings to the pasta.)

4. Transfer the pasta to a serving dish or individual bowls, sprinkle with Parmesan, if desired, and serve with more chili paste. If making ahead, as with any pasta you're transforming into a pasta salad, cover for up to 2 hours and toss with a drizzle of olive oil before serving.

TIP: Since the garlic is raw, we felt that one clove was sufficient, but if you love garlic, up it to two cloves. If you're very sensitive to the bite of raw garlic, you can blanch the clove in the boiling water for a few minutes right along with the rabe to soften the flavor before pureeing it into the pesto.

NOTE: Using a food processor will yield the most traditional pesto texture—well combined but with individual components still visible. If you use a blender, the pesto will be smoother and more velvety. You can use an immersion blender, but you may need to add a little extra olive oil to make sure it holds together well.

CRISPY GNOCCHI SALAD WITH PRESERVED LEMON–TOMATO DRESSING

SERVES 4 TO 6 • TOTAL TIME: 35 MINUTES • DEVELOPED WITH NATHALIE CHRISTIAN

You didn't think I'd do an entire chapter on pasta salads and not include a crispy gnocchi recipe, did you? Crispy gnocchi is so good! Wait until the last second to dress the gnocchi to preserve its crisp for those first few bites. Still, no matter what you do, that crisp will fade. Such is life. Try not to dwell on what you cannot get back, and instead appreciate the dish's many seasons, how the gnocchi's texture and flavor evolve as it soaks up the dressing and turns juicy and chewy, with a faint hint of toasty crisp remaining. Like the late summer sun dipping below the tree line, casting its golden hues on the leaves, it's a bittersweet reminder that shorter days and cooler air are coming, bringing an end to ecstasy, but also a reprieve from the sun's white-hot magnificence.

That's how you eat crispy gnocchi.

This recipe is inspired by a Moroccan starter salad typically made with tomato and preserved lemon, but in place of the more traditional bell peppers, we're using optional spicy pepperoncini.

DRESSING

8 ounces ripe heirloom or beefsteak tomatoes (1 to 2 tomatoes; see tip on page 205)

2 tablespoons extra-virgin olive oil

2 tablespoons finely chopped preserved lemon (see tip on page 114)

2 tablespoons freshly squeezed lemon juice

1 garlic clove, finely grated

1 teaspoon kosher salt

½ teaspoon freshly ground black pepper

¼ teaspoon sugar (optional; add if your tomatoes aren't particularly sweet)

SALAD

3 cups cherry tomatoes (15 ounces), halved (see tip on page 213)

½ small red onion (or ¼ large onion), thinly sliced

3 small, tender celery stalks from the center of the head, leaves attached, thinly sliced diagonally

4 to 6 pepperoncini, thinly sliced (optional)

¼ cup drained capers

2 tablespoons extra-virgin olive oil, plus more as needed

One 16- to 18-ounce package potato gnocchi (see note)

½ cup lightly packed fresh parsley leaves, roughly torn

(continued)

1. For the dressing: Slice ¼ inch off the top of each heirloom tomato and remove the tough core. Place a box grater in a large bowl and use the large holes to shred the cut side of the tomato until the flesh has all been grated off the skin; discard the skins. Transfer the grated tomato to a liquid measuring cup and discard anything over ⅓ cup. Pour the grated tomato back into the bowl, reserving the measuring cup. Add the oil, preserved lemon, lemon juice, garlic, salt, pepper, and sugar, if using, to the grated tomato in the bowl and stir well to combine. Return the dressing to the measuring cup, reserving the bowl.

2. For the salad: Add the cherry tomatoes, onion, celery, pepperoncini (if using), and capers to the reserved bowl. Add ⅓ cup of the dressing and toss to coat. Set aside, reserving the remaining dressing separately.

3. Heat the oil in a large nonstick skillet over medium-high heat until shimmering. Add the gnocchi, breaking up any clumps, and cook, stirring often and adjusting the heat if the gnocchi start to brown too fast, until golden brown all over, 8 to 12 minutes. (If making ahead, pause here, remove the pan from the heat, and set aside for up to 3 hours. When ready to finish the dish, add a sprinkle of olive oil to the pan and toss over medium-high heat until warm.)

4. Add the gnocchi, parsley, and remaining dressing to the bowl with the salad and toss to combine. Transfer to a serving platter or individual plates and serve immediately.

NOTE: This recipe was developed with shelf-stable vacuum-packed gnocchi. If you get the refrigerated or frozen varieties, let them come to room temperature and pat them dry of any moisture before using.

ITALIAN CAFETERIA HOT DOG PASTA SALAD WITH CANNED VEGGIES

SERVES 4 TO 6 • TOTAL TIME: 25 MINUTES

Okay, so there is one pasta salad in here with mayo, and it might be the most authentically Italian recipe in this cookbook. You see, while I know many of us have romantic visions of Italian food prepared lovingly by hand over hours, served in a candlelit restaurant with a view of the Pantheon, the truth is that, like many other people, Italians sometimes just have to get a quick bite during a break from work. They sometimes want to grab lunch at the beach.

And as food writer and cookbook author Katie Parla told me when we met up in Rome, "I think most people don't appreciate how much Italians love hot dogs."

This pasta salad is a variation on a dish you'll see all over Italy in the summertime, especially in cafeteria-style restaurants and beach bars. It's usually made with rice, but as Katie clarifies, "Banish any thoughts of risotto from your mind. This is rinsed rice that's boiled and drained and rinsed again, mixed with canned corn, canned olives, rounds of hot dog, cubes of Swiss cheese, and pickled vegetables that are sold in a mix in a jar." Tuna is a common addition as well. Then you mix it all up with mayo.

"It's not high art," Katie adds, "but it is satisfying."

The details vary from one cafeteria to the next, and I've taken some liberties with it. (I find cubes of Swiss cheese to be hard in an unpleasant way, but that's just me.) You're encouraged to make it your own, but please don't add fresh vegetables, as that would be a violation of the spirit of the dish. You are welcome to add Italian-style pickled vegetables (giardiniera). As long as you have hot dogs in there, you pretty much can't go wrong. Just grab your can opener and enjoy!

2 tablespoons plus ¼ teaspoon kosher salt or more if desired

1 pound rigatoni (or shells, fusilloni, or whatever you have, including a mixture of shapes)

4 hot dogs

One 15.25-ounce can whole-kernel sweet corn, drained

One 14- to 16-ounce can or jar whole pearl onions (a.k.a. Holland-style onions), drained

Two 4-ounce cans Italian tuna in olive oil, lightly drained

One 3.8-ounce can sliced black olives, drained

3 tablespoons extra-virgin olive oil

3 tablespoons mayonnaise, plus more if desired

2 tablespoons white wine vinegar (or red wine vinegar)

½ teaspoon freshly ground black pepper

1. Bring 4 quarts of water and 2 tablespoons of the salt to a boil in a large pot. Add the pasta and hot dogs and cook until the pasta is just al dente (the low end of the package instructions). Use tongs to remove the hot dogs and transfer them to a cutting board. Drain the pasta, shaking off the excess water, and return it to the pot. Slice the hot dogs into disks and return them to the pot. Add the corn, onions, tuna, olives, oil, mayonnaise, vinegar, pepper, and remaining ¼ teaspoon of salt and stir until evenly combined. Taste and add more mayo and/or salt if desired.

2. Transfer to a serving bowl or individual bowls and serve.

TO THE FORNO!: BAKED PASTA DISHES

7

PESTO RICOTTA BAKED CAVATAPPI WITH HALF VEGGIES

SERVES 4 TO 6 (SEE TIP) • TOTAL TIME: 1 HOUR 15 MINUTES, PLUS COOLING • DEVELOPED WITH KATIE LEAIRD

I didn't intend for this to become my signature dish. A few years back we were having a family gathering and I needed something I could assemble in advance, then pop in the oven when it was time for dinner. Something that would feed a bunch of adults and kids, all in one dish.

I decided to make baked ziti, but because of my aforementioned aversion to ziti and penne (see page 153), I made it with rigatoni. Typically baked ziti has a lot of ricotta, which is creamy but bland, so I kept adding pesto and grated Parmesan to the ricotta until it tasted amazing on its own—less like pesto, more like an incredibly savory, flavorful cheese spread. I sautéed mushrooms and spinach but put them in only half the dish, leaving a plain side for the kids.

It was such a huge hit that now I'm asked to make it for every family gathering. It's the dish Emily and Becky request each year for their birthday parties, and it's so popular at those parties that one of Becky's friends asked me to make it for *her* birthday party. I obliged.

Over the years I've tweaked it, switching to cavatappi (corkscrew tubes with ridges on the outside), which are more interesting and festive.

2 tablespoons plus 1 teaspoon kosher salt

2 tablespoons extra-virgin olive oil

One 8-ounce package sliced cremini (a.k.a. baby bella) mushrooms (see note)

5 ounces (about 5 cups) baby spinach

1 pound cavatappi (a.k.a. cellentani; or use rigatoni)

One 24- to 25-ounce jar tomato sauce (see tips on page 30)

16 ounces (2 cups) whole-milk ricotta

1 cup (4 ounces) finely grated Parmesan

One 6.3- to 7-ounce container prepared basil pesto (or ¾ cup homemade pesto, page 21)

¼ teaspoon freshly ground black pepper

4 ounces whole-milk mozzarella cheese, shredded (1 cup)

Sriracha, for serving (optional)

Garlic Bread Pangrattato (page 27), for serving (optional)

1. Bring 4 quarts of water and 2 tablespoons of the salt to a boil in a large pot.

2. Heat the oil in a large skillet (for a double portion use a large pot or Dutch oven) over medium heat until shimmering. Add the mushrooms and the remaining 1 teaspoon of salt and cook, stirring occasionally, until the liquid has evaporated

(continued)

TIP: Of course you can double any recipe in this book, and baked pasta dishes are especially good for a crowd, but I really want to highlight the double-ability of this one. I always double it, using an extra-deep baking dish that Janie got me just for this purpose.

and the mushrooms begin to brown, 7 to 9 minutes. Add the spinach and cook, stirring often, until mostly wilted, 1 to 2 minutes. Transfer the mushroom-spinach mixture to a colander and let drain for at least 15 minutes; return to the empty pan and set aside, reserving the colander.

3. Meanwhile, if baking right away, place an oven rack in the middle position and a second rack 4 to 5 inches from the broiler element; heat the oven to 350°F. Add the pasta to the boiling water and cook for 3 minutes less than the low end of the package instructions. Drain the pasta in the reserved colander, shaking off the excess water, then return it to the pot and stir in the tomato sauce; set aside.

4. In a medium bowl, stir together the ricotta, ¾ cup of the Parmesan, the pesto, and pepper. Spread half of the pasta mixture in the bottom of a 9- by 13-inch broiler-safe baking dish. Dollop half of the ricotta mixture over the pasta and use your fingers or a rubber spatula to spread it into a roughly even layer. Set aside a few mushrooms and spinach leaves, then distribute the remaining vegetables over half of the dish (see photo). Top with the remaining pasta mixture, followed by the remaining ricotta mixture, spreading them into an even layer. Sprinkle evenly with the mozzarella, followed by the remaining ¼ cup of Parmesan. Arrange the reserved mushrooms and spinach on the side of the dish with the vegetables underneath. (At this point the dish can sit, covered, at room temperature for up to 3 hours or be refrigerated for up to 24 hours before baking. If refrigerating, increase the baking time in step 5 to 40 minutes.)

5. Transfer the dish to the middle rack and bake until fully heated through and the cheese is melted, about 30 minutes. Transfer the dish to the higher rack, heat the broiler to high, and broil until the cheese is bubbling and browned, 2 to 5 minutes. (Watch closely while broiling to prevent the cheese from burning.) Let sit for 10 minutes.

6. Serve with Sriracha and/or garlic bread pangrattato, if desired.

NOTE: If your grocery store doesn't sell pre-sliced cremini mushrooms, buy 8 ounces of whole mushrooms, clean, then trim a bit off the stem (but leave it intact) and slice them. Also note that pre-sliced mushrooms will go bad faster, so if you're buying the mushrooms several days before you're making this recipe, go with whole ones.

A partially assembled Pesto Ricotta Baked Cavatappi, which is designed to please everyone at your party. By layering cooked veggies in half of it, you end up with two variations in one dish. This cuts whining about having to eat vegetables by up to 87 percent.

TANGY LABNE NOODLE KUGEL WITH PERSIMMON RELISH

SERVES 12 (THE RELISH YIELDS 2 CUPS) • TOTAL TIME: 1 HOUR 45 MINUTES • DEVELOPED WITH NATHALIE CHRISTIAN

Throughout my life, noodle kugel has made regular appearances at Jewish holidays and family gatherings. This pasta casserole typically calls for egg noodles and a custard of eggs, cottage cheese, sour cream, cinnamon, and sugar. Sometimes raisins or other fruits.

You may be surprised to find a Jewish dish in a pasta cookbook, but as Leah Koenig points out in *Portico: Cooking and Feasting in Rome's Jewish Kitchen*, pasta has been a part of Roman Jewish cuisine since the Spanish Inquisition, when Sephardi Jews were exiled from Sicily and moved north. Benedetta Jasmine Guetta's *Cooking alla Giudia: A Celebration of the Jewish Food of Italy* even includes a kugel-esque baked pasta dish called masconod, which is made with egg noodles, cheese, cinnamon, and sugar.

That's all nice context, but to my taste, noodle kugel is always too sweet and too dry. And I can't be alone because I don't think I've ever seen a Jew approach any holiday spread, survey the many glorious options before them, and exclaim, "Oh great, noodle kugel!"

I want to change that.

Combining savory and sweet can be wonderful, but it requires a commitment to contrast. (To borrow a phrase from the writer Jim Hightower, there's nothing in the middle of the road but yellow stripes and dead armadillos.) Cottage cheese and sour cream are too mild to elicit oohs and aahs on their own, leaving the middling sweetness of most kugels with no counterweight.

Inspired by a labne appetizer with persimmon mostarda at one of my favorite New York restaurants, chef Ayesha Nurdjaja's Shuka, I had an idea: replace the cottage cheese in kugel with labne, the tangy, thick, strained yogurt that's used across the Middle East. Then drizzle the whole thing with a dreamy fruit relish, to provide the dish's traditional sweetness while ensuring there is no chance my kugel comes out dry.

After one test it still wasn't tangy enough for me, so I added buttermilk and completely removed the sugar from the kugel itself, leaving the relish to provide the sweetness. We also put a lot of thought into the instructions for how to know when to take your noodle kugel out of the oven, so you won't overcook it.

When I made this dish for a family Hanukkah party, the reactions came swiftly:

"Why are you messing with kugel by putting a sauce on it?" cried Janie.

"It's wrong," added my sister-in-law Beth.

Eventually, begrudgingly, Janie came around. And after Beth tasted it, she said, "The fruit sauce adds flavor to the kugel, which I didn't realize was dry. But it's not dry with the sauce. It's actually really good."

I love it. Instead of vaguely savory with slightly sweet, you have salty tang mashed up with syrupy goodness. And there's great textural variation, with the crispy bits of browned surface noodles and the creamy, custardy interior. The contrasting elements of this kugel take strong stands in your mouth, setting off fireworks of sensation that may give bagels and lox a run for its money.

For the first time in my life, I'm excited to eat kugel.

(continued)

2 tablespoons plus 2½ teaspoons kosher salt

5 tablespoons extra-virgin olive oil

1 pound extra-wide or wide egg noodles (see note)

8 large eggs

16 ounces (2 cups) sour cream

16 ounces (2 cups) plain whole-milk labne or Greek yogurt

1 cup buttermilk

2 tablespoons freshly squeezed lemon juice

1½ pounds ripe but firm Fuyu persimmons (4 to 6 persimmons; or other fruit, see note)

2 tablespoons honey

1 tablespoon finely grated fresh ginger (or 1½ tablespoons tubed ginger)

1½ teaspoons unsalted butter

1 teaspoon kosher salt

¼ teaspoon freshly ground black pepper

2 tablespoons freshly squeezed lemon juice

½ teaspoon Dijon mustard

1. For the kugel: Bring 4 quarts of water and 2 tablespoons of the salt to a boil in a large pot. If baking right away, place an oven rack in the middle position and heat the oven to 325°F. Coat the bottom and sides of a 9- by 13-inch baking dish with 1 tablespoon of the oil and set aside. Add the noodles to the boiling water and cook for 3 minutes less than the low end of the package instructions, stirring occasionally to prevent sticking. Drain and let cool for at least 5 minutes.

2. Meanwhile, in a very large bowl, combine the eggs, sour cream, labne, buttermilk, remaining 4 tablespoons (¼ cup) of oil, the lemon juice, and the remaining 2½ teaspoons of salt and use an immersion blender to puree the mixture until completely smooth. (Alternatively, blend the ingredients in a blender or food processor and transfer to a very large bowl. You can also whisk vigorously by hand, but the other options yield silkier results.) Add the noodles to the bowl with the custard mixture and stir well to coat. (It will be very loose and soupy at this point.) Transfer to the prepared dish, scraping out the bowl, and spread into an even layer. (At this point the kugel can sit, covered, at room temperature for up to 2 hours or be refrigerated for up to 12 hours. If refrigerating, allow the kugel to sit on the counter for 1 hour to take the chill off before baking, and note that it may take longer to cook.)

3. Bake until slightly puffed and a paring knife or toothpick inserted near the center of the kugel comes out mostly dry with a few curds or streaks of dairy, 40 to 50 minutes. (The center of the kugel should register 160° to 165°F.) Leaving the kugel on the middle rack, heat the broiler to high and broil until the pieces of pasta sticking up are golden brown, 2 to 4 minutes (watch closely while broiling to prevent burning). Let cool for at least 20 minutes before slicing and serving.

4. While the kugel bakes, make the relish: Peel the persimmons, removing the leaves and any tough pieces around the stem and core, then chop the flesh into ½-inch pieces (you should have about 2 cups). In a medium saucepan, combine ¾ cup water, the persimmons, honey, ginger, butter, salt, and pepper and bring to a simmer over medium heat. Simmer, stirring and adjusting the heat as necessary to prevent scorching, until the liquid has thickened and become syrupy and the persimmons are tender but still hold their shape, 15 to 20 minutes. Remove the pan from the heat and stir in the lemon juice and mustard. Serve warm with the kugel. (The relish can be made up to 3 days in advance; just warm it in a pan or microwave before serving.)

PASTA NOTE: Some egg noodles are sold in 1 pound (16-ounce) packages, but they're often sold in 12-ounce packages. I don't know why, but it's annoying. While some kugel recipes call for 12 ounces, I think 16 ounces is better because it means more pasta will pile up above the liquid line in the baking pan, and those are the bits of pasta that will turn crispy golden brown in the oven. If all the pasta is submerged, you don't get that. And if you reduce the amount of liquid, the kugel will lose height and be more prone to drying out. So you really want 16 ounces of pasta, and if it means you have to buy two 12-ounce packages, you'll find a use for the extra 8 ounces. Egg noodles cook very quickly, so you can drop them raw into any soup or stew and they'll be ready almost instantly.

PERSIMMON NOTE: Fuyu persimmons can be replaced with a similar variety of persimmon known as Sharon fruit, but don't use Hachiya persimmons (the taller oblong ones shaped more like Red Delicious apples), which are very astringent and take forever to ripen. You can also replace the persimmons with stone fruit like peaches, plums, apricots, mangoes, or cherries, or berries, apples, pears, or even dried fruit, but you may need to make some adjustments. If using dried fruit, you'll need more water; tart fruit may need more honey and less lemon juice; and pay attention to the visual cues in the recipe more than the actual time: a softer fruit like apples may not need the full 15 to 20 minutes to soften. The good news is, this recipe is very forgiving and you can taste and adjust as you go.

PASTA PIZZA

SERVES 4 TO 6   •   TOTAL TIME: 1 HOUR

This one came to me in a vision while I was driving.

I had been looking through Ali Slagle's creative cookbook, *I Dream of Dinner (so You Don't Have To),* and she has a recipe for a baked pasta dish done with a short shape on a sheet pan, which creates crispy pasta edges all around. I thought that was genius, and I started wondering: What if I did that with a long shape, all the strands intertwining, so that the pasta formed a doughy, crispy, cohesive whole on the sheet pan? It would sort of function like a pizza crust. So then, could I top it like a pizza? And would it be possible to crisp the entire bottom well enough that it would not only hold together as a unit but that you could cut off a square, pick it up, and eat it with your hands like a slice of pizza, without it flopping or falling apart?

I told Emily I had an idea for something called "pasta pizza," and she replied, "Pasta pizza? That's really all I need to know. If I ask you to explain it, I know you're gonna go into a whole hour-long speech about it, so I'm just gonna avoid that."

After seven trials, I am pleased to report that my vision is not only possible, but magical. (You can hear the exact moment this idea came to me in the car, as well as the highlights of the testing process, in *The Sporkful* podcast series about the making of this cookbook.)

When I served the seventh version, which I declared to be the final recipe, Becky said, "The pasta has the perfect amount of crunchiness and softness. It's the perfect kind of balance, but to be honest, this is kind of bittersweet because it's like, now if you don't keep making new versions, I can't keep eating them, and I'm never gonna eat it again." (For the record, we've eaten it multiple times since.)

You can top your pasta pizza with anything you'd put on any other pizza—just be sure veggies that tend to release a lot of water when heated (like mushrooms and onions) are pre-cooked so they don't prevent your pasta crust from crisping. Avoid fresh mozzarella for the same reason. And always put the cheese on first, before any sauce (see tip on page 236)!

2 tablespoons kosher salt

4 tablespoons (¼ cup) extra-virgin olive oil

1 pound fettuccine

2 large eggs

16 ounces whole-milk mozzarella, shredded (4 cups)

2 cups (16 ounces) jarred tomato sauce, warmed

1. Bring 4 quarts of water and the salt to a boil in a large pot. Place an oven rack in the lowest position and heat the oven to 425°F. Spread 3 tablespoons of the oil on a rimmed sheet pan, making sure to coat the entire surface, including the edges and corners. Add the pasta to the boiling water and cook for 1 minute less than the low end of the package instructions, stirring often, especially at first, to prevent sticking.

2. Meanwhile, whisk the eggs in a large bowl until smooth and consistent.

3. Drain the pasta, shaking off the excess water, then immediately return it to the pot and stir in the remaining 1 tablespoon of oil. Add the pasta to the bowl with the eggs and toss until evenly coated.

4. Transfer the pasta mixture to the prepared sheet pan and spread it into an even layer, making sure it reaches the edges and corners and covers the entire surface of the pan with no big gaps. Transfer to the oven and bake until the edges of the pasta are light golden brown, 15 to 18 minutes.

5. Remove the pan from the oven and sprinkle the pasta evenly with the mozzarella (see tip on page 236). Add the tomato sauce and use the back of a spoon to spread it over the cheese. Return to the oven and bake until the cheese is melted and the edges of the pasta are dark brown all around, 15 to 18 minutes.

6. Remove the pan from the oven and let it sit for 3 minutes. Run an inverted thin metal spatula around the edges of the pan, loosening the pasta from the pan if necessary. With the spatula still inverted, scrape underneath the pizza to release it completely from the pan. When the entire bottom surface has been released, tilt the pan over a large cutting board and use the spatula to lift and slide the pizza out of the pan and onto the cutting board. Slice into squares and serve.

Charred Broccoli
and Chili Crisp Pasta
Pizza (page 236)

Artichoke, Feta,
and Za'atar Pasta
Pizza (page 236)

*Pasta Pizza
(page 232)*

CHARRED BROCCOLI AND CHILI CRISP PASTA PIZZA

2 tablespoons plus ¼ teaspoon kosher salt

6 tablespoons extra-virgin olive oil

1 pound fettuccine

2 large eggs

16 ounces whole-milk mozzarella, shredded (4 cups)

1 pound broccoli crowns, florets cut into 1-inch pieces, stems thinly sliced

¼ to ½ cup Lao Gan Ma chili crisp (or more depending on desired spiciness, see page 102)

Follow the instructions for Pasta Pizza; while the pasta is baking in step 4, toss the broccoli in a large bowl with the remaining 2 tablespoons of oil and ¼ teaspoon of salt. Top the pizza with the cheese as in step 5, then top with the broccoli and return to the oven and bake as directed. Remove from the oven and drizzle the chili crisp on top, spreading it gently over the cheese with the back of a spoon. (It's okay if it's uneven in spots and doesn't cover the entire surface.) Return to the oven and bake 1 to 2 minutes to warm the chili crisp, especially if it was in the fridge.

ARTICHOKE, FETA, AND ZA'ATAR PASTA PIZZA

2 tablespoons kosher salt

4 tablespoons (¼ cup) extra-virgin olive oil, plus more for serving

1 pound fettuccine

2 large eggs

8 ounces whole-milk mozzarella, shredded (2 cups)

Three 14-ounce cans artichoke hearts, drained, squeezed dry, and roughly chopped

6 ounces (1½ cups) feta cheese, crumbled (see tip on page 85)

2 tablespoons za'atar

1 teaspoon flaky sea salt

Follow the instructions for Pasta Pizza; after adding the mozzarella, top evenly with the artichokes, then sprinkle with the feta, za'atar, and flaky salt. Return to the oven and bake as above in step 5. Drizzle lightly with oil before slicing and serving.

TIP: New York pizza legend Patsy Grimaldi once told me he always puts the cheese on the pizza first, then the sauce on top, so the cheese fuses to the crust and doesn't slide off in a sheet when you bite into it. I recommend making pasta pizza the same way, not only for the reason Patsy says but also because the cheese acts as a seal, preventing sauce from seeping through the pasta, down onto the sheet pan, and turning your crust soggy. See the end of the Foreword (page xi) for another cheese tip for this dish!

CAULIFLOWER AND BEER CHEESE MAC WITH RITZ CRACKER AND CHIVE PANGRATTATO

SERVES 6 TO 8 • TOTAL TIME: 1 HOUR 45 MINUTES • DEVELOPED WITH ASHA LOUPY

This ultra-cozy baked mac 'n' cheese is inspired by one of my favorite bar snacks: a soft pretzel with beer cheese and extra mustard. So this cheese sauce gets a double dose of layered mustard flavor from sharp, bright Colman's mustard powder and more subtle, tangy whole-grain mustard. It's perfect for game day and every day, whether you care about the game or not.

As an added bonus, this dish contains a whole head of cauliflower, so it's probably extremely healthy.* If you want to have a better chance of sneaking the cauliflower past your kids, chop it into smaller florets and let it boil for a few extra minutes to soften it more. You could also abandon all pretense of getting your life together and instead replace the cauliflower with half-moons of kielbasa or spicy andouille sausage. I'm not gonna judge you.

This may not be true.

Ritz Cracker and Chive Pangrattato (page 26)

2 tablespoons plus 1½ teaspoons kosher salt

8 tablespoons (1 stick) unsalted butter

1 large shallot, minced

2 garlic cloves, minced

6 tablespoons all-purpose flour

2 tablespoons dry mustard powder (see note)

5 cups (40 ounces) whole milk

1 cup medium-bodied lager or ale (see note)

2 tablespoons whole-grain mustard

½ teaspoon freshly ground black pepper

16 ounces sharp Cheddar, shredded (4 cups)

8 ounces smoked Gouda, shredded (2 cups)

1 pound cestini pasta (or vesuvio, cascatelli, quattrotini, or radiatore)

1 medium cauliflower head, cut into small florets, stem diced (about 5 cups)

½ cup heavy cream

Crystal, Cholula, or other vinegar-based hot sauce, for serving (optional)

1. Make the pangrattato and set aside.

2. Bring 4 quarts of water and 2 tablespoons of the salt to a boil in a large pot. Heat the oven to 400°F.

3. Melt the butter in a large saucepan over medium heat. When it starts to foam, add the shallots and garlic and cook until the shallots are translucent, 3 to

5 minutes. Whisk in the flour and mustard powder and cook, whisking constantly, until darkened a shade, 2 to 4 minutes. While whisking constantly, very slowly add the milk and beer, then whisk in the whole-grain mustard, remaining 1½ teaspoons of salt, and the pepper. Increase the heat to medium-high and bring to a boil, then return the heat to medium and simmer, stirring occasionally, until the sauce thickens and holds a line when you drag your finger across the back of the spoon, 5 to 8 minutes. Reduce the heat to low and, working one handful at a time, add 3½ cups of the Cheddar and 1½ cups of the Gouda, whisking thoroughly to incorporate between each addition. Stir until the cheeses are fully melted. Cover and remove from the heat.

4. Add the pasta to the boiling water and cook for half of the low end of the package instructions. One minute before that time, add the cauliflower to the pot. Drain the pasta and cauliflower and immediately return them to the pot. Add the cheese sauce and cream and stir to coat, then transfer to a 9- by 13-inch baking dish. (At this point the mac can sit, covered, for up to 2 hours. Uncover before proceeding with the recipe, and note that you may have to increase the baking time in step 5.)

5. Sprinkle the pasta evenly with the remaining ½ cup each of Cheddar and Gouda. Place the baking dish on a rimmed sheet pan and bake until bubbling and golden on top, 18 to 22 minutes. (For more color, broil on high for 1 to 3 minutes at the end.)

6. Let sit for at least 10 minutes, then sprinkle evenly with the pangrattato and serve. Enjoy with a couple of dashes of your favorite vinegar-based hot sauce, if desired.

MUSTARD POWDER NOTE: Mustard powder can be found in the spice section of the grocery store, not the condiments section. I strongly recommend using Colman's mustard powder, my absolute favorite, but any one will work. If you don't have mustard powder, you can use a spoonful of Dijon or just a little extra whole-grain mustard to taste.

BEER NOTE: Choose a medium-bodied lager or pilsner. Avoid light beers, stouts, and anything too hoppy. Also, just like wine, cook with something you'd drink—the recipe only calls for a cup of beer, so the rest is for you, Chef.

SPINACH ARTICHOKE DIP LASAGNA PINWHEELS

SERVES 4 TO 6 (SEE TIP) • TOTAL TIME: 2 HOURS 30 MINUTES • DEVELOPED WITH ASHA LOUPY

I am on record as saying that traditional lasagna is not worth the effort. You go through the painstaking process of layering it just so, only to watch those layers collapse as it makes its way from the pan, to your plate, to your mouth. You could combine the same ingredients in a fraction of the time if you just made baked ziti.

On top of that, lasagna is usually so heavy that if spending all that time assembling it doesn't make you question your life choices, eating it sure will.

This recipe requires just as much effort as a traditional lasagna, but with a showstopping payoff that makes the work worthwhile, and a flavor that will have you ready to run back into the kitchen to do it all over again. (Becky also pointed out one of the advantages of a long recipe: "Even if we didn't like it, we wouldn't criticize it because it took you two and a half hours to make.")

We take inspiration from the best spinach artichoke dips, which, as the name suggests, are mostly spinach and artichokes. The only cheese you'll find here is a healthy dose of Parmesan, which brings just enough nutty, sharp, cheesy flavor to complement the vegetables. (If you're really craving some extra cheese, you can sprinkle 1 cup of shredded low-moisture mozzarella over the top when the foil is removed.) A lemon béchamel adds a sunny, saucy lusciousness without weighing it down.

In response to an early test, Emily suggested, "There should be a way to make it hold together easier because when I cut it, it kinda all falls apart. But when it's in my mouth, it's really good." So we increased the amount of lemon béchamel to hold it all together and put more emphasis on that sauce—this dish's secret weapon.

2 tablespoons plus 5 teaspoons kosher salt

30 to 32 ounces frozen chopped spinach, thawed (see note)

8 tablespoons (1 stick) unsalted butter

2 tablespoons extra-virgin olive oil

2 medium white or yellow onions, thinly sliced

6 garlic cloves, minced

Two 14-ounce cans artichoke hearts, drained, patted dry, and roughly chopped

1 pound dried lasagna noodles (not "no boil")

5 tablespoons all-purpose flour

4½ cups (36 ounces) whole milk

1¼ cups (5 ounces) finely grated Parmesan

½ cup good-quality prepared basil pesto

3 tablespoons finely grated lemon zest (from about 3 lemons)

(continued)

1. Bring 4 quarts of water and 2 tablespoons of the salt to a boil in a large pot.

2. Working with a handful at a time, squeeze out all the liquid from the spinach and transfer it to a large bowl, discarding the liquid; set aside.

3. Heat 2 tablespoons of the butter and the oil in a large, high-sided ovenproof skillet over medium-high heat until the butter melts and begins to foam. Reduce the heat to medium, add the onions and 1 teaspoon of the salt, and cook, stirring occasionally, until the onions are softened and golden around the edges, 10 to 14 minutes. Add the garlic and cook, stirring, until fragrant and beginning to color, 1 to 3 minutes. Stir in the spinach and artichokes, reserving the bowl, along with 1½ teaspoons of the salt and cook, stirring often, until the vegetables are evenly combined and heated through and any residual liquid has evaporated, 2 to 4 minutes. Transfer the artichoke-spinach mixture to the reserved bowl; reserve the skillet.

4. Add the noodles to the boiling water and cook until just pliable, 5 to 7 minutes, stirring to prevent sticking. Drain well, then lay them out on a rimmed sheet pan (it's okay if they overlap), cover loosely with aluminum foil, and set aside.

5. Return the reserved skillet to medium heat and add the remaining 6 tablespoons of butter. When the butter begins to foam, whisk in the flour and cook, whisking often, until the roux has darkened a shade, 2 to 4 minutes. Slowly whisk in the milk and remaining 2½ teaspoons of salt, increase the heat to high, and bring to a boil. Reduce the heat to medium and simmer, whisking often and adjusting the heat as necessary to maintain a medium simmer, until the sauce thickens and holds a line when you drag your finger across the back of the spoon, 4 to 8 minutes. Add 1 cup of the sauce to the artichoke-spinach mixture along with 1 cup of the Parmesan and the pesto; stir to combine. Transfer the remaining sauce to a second bowl and stir in the lemon zest. Reserve the skillet, wiping it out if necessary.

6. If baking right away, heat the oven to 375°F. Spread ½ cup of the sauce in the bottom of the reserved skillet. Working with one noodle at a time, mound ⅓ cup of the artichoke-spinach mixture in the center, spread it into an even layer, and roll the noodle into a cylinder starting at one of the short ends. Transfer to the skillet, standing on end with the frilly edges up. Repeat with the remaining noodles and filling, arranging the rolls in concentric circles in the pan (once you have a few made, it becomes easier to keep them standing up). Spoon the remaining sauce over the tops of the rolls, then cover the pan tightly with aluminum foil and bake for 20 minutes. (If making ahead, cover with foil and set aside for up to 1 hour or refrigerate for up to 6 hours. If refrigerating, increase the baking time to 25 minutes.)

7. Remove the pan from the oven and increase the heat to 425°F. Remove the foil (if some of the sauce sticks to the foil, scrape it back onto the pasta) and sprinkle the rolls with the remaining ¼ cup of Parmesan. Return to the oven and bake until golden in spots and some of the noodles have browned at the edges, 15 to 17 minutes. (For extra crispiness, broil on high for 2 to 4 minutes.)

8. Let cool for 5 minutes before serving.

TIP: If you double this recipe, it probably won't all fit in one skillet, so be sure to rotate the two skillets halfway through baking.

NOTE: Packages of frozen chopped spinach vary in size from 10 to 16 ounces. You can use three 10-ounce packages or two 16-ounce packages. To thaw, either leave the packages in the fridge overnight or cook following the microwave instructions on the package but deduct 2 to 3 minutes from the total time. This latter method will thaw the spinach but leave it cool enough to squeeze out all the excess liquid with your hands.

PASTA FRITTATA

SERVES 4 TO 6 • TOTAL TIME: 45 MINUTES • DEVELOPED WITH KATIE LEAIRD

Every so often someone on social media asks, "Why is there no breakfast pasta???" and it gets a lot of likes and I get tagged, because I guess I'm a Pasta Influencer now. First off, carbonara is a breakfast pasta—it's essentially bacon, eggs, and cheese. So is cacio e uova (cheese and egg), which you can find on page 36. But if that doesn't satisfy you, I give you the pasta frittata, which is traditionally made with leftover spaghetti. Italians often whip it up in the morning and fill it with whatever meats, cheeses, and/or veggies they have on hand from the night before. While they usually wait until the afternoon to eat it, a slice does make for a perfect breakfast—or, as they do in Campania, a portable lunch to take to the beach.

Emily's review: "I give it 1, 2, 3, 4, 5, 6, 7, 8, 9, 10. Million thumbs-up." Just don't skip the nutmeg, it takes the flavor of this frittata to the next level!

For the record, I realize this is the one recipe in this chapter that is not actually baked, but I put it in here because it FEELS like a baked pasta dish. It's a cohesive whole that puffs up when you cook it, then you slice it into portions to serve it. That it doesn't actually go into an oven seems beside the point. Ovens are just a state of mind, man.

This recipe does not call for any fillings, but you can add pretty much anything you might put in an omelet—just make sure it's already cooked, chop it into small pieces, and add it to the whisked egg mixture.

2 tablespoons plus 2 teaspoons kosher salt

5 large eggs

1 cup (4 ounces) finely grated Parmesan

¼ cup heavy cream or whole milk

3 tablespoons extra-virgin olive oil

½ teaspoon freshly ground black pepper

¾ teaspoon freshly grated nutmeg (or ¼ teaspoon ground nutmeg)

1 pound spaghetti (see note)

Hot sauce, for serving (optional)

1. Bring 4 quarts of water and 2 tablespoons of the salt to a boil in a large pot.

2. In a large heatproof bowl, whisk the eggs, Parmesan, cream, 1 tablespoon of the oil, the pepper, nutmeg, and remaining 2 teaspoons of salt until combined. Add the pasta to the boiling water and cook for 1 minute less than the low end of the package instructions. Drain the pasta, shaking off the excess water, and add it to the bowl with the egg mixture. Stir until the pasta is evenly coated.

(continued)

3. Heat 1 tablespoon of the oil in a 10-inch nonstick skillet over medium-low heat until shimmering. Add the pasta-egg mixture and use a rubber spatula to spread into an even layer. Cover and cook until the bottom of the frittata is golden brown and the eggs are just set, 5 to 8 minutes. (The surface may still appear wet in the center. Check the color by using the spatula to gently lift an edge and peek underneath.)

4. Remove the pan from the heat and run the spatula around the edge of the frittata to loosen it. Using oven mitts or towels, invert a large plate on top of the skillet and use both hands to carefully flip the skillet and plate, releasing the frittata onto the plate.

5. Add the remaining 1 tablespoon of oil to the empty skillet, increase the heat to medium-high, and heat until shimmering, about 30 seconds. Carefully slide the frittata back into the skillet, browned side up, and use the spatula to nudge it into place and tuck the edges under. Cook, uncovered, until the bottom is browned and crisp, 3 to 5 minutes.

6. Invert the frittata onto a serving platter or cutting board, slice it into wedges, and serve hot or at room temperature with your favorite hot sauce, if desired. You can also slice it up and take it to go—it's handheld pasta!

NOTE: You can use almost any pasta shape you want except tubes. If you don't get the egg mixture inside the tubes, you end up with big air pockets inside the frittata, which I find suboptimal. If you're using leftover pasta, it's okay if you have less than a pound—you'll just have an eggier frittata. You can also remove one egg from the recipe if you prefer. I do recommend warming leftover pasta in the microwave first, which makes it more pliable and helps jump-start the egg-cooking process.

SMOKED CHEDDAR AND CHICKEN MANICOTTI "ENCHILADAS"

SERVES 4 • TOTAL TIME: 1 HOUR 45 MINUTES (45 MINUTES' ACTIVE TIME) • DEVELOPED WITH ASHA LOUPY

Enchiladas, but with pasta. What more do I need to tell you? Instead of the traditional corn tortillas, we start with giant tubes of pasta (manicotti or cannelloni), fill them with cheesy chicken and Mexican crema, coat them in a red chile sauce, and top it all off with an ooey-gooey layer of broiled cheese. And we do it all using store-bought enchilada sauce and rotisserie chicken! (Insert infomercial-style applause here.)

If you double this recipe, use a second baking dish so the stuffed manicotti remain in a single layer, to maintain surface area for the cheesy topping. Rotate the dishes halfway through baking.

Canola or other neutral oil, for greasing

3 cups diced rotisserie chicken, skin and bones removed (about 1 pound, see note)

8 ounces smoked Cheddar, shredded (2 cups)

8 ounces (about ¾ cup) jarred or canned chopped Hatch chiles (see note)

½ cup roughly chopped fresh cilantro leaves and tender stems, plus more for serving

½ cup Mexican crema, plus more for serving

1¼ teaspoons kosher salt

One 8- or 8.8-ounce package dried manicotti or cannelloni shells

One 15- to 19-ounce jar or can good-quality red enchilada sauce

6 ounces Monterey Jack, shredded (1½ cups; or low-moisture mozzarella; see note)

Sliced avocado, for serving

Finely diced red onion, for serving (optional)

1. If baking right away, place an oven rack in the middle position and heat the oven to 375°F. Lightly grease a 9- by 13-inch baking dish.

2. In a large bowl, combine the chicken, Cheddar, ½ cup of the chiles, the cilantro, crema, and salt. Stir and mash together until well combined.

3. Working with one pasta shell at a time, use a small spoon or your fingers to scoop the chicken mixture into the shell, tamping it down with the end of the spoon or your finger (a chopstick also works well), repeating until the filling reaches the top edge. Rotate the shell and repeat on the other end to fill the shell from end to end. Transfer to the prepared baking dish and repeat with the remaining shells and filling. (If you have extra filling, nestle it around the manicotti in the pan. At this point the dish can sit, covered, for up to 1 hour. Proceed with step 4 when you're ready to bake.)

(continued)

4. Pour ½ cup of water evenly over the manicotti, followed by the enchilada sauce. Sprinkle with the Monterey Jack, leaving a ½-inch border around the edge of the pan, then top with the remaining chiles. Cover the dish first with parchment paper (if you have it), then tightly with aluminum foil, and bake until the pasta is easily pierced with a paring knife, 40 to 45 minutes.

5. Uncover the dish and return it to the middle rack, then heat the broiler to high and broil until the cheese is golden, 3 to 6 minutes (watch closely while broiling to prevent burning). Let cool for 10 minutes.

6. Sprinkle with extra cilantro and serve with more crema, avocado, and onion, if desired.

CHICKEN NOTE: For a 2-pound rotisserie chicken, this quantity works out to about three-fourths of the chicken, but since the size of rotisserie chickens can vary, stick with the 3-cup measurement. You can also use leftover roast chicken. Be sure to dice the chicken smaller than the diameter of the opening of your manicotti—otherwise it won't fit inside.

HATCH CHILES NOTE: One of the nice things about Hatch chiles is that they come in mild, medium, and hot, and either red or green. Choose your own adventure! I prefer jarred chiles and used Zia brand hot Hatch chiles in this dish. In a pinch, go for Hatch brand 4-ounce cans.

MONTEREY JACK NOTE: For best results buy Monterey Jack cheese in a block and shred it by hand on the large holes of a box grater. Preshredded Mexican cheese blend has a powdery coating that prevents it from getting quite as perfectly melty, but it will work in place of the Monterey Jack.

EGGPLANT TIMPANO

SERVES 6 • TOTAL TIME: 2 HOURS 45 MINUTES (1 HOUR 45 MINUTES' ACTIVE TIME) • DEVELOPED WITH ASHA LOUPY

This dish takes time, and the technique and presentation may look intimidating, but the recipe is actually very forgiving. I promise it'll come out great, and the end result may even earn you a trophy like the one in the photo.

You may recognize timpano—also known as timbale—from the beloved movie *Big Night,* starring Stanley Tucci and Tony Shalhoub. The timpano featured in the film is a stunning, deep-dish version that layers rigatoni with homemade ragù, multiple cheeses, peas, meatballs, eggs, and salami, all encased in a thin pastry crust. When it comes out of the oven, it's the size of a small tire.

That timpano's magnitude reminds me of the time, years ago, when I had a brief viral moment with a dish I invented called the Veggieducken—sweet potatoes stuffed inside leeks stuffed inside a giant squash. My goal was to create a centerpiece-worthy entrée for vegetarians to make at the holidays, and I know vegetarians and omnivores alike had a lot of fun making it. So I decided to think of my timpano as the Bride of Veggieducken.

At its essence, timpano typically consists of sauced pasta, cheese, and meat, encased in pastry, bread, or even slices of cooked vegetables. Our simpler, vegetarian version stars eggplant in two ways—thinly sliced and breaded to form the outer crust, and cubed in the filling. Add in frozen peas, smoked mozzarella, and hard-boiled eggs and you won't miss the meat.

To partially make ahead: the eggplant slices can be salted and roasted, and the cubed eggplant can be salted and sautéed up to 2 days in advance. This will save you about an hour when you go to make the finished dish.

3 medium to large globe eggplants (about 2½ pounds total), ends trimmed (see tip)

3½ teaspoons plus 1 tablespoon kosher salt

12 tablespoons (¾ cup) extra-virgin olive oil, plus more as needed

4 large eggs

8 ounces (about 2 cups) anellini (or anelli sor anelletti) pasta

One 24- to 25-ounce jar good-quality tomato sauce

6 ounces smoked mozzarella, cut into ½-inch cubes

1 cup frozen peas

3 tablespoons unsalted butter, melted

½ cup Italian seasoned bread crumbs

Calabrian chili paste (bomba sauce; see note on page 205) or sambal oelek, for serving (optional)

1. Slice 2 of the eggplants lengthwise into ¼-inch-thick oblong slices (doing your best to make the slices an even ¼ inch thick) and transfer the slices to a large bowl. Sprinkle with 2 teaspoons of the salt and toss to coat; let sit for 15 to 30 minutes,

(continued)

tossing occasionally. Dice the remaining eggplant into ½-inch cubes, transfer to a second bowl, and toss with 1½ teaspoons of the salt; set aside.

2. Place oven racks in the upper- and lower-middle positions and heat the oven to 400°F.

3. Divide the eggplant slices between two rimmed sheet pans, spreading them into a single layer and reserving the bowl. Pat the slices dry on both sides with paper towels. Using 8 tablespoons (½ cup) of the oil, brush both sides of each eggplant slice (the slices should be liberally coated; use an extra tablespoon or two of oil if necessary).

4. Roast the eggplant until tender and golden on one side, 22 to 30 minutes, flipping the slices and rotating the pans from top to bottom and front to back halfway through. Remove the pans from the oven and reduce the temperature to 375°F.

5. While the eggplant roasts, bring 2½ quarts of water to a boil in a large saucepan.

6. Heat the remaining 4 tablespoons (¼ cup) of oil in a large nonstick skillet over medium-high heat until shimmering. Add the cubed eggplant, stirring to coat, and cook, stirring occasionally, until tender and golden, 10 to 15 minutes; remove the pan from the heat.

7. In the reserved bowl, combine about 2 cups of ice and 3 cups of cold water. Add the eggs to the boiling water and cook for 7 minutes, then use a slotted spoon to transfer the eggs to the ice bath and let sit for 10 minutes.

8. Add the remaining 1 tablespoon of salt to the water in the pot and return to a boil if necessary. Add the pasta (remember, it's only half the package!) and cook for half of the low end of the package instructions. (Because this shape is often used in baking, some packages may offer only a "precooking" or "prebaking" time. If that's the case, use that precooking time.) Drain, shaking off the excess water, and return to the pot (off the heat). Add the tomato sauce, mozzarella, peas, and eggplant cubes and gently stir to combine.

9. Peel and halve the eggs (they may be a little runny at this point, so try not to spill any yolk—they'll continue to cook in the timpano).

10. Brush the bottom and sides of a 9-inch-round, 2-inch-high cake pan with 2 tablespoons of the butter, then coat with ¼ cup of the bread crumbs, tilting and rotating the pan until the sides and corners are completely coated. Arrange about

(continued)

Eggplant Timpano
under construction

three-quarters of the roasted eggplant slices so they are radiating out from the center of the pan, overlapping slightly so the bottom and sides of the pan are fully covered. (If your slices are very long, an inch or so might hang over the top edge of the pan, which is fine. End pieces should be placed cut side down, skin side up.) Add one-third of the pasta mixture and spread it into an even layer. Arrange 6 of the egg halves cut side down in a circle, about an inch in from the edge, spacing them about 1 inch apart, then place the remaining 2 halves in the center (see photo).

11. Spoon the remaining pasta mixture over the top, making sure to completely fill the space around each egg, and smooth it into an even layer. Arrange the remaining eggplant slices on top (with any end pieces placed skin side down, cut side up). Do your best to slightly overlap them so everything is covered (it's okay if a few small bits are exposed), then fold any overhanging pieces in to encase the filling. Brush the top with the remaining 1 tablespoon of butter and sprinkle with the remaining ¼ cup of bread crumbs.

12. Place on a rimmed sheet pan and bake on the upper-middle rack until most of the top is deep golden, 40 to 45 minutes.

13. Let cool in the pan on a wire rack for 20 minutes. Carefully run a paring knife or offset spatula around the edge of the pan, then invert a large plate on top of the pan and use both hands to flip the pan and plate. Carefully lift the pan, jiggling gently as you go, to unmold the timpano.

14. Slice and serve warm or at room temperature with Calabrian chili paste or sambal oelek, if desired.

TIP: Look for eggplants with tight, shiny skin that are very firm to the touch and feel heavy for their size.

RECIPES BY CATEGORY

45 MINUTES OR LESS, 5 INGREDIENTS OR FEWER, MAKE AHEAD, VEGETARIAN

45 MINUTES OR LESS

CLASSIC COMFORT: HUGS ON A PLATE (PAGE 34)

Cacio e Uova (Pasta with Pecorino and Eggs)

Tagliatelle with Prosciutto, Nutmeg, and Parmesan

Shells with Miso Butter and Scallions

Casarecce alla Vodka with Tomato Achaar

Ssamjang Aglio Olio

Thai Curry Quattrotini Mac 'n' Cheese

Spaghettoni alla Tadka

CARBY AND CRISPY: ADVENTURES IN TEXTURE (PAGE 67)

Cacio e Pepe e Chili Crisp

Ciceri e Tria (Fried and Boiled Noodles with Chickpeas)

Orecchiette with Salami, Fennel, Manchego, and White Wine

Chili Crisp Tahini Pasta with Fried Shallots

ZING: FLAVOR BOMBS, NOT BELLY BOMBS (PAGE 108)

Cavatelli with Roasted Artichokes and Preserved Lemon

Swordfish with Salsa Verde Sagne a Pezzi

Pappardelle with Arugula and Olives

Kimchi Carbonara

Kimchi alla Gricia

Larb-ish Cascatelli

Gnocchi with Bacon and Sauerkraut

Caramelized Endive and Radicchio with Savory Bagna Cauda

STEWS, ROUXES, AND RAGÙS: THICK AND HEARTY, WARM AND TOASTY (PAGE 158)

Mapo Tofu Cascatelli

Cajun Crawfish Carbonara with Cascatelli

Shrimp and Andouille Mac 'n' Cheese

Tortellini in Kimchi Parmesan Brodo

Tteokbokki Bolognese (Korean Rice Cakes in Meat Sauce)

PASTA SALADS REDEEMED: FRESH AND BRIGHT, HOLD THE MAYO (PAGE 198)

Lemony Tuna with Olives, Capers, Green Beans, and Parsley

Raw Heirloom Puttanesca with Fish Sauce and Calabrian Chili

Conchiglie with Corn, Avocado, and Fried (or Grilled) Halloumi

Cavatelli with Crunchy Fresh Corn, Tomatoes, Ricotta Salata, and Mozzarella

Cascatelli with Spicy Broccoli Rabe Pesto

Italian Cafeteria Hot Dog Pasta Salad with Canned Veggies

Crispy Gnocchi Salad with Preserved Lemon–Tomato Dressing

TO THE FORNO!: BAKED PASTA DISHES (PAGE 222)

Pasta Frittata

258

5 INGREDIENTS OR FEWER

Does not include the pasta itself or staples (eggs, oil, butter, salt, and black pepper)

CLASSIC COMFORT: HUGS ON A PLATE (PAGE 34)

Cacio e Uova (Pasta with Pecorino and Eggs)

Tagliatelle with Prosciutto, Nutmeg, and Parmesan

Shells with Miso Butter and Scallions

Ssamjang Aglio Olio

Thai Curry Quattrotini Mac 'n' Cheese

Spaghettoni alla Tadka

CARBY AND CRISPY: ADVENTURES IN TEXTURE (PAGE 67)

Cacio e Pepe e Chili Crisp

Ciceri e Tria (Fried and Boiled Noodles with Chickpeas)

Orecchiette with Salami, Fennel, Manchego, and White Wine

Scallion Oil Bucatini with Runny Eggs

Spaghetti all'Assassina (Assassin's Spaghetti)

Spaghetti all'Assassina con Cime di Rapa (with Broccoli Rabe)

ZING: FLAVOR BOMBS, NOT BELLY BOMBS (PAGE 108)

Cavatelli with Roasted Artichokes and Preserved Lemon

Pappardelle with Arugula and Olives

Creste di Gallo with Fava Beans and Dandelion Greens

Kimchi Carbonara

Kimchi alla Gricia

Linguine with Miso Clam Sauce

Busiate with Roasted Tomato Butter and Gim

Gnocchi with Bacon and Sauerkraut

STEWS, ROUXES, AND RAGÙS: THICK AND HEARTY, WARM AND TOASTY (PAGE 158)

Tteokbokki Bolognese (Korean Rice Cakes in Meat Sauce)

PASTA SALADS REDEEMED: FRESH AND BRIGHT, HOLD THE MAYO (PAGE 198)

Cascatelli with Spicy Broccoli Rabe Pesto

TO THE FORNO!: BAKED PASTA DISHES (PAGE 222)

Pasta Pizza

Pasta Frittata

RECIPES BY CATEGORY   **259**

MAKE AHEAD

Most of these recipes will have you wait to cook the pasta, leaving about 15 to 20 minutes of work just before you serve it. To get more done ahead of time, you can cook the pasta in advance—just see the tips on page 15.

VEGETARIAN

MEET THE TEAM

THE RECIPE DEVELOPERS

As I said at the outset, I'm not a chef. And while I am a pretty good home cook, I've known since the start of this project that if I was going to create the kind of cookbook I envisioned, I would need to collaborate with culinary pros to do it. I didn't necessarily set out, however, to assemble a team of absolute superstars. Still, that's what ended up happening, and I am so grateful that each of these folks shared their unique talents for this project.

In some cases the recipe developers took an idea I had and made it better. In other cases they contributed their own ideas that we refined together.

(If no developer is credited on a recipe, I did that one myself.) In all cases the process was guided by recipe editor Rebeccah Marsters, who provided crucial feedback, cross-tested every single recipe to confirm it was right, and made sure none of the teaspoons accidentally became tablespoons.

I urge you to follow each of these folks on social media, watch their videos, cook their recipes, buy their books, take their cooking classes, subscribe to their newsletters, and generally become fans of theirs, just as I have!

ASHA LOUPY

Asha Loupy is an Oakland-based writer and freelance recipe developer. She is also the recipe editor for Diaspora Co., a company that equitably sources spices from India and Sri Lanka. Asha has spent over a decade in the specialty food industry, from cheesemonger to grocery buyer and e-commerce manager. You can find her work in *Bon Appétit*, Food52, Martha Stewart, Kitchn, and Epicurious, and you can follow her on Instagram @fromheadtotable. When she's not cooking, you can find her exploring Oakland in search of the perfect negroni.

KATIE LEAIRD

Katie Leaird is a recipe developer, food writer, and pasta maker located on Martha's Vineyard. She earned culinary degrees in New York and Italy, as well as a pastry degree in San Francisco, and has cooked at restaurants in Italy, Napa, and Martha's Vineyard. She spent five years at America's Test Kitchen, and now contributes recipes and equipment reviews to Serious Eats, Kitchn, and other food media outlets. Katie also spent over a decade making wedding cakes and teaching kids and adults how to cook and bake, and she currently teaches classes on making fresh pasta.

JAMES PARK

James Park is a culinary producer and food content creator based in Brooklyn. He trained professionally at International Culinary Center and has worked with various food media brands, including Kitchn, Eater, Food52, and BuzzFeed, where he shares his love and passion for Korean cuisine and culture, fried chicken, chili crisp, and more. His first cookbook, *Chili Crisp*, came out in 2023, and you can find him eating and cooking his feelings at @jamesyworld on social media. Together with fellow contributor Irene Yoo, he cohosts the YouTube channel KA KA Studio, which shares their unique Korean American experiences and perspectives through Korean food, culture, and travel.

DARNELL REED

Darnell Reed is the chef and owner of Luella's Southern Kitchen in Lincoln Square, Chicago, which also has a stand at Soldier Field, home of the Chicago Bears. Luella's specializes in southern cuisine and is recognized as one of Chicago's premier southern/soul restaurants. In 2022 Darnell was a James Beard Award semifinalist. His great-grandmother, Luella Funches, is the inspiration for the food he serves today. Darnell is also the owner of Luella's Southern Popcorn, which ships nationwide.

IRENE YOO

Irene Yoo, also known as Yooeating, is a chef, recipe developer, writer, and culinary historian focused on Korean and Korean American home cooking, street food, and culinary history. She has contributed to Food52, Food Network, and *Bon Appétit*, and previously presented at the Korea Society and the Museum of Food and Drink. Together with fellow contributor James Park, she cohosts the YouTube channel KA KA Studio, which shares their unique Korean American experiences and perspectives through Korean food, culture, and travel.

REBECCAH MARSTERS

A Massachusetts native, Rebeccah Marsters has more than a decade's experience in the Boston food industry, from honing recipe development and editing skills at America's Test Kitchen and Christopher Kimball's Milk Street to managing social media for local restaurants and working wine retail. She is now a full-time freelancer out of her home in Gloucester, Massachusetts, where she lives with her husband, stepdaughter, and French bulldog. When she's not in the kitchen, she can probably be found on the yoga mat, the hiking trail, or the couch, sipping a cocktail and doing a crossword puzzle.

NATHALIE CHRISTIAN

Nathalie Christian is a Northern California–based freelance recipe developer, tester, and editor. Since switching careers to train at the San Francisco Cooking School, she has had the enormous pleasure of helping both her culinary heroes as well as industry newbies advance their cookbooks from concept to hardcover. Nathalie loves developing accessible recipes for print and online publication as well as helping startups find and leverage market fit for new and exciting products. Social and environmental justice activism take up what time she doesn't devote to cooking and family.

ADDITIONAL THANKS TO **Andrea Nguyen** and **Andrew Janjigian**, who each contributed one recipe, and to my mom, **Linda Pashman**, who contributed two recipes, provided feedback on several others, and shared her many opinions on the optimal method for tahini storage.

THE PHOTOGRAPHY TEAM

I hope that at points in this book, you looked at a photo of a dish and felt not only that you would very much like to eat it, but also that you'd been transported to a real place where real people were eating it already. All you had to do to join us was to start cooking. If so, all credit goes to our incredibly creative and talented photography team, who brought these recipes to life under a tight deadline, yet always with smiles and laughter. In some photos you'll see their hands alongside or instead of mine, which we did to represent and underscore just how many hands went into creating this book. The photo team is (left to right):

Nelson Lau, digital technician and first assistant
Dan Liberti, photographer
Malina Syvoravong, food stylist
Jillian Knox, art director and food and prop stylist
Additional food styling and prop assistance was provided by Elvis Santoyo, Marina Freytes, Caitlin Beyer, and Royce Burke.

ADDITIONAL ACKNOWLEDGMENTS

I'm fortunate to work with an incredibly talented and dedicated team on *The Sporkful*, and their excellent work crafting our "Mission: ImPASTAble" series was a big part of cascatelli's success. (The *New York Times* named the series one of the Ten Best Podcasts of 2021—it's still publicly available if you want to check it out.) And while it hasn't been created yet as I write this, I'm sure the series about the making of this cookbook will also be great! Thank you to all the key contributors to these two series: senior producer Emma Morgenstern, producer Andres O'Hara, editor Tracey Samuelson, executive producers Nora Ritchie and Daisy Rosario, and engineer Jared O'Connell, as well as Anne Saini, Ngofeen Mputubwele, Chris Bannon, Peter Clowney, Colin Anderson, Gianna Palmer, Abigail Keel, Hali Bey Ramdene, Harry Huggins, Daphne Chen, Casey Holford, Andrea Kristinsdottir, and Niña Cayaban.

Special thanks to Emma Morgenstern, who was the lead producer on the "Mission: ImPASTAble" series and who also brought her steady hand and keen insights to this book, contributing research and additional editing.

On the pasta front, I also want to thank Scott Ketchum and Steve Gonzalez from Sfoglini Pasta, as well as the die makers Chris Maldari of D. Maldari and Sons and Giovanni Cannata of De Mari Pasta Dies. And shout out to Katie Kimmel, who designed the Linguini and Clams T-shirt I'm wearing on page 139!

My editor, Cassie Jones, brought the ideal combination of pragmatism and weirdness to the creation of this book, and always responds to emails promptly, which is probably too important to me. Thank you also to the many others at William Morrow who helped make this book: Ploy Siripant, Jill Zimmerman, Shelby Peak, Jennifer Eck, Renata de Oliveira, Anna Brower, Sarah Falter, Tavia Kowalchuk, and Taylor Turkington.

My literary agent, Anthony Mattero at CAA, got behind the idea for this book the first time I pitched it to him, even though others were skeptical (because not so many people bought my first book!). More important, Anthony stayed behind it throughout. Thanks also to everyone else at CAA including Jim Nicolay, Josh Lindgren, Kate Childs, and Khalil Roberts. And thank you to Eva Karagiorgas, Vanessa Santos, Ella Stearns, and everyone at Mona Creative for their great work!

I learned so much during my travels in Italy, which deepened and changed my understanding of pasta. Thank you to my guide in Rome, Katie Parla, who also contributed research to this book—check out her fantastic cookbooks, and if you're in the area, take one of her tours! I got additional help and guidance from Maureen Fant, Evan Kleiman, Sophie Minchilli, Katie Quinn, Rachel Roddy, Roberta Bourassa, Massimo Dell'Erba, Antonello Di Bari, and Silvestro Silvestori of the Awaiting Table Cookery School in Lecce.

While the developers did the heavy lifting on the recipe front, I'm lucky to have many friends who were kind enough to cook and/or eat pasta dishes and share their feedback with me. Thank you to the Delaney-Fans, Englands, Ehlerses, Goulds, McCloskeys, Noahs, Post-Gottliebs, Rathbuns, Risingers, Roers, Saylors, and everyone who was at the Hamiltons' 2022 holiday party.

Thank you to my friend Kenji López-Alt, whose work I have admired for many years, who was kind enough to write the foreword for this book. I'm also indebted to all the others in the worlds of food and audio who have supported and encouraged me over the years and whose work has inspired me to continue to refine my craft. And thank you to YOU—yes, you—and all those who've taken the time to engage with my work over the years. Putting something out into the world and finding that it has connected with others is the most rewarding part of my job.

I'm so fortunate to have an incredibly supportive family. Thank you to my parents, Linda and Louis, who instilled in me a love of eating. And while my mom got more attention throughout this book, please know that my dad was instrumental in washing dishes after my mom tested recipes. He did also try each dish she made, but his palate is less discerning. (There's a reason why, when we were kids, my brother Howard and I nicknamed him The Human Garbage Disposal.) Thank you also to my in-laws, Alice and Gene Fossner, who are always there for our family, and to Howard, Manya, Max, and Rose Pashman, and Dan, Beth, Gabriel, and Noa Fossner.

Finally and most importantly, thank you to Janie, Emily, and Becky, whose hands also appear in a few photos in this book. I joke about Janie's skepticism, but she has always supported my projects, no matter how unlikely their success seemed at the start. She is my best PR agent and biggest booster, whether that means making extra trips to the grocery store for my recipe testing or hitting the floor of the Fancy Food Show in New York to hawk cascatelli herself. This cookbook and everything that led up to it are as much Janie's success as mine. And Becky and Emily, this cookbook really feels like a project our whole family contributed to, which makes it even more meaningful, and a memento of a time in our lives that I'm so glad we'll always have. Also, now you'll know how to make these dishes for yourselves. But I'll still make them for you anytime.

UNIVERSAL CONVERSION CHART

OVEN TEMPERATURE EQUIVALENTS

250°F = 120°C

275°F = 135°C

300°F = 150°C

325°F = 160°C

350°F = 180°C

375°F = 190°C

400°F = 200°C

425°F = 220°C

450°F = 230°C

475°F = 240°C

500°F = 260°C

MEASUREMENT EQUIVALENTS

Measurements should always be level unless directed otherwise.

⅛ teaspoon = 0.5 mL

¼ teaspoon = 1 mL

½ teaspoon = 2 mL

1 teaspoon = 5 mL

1 tablespoon = 3 teaspoons = ½ fluid ounce = 15 mL

2 tablespoons = ⅛ cup = 1 fluid ounce = 30 mL

4 tablespoons = ¼ cup = 2 fluid ounces = 60 mL

5⅓ tablespoons = ⅓ cup = 3 fluid ounces = 80 mL

8 tablespoons = ½ cup = 4 fluid ounces = 120 mL

10⅔ tablespoons = ⅔ cup = 5 fluid ounces = 160 mL

12 tablespoons = ¾ cup = 6 fluid ounces = 180 mL

16 tablespoons = 1 cup = 8 fluid ounces = 240 mL

INDEX

Note: Page references in *italics* indicate photographs.

HarperCollins books may be purchased for educational, business, or sales promotional use. For
information, please email the Special Markets Department at SPsales@harpercollins.com.

FIRST EDITION

DESIGNED BY RENATA DE OLIVEIRA

Photographs by Dan Liberti except the following: pages 9, 76, 77, 87, 90, 91, 175, 262, 263 (lower
right), and 267 by Dan Pashman; page 11 by Scott Gordon Bleicher; page 130 (lower right) by
Katie Parla; page 263 (upper left) courtesy of Asha Loupy; page 263 (lower left) by Heami Lee;
page 263 (upper right) by Jocelyn Filley; page 264 (upper left) by Nick Surette; page 264 (lower
left) courtesy of Rebeccah Marsters; page 264 (right) courtesy of Nathalie Cristian

Art direction and food styling by Jillian Knox

Library of Congress Cataloging-in-Publication Data has been applied for.

ISBN 978-0-06-329112-6

24 25 26 27 28   TC   10 9 8 7 6 5 4 3 2